Capodimonte and I Vergini

Decumano Maggiore

Spaccanapoli

Toledo and Castel Nuovo

CAPODIMONTE AND I VERGINI
Pages 90–101

DECUMANO MAGGIORE
Pages 74–89

SPACCANAPOLI
Pages 60–73

0 meters	500
0 yards	500

NAPLES

WITH POMPEII & THE
AMALFI COAST

EYEWITNESS *TRAVEL GUIDES*

NAPLES
WITH POMPEII & THE AMALFI COAST

DK PUBLISHING, INC.

A DK PUBLISHING BOOK

Produced by Fabio Ratti
Editoria Libraria e Multimediale
Milano, Italy

PROJECT EDITOR Giovanni Francesio
EDITORS Barbara Cacciani, Giorgia Conversi,
Elena Marzorati, Michele Di Muro
DESIGNERS Paolo Gonzato, Carlotta Maderna, Stefania Testa
MAPS Paul Stafford
PICTURE RESEARCH Emilia Marchi, Riccardo Villarosa

Dorling Kindersley Ltd
PROJECT EDITOR Fiona Wild
EDITORS Francesca Machiavelli, Naomi Peck, Rosalyn Thiro
US EDITOR Mary Sutherland
DTP Cooling Brown
DTP DESIGNER Ingrid Vienings
PRODUCTION David Proffit
MANAGING EDITOR Georgina Matthews
MANAGING ART EDITOR Annette Jacobs
SENIOR MANAGING EDITOR Vivien Crump
DEPUTY ART DIRECTOR Gillian Allan

CONTRIBUTORS
Emilia Marchi, Daniela Lepore, ed. by (Napoli)
Practical information by Ciro Cacciola,
Angela Catello and Kirsi Viglione
Additional contributions from Patrizia Antignani,
Mariella Barone, Beatrice Vitelli

ILLUSTRATORS Giorgia Boli, Paola Spampinato, Nadia Viganò
•
ENGLISH TRANSLATION Richard Pierce
•
Film outputting bureau Press Data (London)
Reproduced by Lineatre Service (Milano)
Printed and bound by A Mondadori (Italy)

First American Edition, 1998
2 4 6 8 10 9 7 5 3

Published in the United States by
DK Publishing, Inc.,
95 Madison Avenue, New York, New York 10016

Copyright © 1998 Dorling Kindersley Limited, London
Visit us on the World Wide Web at http://www.dk.com

Library of Congress Cataloging-in-Publication Data
Naples. –– 1st American ed.
p.   cm. –– (Eyewitness travel guides)
Includes index.
ISBN 0-7894-2752-4
1. Naples (Italy)–– Guidebooks.   I. Series.
DG842.N27 1998   97-32279
914.5'7304929 –– dc21   CIP
•

Every effort has been made to ensure that the information in this
book is as up-to-date as possible at the time of going to press.
However, details such as telephone numbers, opening hours, prices,
gallery hanging arrangements, and travel information are liable to
change. The publishers cannot accept responsibility
for any consequences arising from the use of this book.

We would be delighted to receive any corrections and
suggestions for incorporation in the next edition. Please write to:
Senior Editor, Eyewitness Travel Guides,
DK Publishing, Inc., 95 Madison Avenue, New York, New York 10016.

CONTENTS

HOW TO USE THIS GUIDE 6

The Farnese Hercules

INTRODUCING NAPLES

The Spaccanapoli district

◁ **Overview of the city with the distinctive dome of San Francesco di Paola in Piazza del Plebiscito**

Panoramic view of the Forum at Pompeii, with Vesuvius in the background

Outdoor eating, Bay of Naples

Pizza Napoletana

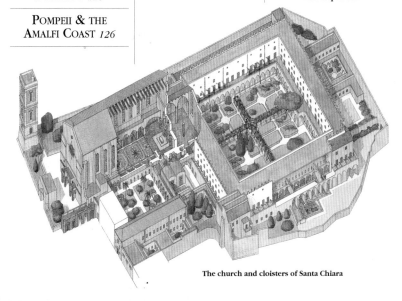

The church and cloisters of Santa Chiara

HOW TO USE THIS GUIDE

THIS GUIDE helps you get the most out of your visit to Naples. It provides both expert recommendations and advice as well as useful practical information. The first chapter, *Introducing Naples*, sets the city in its rich and varied geographical and historical context. *Naples at a Glance* gives you a brief overview of the main sights in the city, as well as cultural background. *Naples Through the Year* describes events and festivals season by

season. *Naples Area by Area* describes the main sightseeing areas in detail, with maps, illustrations, and photographs. *Pompeii and the Amalfi Coast* covers this region's splendid archaeological sites and also features an itinerary for a coastal boat trip. Information on hotels, shops, restaurants, and bars is covered in *Travelers' Needs*, while the *Survival Guide* contains practical advice – for example, how to use the local transporation networks.

FINDING YOUR WAY AROUND THE SIGHTSEEING SECTION

The city has been divided into six color-coded areas, each with its own chapter. A description of the history and features of each area is followed by a Street-by-Street

map focusing on the main attractions. The sights are numbered for easy reference. The most important sights in each area are described in detail in two or more pages.

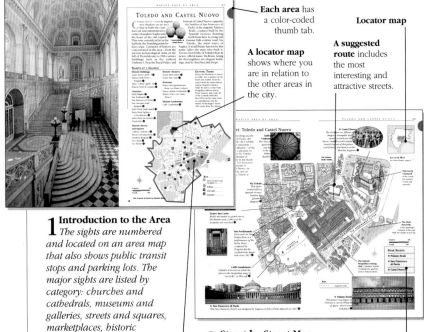

Each area has a color-coded thumb tab.

Locator map

A locator map shows where you are in relation to the other areas in the city.

A suggested route includes the most interesting and attractive streets.

1 Introduction to the Area
The sights are numbered and located on an area map that also shows public transit stops and parking lots. The major sights are listed by category: churches and cathedrals, museums and galleries, streets and squares, marketplaces, historic buildings, parks and gardens.

The area shaded pink is shown in greater detail on the Street-by-Street Map on the following pages.

2 Street-by-Street Map
This gives a bird's-eye view of the heart of the sightseeing area. The numbers refer to the fuller descriptions provided on the following pages.

The list of star sights indicates places no visitor should miss.

NAPLES AREA MAP

The colored areas on this map *(see inside front cover)* correspond to the six main sightseeing areas. Each area is covered in full in the *Naples Area by Area (see pp44–125)* section. The map showing the center of Naples *(pp12–13)* also locates all of the major sights and monuments in the city.

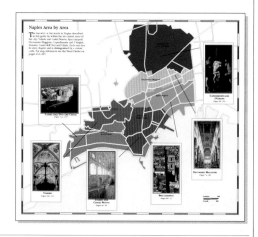

Numbers refer to each sight's position on the area map and its place in the chapter.

Practical Information provides all the information you need to visit the sights, including map references to the *Street Finder (see pp212–27).*

The Visitors' Checklist provides all the practical information needed to plan your visit.

3 Detailed Information on Each Sight

All the most important sights in Naples are described individually. They are listed in order, following the numbering on the area map, which appears at the beginning of each chapter. The key to the symbols used is shown on the back flap for easy reference.

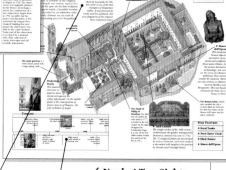

4 Naples' Top Sights

Historic buildings are dissected to reveal their interiors. Museums and galleries have color-coded floor plans to help you locate the major exhibits.

The timeline lists the most important events in the history of the building.

Stars indicate the features you should not miss.

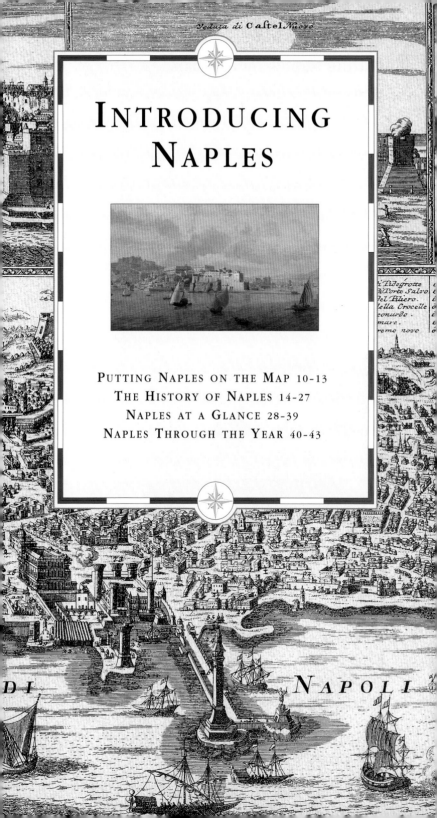

INTRODUCING
NAPLES

DI NAPOLI

Putting Naples on the Map

NAPLES IS THE third largest city in Italy after Milan and Rome, and the largest city in Southern Italy. The population of the city proper *(see pp12–13)* is 1,250,000, rising to almost three million when the suburbs are taken into account. The city faces the great sweep of the splendid Bay of Naples, extends into the fertile Campania plain, and occupies high ground and hollows formed by ancient volcanic craters.

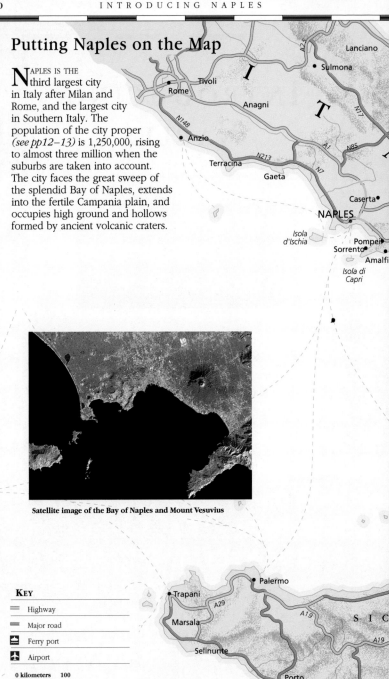

Satellite image of the Bay of Naples and Mount Vesuvius

KEY

▬	Highway
▬	Major road
⚓	Ferry port
✈	Airport

0 kilometers   100

0 miles   100

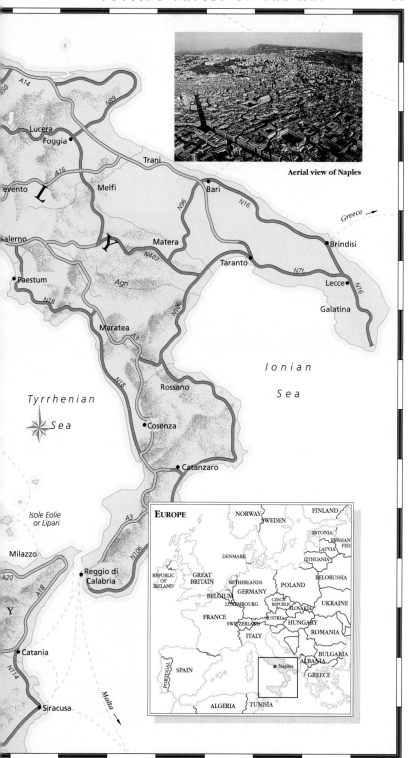

Aerial view of Naples

A14

N89

Lucera

Foggia

Trani

evento

A16

Melfi

Bari

N96

N16

Greece

alerno

Matera

N407

Brindisi

Paestum

Agri

Taranto

N7t

N18

Lecce

N16

Maratea

A3

N106

Galatina

Ionian

Sea

Tyrrhenian

Rossano

Sea

N18

Cosenza

Catanzaro

Isole Eolie
or Lipari

A3

Milazzo

N106

EUROPE   NORWAY   SWEDEN   FINLAND

A20

A18

ESTONIA

RUSSIAN
FED

DENMARK   LATVIA

LITHUANIA

Reggio di
Calabria

REPUBLIC
OF
IRELAND   GREAT
BRITAIN   BELORUSSIA

Y   NETHERLANDS   POLAND

GERMANY

BELGIUM   UKRAINE

LUXEMBOURG   CZECH
REPUBLIC   SLOVAKIA

Catania   FRANCE   AUSTRIA   HUNGARY

SWITZERLAND

N114   ITALY   ROMANIA

Siracusa   BULGARIA

Malta   PORTUGAL   SPAIN   ALBANIA

Naples   GREECE

ALGERIA   TUNISIA

Central Naples

THE OLD TOWN is divided into six distinct areas. From the 16th century on, the administrative and commercial center of Naples developed around Toledo and Castel Nuovo. The old city center is described in the chapters on Spaccanapoli and Decumano Maggiore. The Vergini district, immediately north of the Foria gorge, leads to the park of Capodimonte with its Royal Palace. The Certosa di San Martino and Castel Sant'Elmo dominate the Vomero hill. In the Chiaia area, a few steps from the most elegant stores in Naples, places such as Castel dell'Ovo and Mergellina are surrounded by greenery and the sea. To the west are the lovely inlets and villas of Posillipo.

The Certosa di San Martino, on the Vomero

The Cappella Caracciolo di Vico in San Giovanni a Carbonara

Castel Nuovo, known locally as Maschio Angioino

Reggia di Capodimonte

NDO IMONTE

CAPODIMONTE E I VERGINI

PIAZZA S. EFRAMO VECCHIO

PIAZZA SANSEVERO

PIAZZA A SANITÀ

NICLO DIMONTE

ORTO BOTANICO

PIAZZA CARLO III

CORSO GARIBALDI

FORIA

L.GO MIRACOLI

PIAZZA MIRACOLI

VIA

S. Giovanni a Carbonara

P.ZA TEATRO S. FERDINANDO

P.ZA VOLTURNO

P.ZA PAGANO

P.TTA S. CARLO ALL'ARENA

P.TTA DEI LEPRI

P.ZA STELLA

P.TTA SETTEM- BRINI

P.ZA S. ANNA A CAPUNA

PIAZZA CAVOUR

PIAZZA DE NICOLA

PIAZZA PRINCIPE UMBERTO

The tiled cloister of Santa Chiara

Museo Archeologico Nazionale

P.TTA S.ANDREA D. DAME

LARGO DONNAREGINA

MANO GIORE

L.GO REGINA COELI

VIA

Duomo

PIAZZA SISTO RIARIO SFORZA

S. Lorenzo Maggiore

PIAZZA S. GAETANO

P.ZA MIRAGLIA

P.ZA BELLINI

P.ZA. CALENDA

PIAZZA S. MARIA LA SCALA

S. Gregorio Armeno

IAZZA ANTE

S. Domenico Maggiore

P.ZA S. DOMENICO NILO MAGGIORE

DUOMO

VIA UMBERTO I

PIAZZA NICOLA AMORE

P.TTA SCACCHI

P.TTA DE OMO

P.TTA S. ELIGIO

PIAZZA MERCATO

Gesù Nuovo

P.ZA DEL GESÙ NUOVO

Santa Chiara

PIAZZA MASANIELLO

SPACCANAPOLI

P.ZA PORTA- NOVA

NUOVA MARINA

P.TTA PRINCIPESSA MARGHERITA

P.TTA PORTO

VIA

The fountain of *Christ and the Samaritan* in the cloister of the convent of San Gregorio Armeno

PIAZZA BOVIO

CALATA PORTA DI MASSA

MOLO C. PISACANE

EDO E L NUOVO

VIA C. COLOMBO

NUOVA CALATA PILERO

0 meters   500

0 yards   500

PIAZZA MUNICIPIO

Castel Nuovo

lazzo Reale

MOLO ANGIOINO

GIARDINI PUBBLICI

MOLO SIGLIO

N. SAURO

Castel dell'Ovo, seen from the bay

KEY

- Major sight
- **M** Metro station
- Ferry port
- Funicular
- **P** Parking lot
- Tourist information
- Hospital/emergency room
- Police station
- Church
- Synagogue
- Post office

THE HISTORY OF NAPLES

IN GREEK MYTHOLOGY, Naples was built where the Siren Parthenope was washed ashore after she had been rejected by Odysseus. Greek colonists, perhaps from Rhodes, may have founded a colony at this point as early as the 10th century BC, but this too may be the stuff of legend. What is certain is that Greeks from Cumae built a new city nearby, calling it *Neapolis* (new city); the original town was renamed *Palaeopolis*, or old city. Neapolis was a leading commercial center and the Greek language and customs survived during the Roman period, when it was a favorite area of the elite.

Gorgon, 6th-century BC Cumaean antefix

After the fall of the Roman Empire and a wave of invasions, the city came under Byzantine influence and went through a period of rebirth. Naples, as a duchy, largely retained its independence. In the 10th century the invading Normans conquered the whole of Southern Italy, a kingdom initially ruled from Palermo, under Roger II. Norman rule finally came to an end in 1189. With the Angevin (French) and Aragonese (Spanish) dynasties, Naples itself became a capital, and the court began to attract famous artists. The 15th century was a golden era for Naples, but there then followed two disastrous centuries of direct rule by Spain. The Spanish viceroys were oppressive rulers, and the era is remembered for unjust taxation, the Inquisition, plague, overpopulation, and the rebellion of Masaniello. However, creativity flowered despite widespread poverty.

In 1734 Charles III began the period of Bourbon hegemony. With the exception of the short-lived republican government in 1799 and the subsequent decade of French dominion, the Bourbons ruled Naples until 1860.

Since the unification of Italy the city's problems have become national issues – for example the markedly different level of development between Northern and Southern Italy.

Map of Naples in 1790

◁*Paquius Proculus and His Wife*, 1st-century AD wall painting from Pompeii

Greco-Roman Naples

Pompeiian cameo

B Y THE 8th century BC, Greeks had founded a settlement at Cumae, one of the earliest Greek colonies in Italy. From there they established a new town on Pizzofalcone hill, known as Parthenope, and trade prospered. Population growth led to the founding of Neapolis, or new city, nearby, and victory over the Etruscans in 474 BC brought further expansion. Neapolis came into contact with the growing power of Rome during the its protracted wars with the Samnites. In the 4th century BC the Neapolis citizens agreed to become an "allied city" of Rome. In AD 79 an erupting Vesuvius buried a number of ancient Roman cities, including Pompeii.

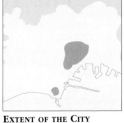
EXTENT OF THE CITY

☐ *8 BC*   ☐ *Today*

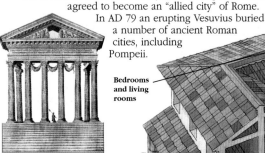

Bedrooms and living rooms

Temple of the Dioscuri
This 16th-century print shows the Roman temple that once stood on the site of San Paolo Maggiore (see p79). The temple façade collapsed in the 1688 earthquake.

Atrium

Via Anticaglia
The "street of ruins" acquired its name from the brick arches connecting the Ancient Roman bath house and the theater (see p84).

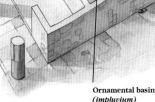

Ornamental basin *(impluvium)*

TIMELINE

1000–900 BC
According to Greek myth, city of Parthenope founded

328 BC War with Rome; Naples is defeated but a treaty sanctions the city's freedom

90–89 BC People of Campania become Roman citizens

900 BC	600 BC	300 BC	100 BC

600 BC
Greeks from Cumae found *Neapolis*, or "new city"

Red-figure vase (5th century BC)

100 BC Tunnel built in Posillipo hill connecting city with Phlegraean Fields area and its trade and military ports

THE HOUSES OF POMPEII

The Roman houses in Pompeii *(see pp146–7)* are among the best-preserved examples of Roman civilization in Campania. This illustration shows a typical patrician house in Pompeii, displaying characteristic features of Roman and Greek domestic architecture. The houses were generally rectangular. To ensure privacy, they faced inward, as can be seen by the few windows on the outer walls. The rooms were built around an atrium, or courtyard, which was the focal point of domestic life. Wealthier houses were richly decorated.

The garden was surrounded by columns, known as a "peristyle."

The kitchen and dining room (*triclinium*) were in this part of the house.

The Greek Walls
Made of large tufa blocks, the city walls date from the 5th century BC. Remnants can be seen in present-day Piazza Bellini (see p78).

WHERE TO SEE GRECO-ROMAN NAPLES

Beneath the cloister *of San Lorenzo* (see p80) *layers of the ancient city are still visible.*

Although not much is left of Greco-Roman *Neapolis*, some traces are visible in Piazza Bellini *(see p78)*, around Santa Chiara *(see pp66–7)*, and under the duomo *(see pp82–3)*. Outside the city, Pompeii and Herculaneum are vivid records of ancient Roman life. The Museo Archeologico Nazionale *(see pp86–9)* in Naples houses rich finds. Amphitheaters survive at Pozzuoli *(see p132)* and Santa Maria Capua Vetere *(see p159)*, and Greek ruins at Cumae *(see p134)* and Paestum *(see pp156–7)*.

The Diadumeno Torso from Castel Capuano

Statue of Aphrodite, Museo Archeologico	**350–400** Christianity gaining in acceptance	**500** Bishop Severus builds the first parish church, now San Giorgio Maggiore *(see p70)*	
AD 1	**AD 300**	**400**	**500**
79 Vesuvius erupts; Pompeii and Herculaneum destroyed	*The Siren Parthenope on a Roman coin*	**476** Romulus Augustulus, last Roman emperor of the West, imprisoned in the *Castrum Lucullanum (see p116)*	**536** Byzantine General Belisarius wins Naples, entering city via the aqueduct

From Byzantine Rule to the Aragonese Dynasty

Angevin lily

IN THE 6TH CENTURY AD, Naples became part of the Byzantine (Eastern Roman) empire. Despite the incursions into Southern Italy by Goths, Lombards, and Saracens, it remained a semi-independent duchy, nominally under Byzantine rule, until it became part of the Norman kingdom of Sicily in the 12th century. By the 13th century the French House of Anjou had taken over, and Naples became the capital of the Angevin kingdom. Ambitious schemes began: land reclamation and building of new castles, churches, and monasteries. In 1421 the last Angevin queen, Joan II, named Alfonso V of Aragon as her successor.

GROWTH OF THE CITY

■ 500   □ Today

Tombs in Santa Chiara
The Angevin rulers were buried in Santa Chiara, which contains superbly crafted tombs such as this one by an unknown artist (first half of the 14th century).

Louis of Anjou took vows after refusing the crown of Naples and was canonized in 1317.

Tomb of Ladislas of Durazzo
This tomb is in San Giovanni a Carbonara (see p96), chosen by Ladislas to house the tombs of the Angevin kings.

The Pietrasanta Bell Tower
This is among the few remaining examples of medieval architecture in Naples (see p78).

TIMELINE

553
Naples again under Byzantine rule

7th-century Byzantine fibula

902
After many attempts to conquer Naples, the Saracens are defeated at Garigliano

600	700	800	900

600
Naples resists Lombard siege and remains an independent duchy

763
The duchy becomes hereditary and independent

Statue of Frederick II, Holy Roman Emperor

Frescoes of the Giotto School

Giotto lived in Naples from 1328–33. His influence can be seen in the frescoes in Santa Maria di Donnaregina Vecchia (1332–5).

The crown Louis is placing on the head of his brother Robert legitimized the Angevin dynasty.

ST. LOUIS OF TOULOUSE

This Gothic portrait was probably painted in 1317, after Louis of Anjou was canonized. Louis is shown as a Franciscan saint crowning his younger brother Robert King of Naples. Simone Martini's masterpiece is now in the Museo Nazionale di Capodimonte *(see pp98–101).*

Robert of Anjou

WHERE TO SEE ANGEVIN AND ARAGONESE NAPLES

Evidence of this period is everywhere in Naples, although successive reconstructions have often obscured the original architectural styles. Rather than civic buildings such as Castel Capuano *(see p81)*, it was the churches that changed the face of the city: Santa Chiara *(see pp66–7)*, San Lorenzo *(see p80)*, San Domenico Maggiore *(see p68)*, and Santa Maria di Donnaregina Vecchia *(see p84)* with its wonderful cycle of frescoes painted by the school of Giotto.

Castel Nuovo, *originally Angevin, also has Aragonese elements (see pp54–5).*

King Roger II

The first great king of Naples is depicted in one of the eight statues placed in the niches of the Palazzo Reale facade in 1888 (see pp50–51).

Bust of Alfonso V

The Spanish Viceroyalty

Masaniello

IN 1503 NAPLES ceased to be an independent kingdom and became a colony of Spain, ruled by a viceroy. The city began to expand, unchecked in the suburbs and beyond the walls. Palazzo Reale was built near Castel Nuovo, and courts assembled at Castel Capuano. With the construction of Via Toledo and the restructuring of Via Chiaia in the mid-1500s, the focus of city development shifted: aristocratic palaces were built along the Riviera and Toledo, and the need to accommodate the troops led to the building of the Quartieri Spagnoli district. New churches and monasteries were built. By now Naples was the largest city in Italy, with the accompanying problems of overcrowding and poverty. A famous figure in this period is Masaniello, the revolutionary who was first considered a hero and then killed by the people who had supported him. Spanish rule came to an end in 1707, when the kingdom of Naples was ceded to Austria.with the Treaty of Utrecht.

GROWTH OF THE CITY

☐ *1500*   ☐ *Today*

Santa Maria del Carmine *(see p73)*, which gave the square its name.

Don Pedro de Toledo
A controversial figure, Don Pedro was viceroy from 1532 to 1553. He promoted new town planning, but also wanted to bring the Inquisition to Naples, triggering a popular revolt.

Masaniello, born Tommaso Aniello in 1620, was an illiterate fisherman.

TIMELINE

1503 Gonzalo Fernández de Cordoba, sent by the King of Spain, enters the city	**1532–52** The first modern town plan of Naples put into effect	**1600** Construction of Palazzo Reale, by Domenico Fontana	The Eruption of Vesuvius by *Philipp Hackert*
			1631 Eruption of Vesuvius

1500			**1600**	

1510 Failure of the viceroy's attempts to bring the Inquisition to Naples	**1536** Via Toledo opened	*Palazzo Reale*	**1606–7** Caravaggio in Naples	**1637–60** Construction of Guglia di San Gennaro to thank the patron saint for saving the city from the Vesuvius eruption

Statue of San Gennaro
The Neapolitans gave their venerated patron saint credit for having stopped the eruption of Vesuvius in 1631.

This memorial stone was to record all the concessions obtained from the viceroy by Masaniello.

MASANIELLO'S UPRISING

This painting by Micco Spadaro depicts Piazza del Carmine *(see p73)* during the 1647 riot. A tax levied on fruit sparked the riot, which rapidly grew into a full-fledged uprising against the aristocracy. However, the attempt was soon crushed; the city's moderates managed to persuade people to rebel against their revolutionary leader, who was killed the same year on July 16.

Giambattista Vico
The famous philosopher and historian, author of La Scienza Nuova (The New Science), *was born in Naples in 1668, the son of a bookseller.*

WHERE TO SEE VICEROYAL NAPLES

The original 17th-century facade of the Palazzo Reale *(see pp50–51)* has changed little over the centuries. The Cappella del Tesoro di San Gennaro *(see pp82–3)* is one of the richest Baroque monuments in Naples. A short distance from the duomo is a small area with a wealth of 17th-century treasures: the Guglia di San Gennaro *(see p81)* and Pio Monte della Misericordia *(see p97)*, which houses the canvas that marked a turning point in 17th-century Neapolitan painting – *The Seven Acts of Mercy* by Caravaggio, who lived in Naples in 1607.

The Certosa di San Martino
(see pp108–11) *was extended and decorated in the late 1500s.*

At San Gregorio Armeno
(see p80), *the cloister is decorated with this fountain.*

1647 Masaniello's uprising

The plague in a painting by Micco Spadaro (detail)

1707 Beginning of Austrian viceroyalty

1723 Pietro Giannone flees to Vienna after publishing his *Civic History of the Kingdom of Naples*, which is banned by the Church

1650

1700

1656 Devastating plague epidemic; Naples loses one-third of population

1688 Earthquake damages most of old city

1701 Failure of the Prince of Macchia's conspiracy in favor of the Austrians

1697 Giambattista Vico becomes professor of rhetoric at Naples University

Bourbon Naples

Portrait of Charles III

IN 1734 THE MUCH-ABUSED kingdom of Naples changed hands once more, with the arrival of the Bourbon king Charles III, who set out to make Naples into a metropolis. He suspended church building in favor of large-scale public works and new industries. He also built a Royal Palace in Caserta modeled on Versailles, which was to be the focal point of an entire city. At the same time, art, antiquities, music, and even the *lazzari* (street urchins) attracted travelers making the Grand Tour. The royal strategy lacked a coherent plan however, and fundamental problems failed to be addressed. Bourbon rule ended in 1860, when Garibaldi arrived in Naples, having won over Sicily and Calabria. In the same year, Naples became part of the new kingdom of Italy.

GROWTH OF THE CITY

▨ *1700*   ☐ *Today*

The Palace of Capodimonte

Charles III's Porcelain
The king was so proud of his porcelain factory that when he returned to Spain, he closed it down and took his best craftsmen with him.

The Beheading of Ettore Carafa
This relief in the Museo di San Martino depicts the execution of one of the martyrs of the Parthenopean Republic on August 17, 1799.

Antonio Genovesi (1713–69)
A leading figure in the Neapolitan Enlightenment movement, he became the first professor of political economics in Italy in 1754.

TIMELINE

Statuette found in Herculaneum

1738 Beginning of excavations at Herculaneum

Ancient finds at Herculaneum transferred to Palazzo degli Studi

1734 Under Charles III Naples becomes an independent kingdom again

1740 Church building suspended

1759 Charles III returns to Spain, his son Ferdinand becomes king

1777 The university moves to the Jesuit College, now a banished society. Ferdinando Fuga turns Palazzo degli Studi into a museum

Cappella di San Gennaro
19th-century Neapolitan painting often featured landscapes and picturesque settings – as seen in this work by Gigante (1806–76), showing the chapel of San Gennaro – as well as the rural scenes of Palizzi (1818–99) and the realism of Morelli (1826–1901).

THE DUKE OF NOJA'S MAP
This was the first modern relief map, the work of Duke Giovanni Carafa di Noja in 1775. The map shows the full extent of the city of Naples and the monumental buildings in the newly developed districts. In this detail the impressive Royal Palace of Capodimonte dominates the city skyline.

Naples appears as a chaotic muddle of buildings here.

WHERE TO SEE BOURBON NAPLES
The most important architectural achievements of the Bourbons are the Teatro San Carlo *(see p53)*, the Palace of Capodimonte *(see pp98–101)* and the Albergo dei Poveri *(see p97)*. Urban projects such as the Foro Carolino and the Villa Reale at Chiaia also date from the Bourbon period. The passion for antiquity inspired collecting and the setting up of the Museo Archeologico *(see pp86–9)*. But Bourbon influence is primarily seen outside the city, where kings built hunting lodges as well as royal palaces such as Caserta *(see pp160–61)*.

The Bourbon court *out hunting in a painting by Jakob Philipp Hackert (1783)*

The Naples-Portici Railway
The first Italian railroad was inaugurated in 1839. The Bayard locomotive took 9 minutes 30 seconds to travel about 7.5 km (4.5 miles). This painting by Salvatore Fergola is kept in the palace at Caserta.

1806 Napoleon gives the role of king of Naples to his brother Joseph Bonaparte

1808 Bonaparte goes to Spain and is replaced by Joachim Murat. The French promote great public works and administrative reforms

1848 Popular revolt restores constitution but is annulled by Parliament in 1849

Giuseppe Garibaldi

1799 Birth of Neapolitan Republic, overthrown six months later by the counterrevolution. Its leaders are executed in Piazza Mercato

1820 Constitution granted but is repealed the following year

1815 Murat executed at Pizzo Calabro. Ferdinand returns to throne as King of the Two Sicilies

1839 First railroad in Italy, Naples–Portici, inaugurated

1860 Garibaldi enters city on October 21; after plebiscite Naples becomes part of newly united Kingdom of Italy

Naples after Unification

The philosopher Benedetto Croce

IN A CROWDED, DENSELY POPULATED CITY, the 1884 cholera epidemic brought ancient problems to a head. An attempt to face them was made with the Urban Renewal Plan. Slum clearance was carried out around the port and new districts were created in the center and toward the hills. However, the Plan failed to solve many basic problems, work took much longer than expected, and triggered a wave of corruption. The Fascist regime contented itself with a new series of public works and the creation of more built-up areas. A leading local figure of the time was the philosopher Benedetto Croce, one of the few Italian intellectuals who openly opposed Fascism.

GROWTH OF THE CITY

☐ *1850*   ☐ *Today*

THE ILVA STEELWORKS IN BAGNOLI

This plant, later known as Italsider, was built near the beach and the ancient hot springs in 1907 *(see p132)*. Renovated for the last time in 1987 and now abandoned, it has become a symbol of modern development carried out with total disregard for the natural context and scenic beauty of the area.

Santa Chiara
Restoration of Santa Chiara was carried out after the 1943 fire, recreating its presumed original appearance.

Matilde Serao (1856–1927)
"Naples must be gutted" declared the prominent author on the eve of the Renewal Plan. A few years later, disappointed by the results, she described Corso Umberto I as a "screen" concealing old and new misery.

TIMELINE

The Mount Vesuvius funicular

1880 Inauguration of Vesuvius funicular, which inspires the famous song *Funiculì Funiculà*

1891 First city funicular connecting Vomero with center becomes operative

1850	1880	1890

1868 Via Duomo begun with first city demolition and finished in late 1800s as part of Urban Renewal Plan

1885 Special law for Urban Renewal Plan: demolition of slum areas begins

1884 Cholera epidemic

The Rettifilo
This eclectic and stately avenue, officially called Corso Umberto I and built after the Urban Renewal projects ended, is a good example of late 19th-century bourgeois Naples.

WHERE TO SEE POST-UNIFICATION NAPLES

The Caffè Gambrinus *(see p52)* was the haunt of Italian avant-garde artists, like the Futurists, as well as such illustrious visitors as Oscar Wilde. During the Urban Renewal period that changed the face of civic Naples, the Art Nouveau style prevailed in the new residential districts and the small villas in Chiaia *(see pp112–19)* and Vomero *(see pp102–11)*. Monumental Fascist architecture is represented by the Palazzo delle Poste e Telegrafi *(see p57)* and the Stazione Marittima (the port). Via Toledo *(see p53)* boasts an important Novecento-style building constructed in 1939 to house the main offices of the Banco di Napoli.

The Caffè Gambrinus *was popular in the early 1900s.*

The Mostra delle Terre d'Oltremare
This huge exhibition and recreational complex was one of the Fascist regime's most notable architectural achievements. Work on the site began in 1937 after the demolition of the Fuorigrotta quarter.

1901 Saredo judicial inquiry reveals government–Camorra rapport

1925–7 Naples incorporates surrounding towns, formerly independent

1940 Mostra delle Terre d'Oltremare, a huge exhibition, recreational, and sports complex built by the Fascist regime

Entrance to Mostra d'Oltremare

1900	1920	1945

Benito Mussolini

1899 First stretch of Cumana railroad built

1922 On October 24, Fascists meet in Naples on eve of "March on Rome"

1928–41 Rione Carità district replaces old San Giuseppe quarter

1944 Last eruption of Vesuvius

1943 *"Quattro giornate"* uprising: Germans driven out of Naples

Present-day Naples

Eduardo De Filippo

AT THE END of World War II the city had to cope with the appalling damage inflicted by all the bombardments. The 1950s and 1960s were marked by the large-scale, indiscriminate building activity promoted by politicians who looked only for short-term gain. The closing down of some large factories in the 1980s aggravated the acute unemployment problem. However, Naples has always distinguished itself by its irrepressible vitality and creativity, especially in the fields of music and theater. Today the city is rediscovering its past, and there is a new commitment to city regeneration, as well as a resurgence of cultural programs.

GROWTH OF THE CITY

◼ *1945*   ☐ *Today*

Mount Vesuvius
This work by Andy Warhol was produced in 1985 for an exhibition held at the Museo di Capodimonte, where the canvas is now on display. It is the American artist's tribute to the most recurrent artistic motif relating to Naples – an erupting Vesuvius.

San Paolo Stadium
Built in the 1960s, this soccer stadium has a seating capacity of 80,000. Famous players for Naples include Dino Zoff and Diego Maradona.

TIMELINE

1945 Eduardo De Filippo writes *Napoli milionaria*. Town council approves reconstruction project

1949 Curzio Malaparte's novel *La Pelle*, set in Naples, causes a scandal with its raw descriptions

1952 Shipowner Achille Lauro, leader of the monarchist party, becomes mayor. Period of building speculation begins

1950

1960

1962 Left of center coalition governs city

1963 Francesco Rosi directs film *Hands over the City (see p36)*

Achille Lauro

Posillipo Today
Among the many examples of reckless building in Naples, Posillipo is one of the most tragic. The hill, known the world over for its ancient history and lovely scenery, has been defaced by unchecked and unscrupulous development.

Pedestrian avenue

Skyscrapers are a novelty in Neapolitan architecture.

CENTRO DIREZIONALE
This district of futuristic administrative office buildings in the heart of the city, near the central train station, is an example of "rational" modernization. The original plan dates from the 1960s, but in 1982 the famous Japanese architect Kenzo Tange began a new design. The layout of the area allows traffic, which runs along underground streets, to be separated from pedestrians.

The underground roads are an attempt to solve serious traffic problems.

Montagna di Sale
Mimmo Paladino's Salt Mountain was installed in Piazza del Plebiscito for New Year's Day 1996. The square, restored for the G7 summit and now a pedestrian zone, has become a symbol of the new Naples.

1975 Inauguration of detour road for fast traffic at edge of old town	**1982** The new Via Marittima, planned in the early postwar period, is finally completed. Kenzo Tange redesigns the Centro Direzionale	**1995–6** Mimmo Paladino's temporary sculpture *Montagna di Sale* is placed in Piazza del Plebiscito
1970	**1980**	**1990**
1972 Town-planning regulations (still partly in force) protect historic old town, considered a cultural heritage	**1980** The earthquake in Campania and Basilicata also causes damage in Naples. Reconstruction includes a plan to revive the outskirts	**1994** G7 summit opens in July in Naples. First stage of hill metro becomes operative

NAPLES AT A GLANCE

APLES IS FILLED with evidence of many centuries of occupation blended into the fabric of the present-day city. This complex heritage, from ancient Greeks and Romans to the dukes, kings and queens of the Middle Ages and beyond, has contributed to a rich store of galleries and museums, ancient amphitheaters and ruins, as well as churches, monasteries, royal palaces, and monuments. While the *Area by Area* section *(pp45–125)* describes the various places of interest in detail, the following ten pages will provide some background and cultural context. Each corner of Naples has something different to offer, but below is a selection of attractions that no visitor to the city should miss.

NAPLES' TOP TOURIST ATTRACTIONS

Castel Nuovo *See pp54–5*

Santa Chiara *See pp66–7*

Museo di Capodimonte
See pp98–101

Certosa di San Martino *See pp108–11*

Mergellina *See p119*

Castel dell'Ovo *See p116*

Museo Archeologico Nazionale
See pp86–9

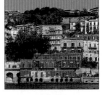

Posillipo
See pp120–25

◁ The waterfront with its historic hotels, Castel dell'Ovo and the Borgo Marinaro

Naples and the Bay

The Faraglioni of Capri

FORMED BY AN IMMENSE CRATER, the Bay of Naples is both sheltered and exposed: sheltered by the curve of hills to the east, which create a natural semicircular amphitheater, but open to the sea. The zone is volcanic, shaped by cones and craters of all ages, some submerged, some still bubbling with thermal springs and jets of steam. Now that Vesuvius is quiet (the last smoke trail was seen in 1944), the most active crater in the region is the Solfatara at Pozzuoli *(see p133)*. The living, breathing quality of the land led Homer to choose the coastline as the setting for parts of the Odyssey. Chaotic development along the coast has not deterred visitors from seeking out and appreciating the beauty of the bay.

Ischia has small, sandy beaches that are a great tourist attraction.

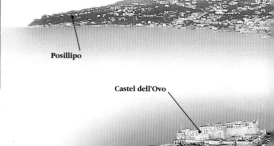

Posillipo

Castel dell'Ovo

Gaiola *is the largest of the three islands facing the Gaiola quarter. The coastline is rocky and precipitous with natural caves.*

THE BAY OF NAPLES

Mount Vesuvius stands guard over a bay that owes its beauty and characteristic curves to the violent and often deadly explosions of a series of volcanoes. The conical shape of Monte Epomeo on Ischia still shows its volcanic origin; one submerged crater now serves as the port of Ischia, and hot springs abound. Capri, once joined to the mainland, is geologically an extension of the Sorrento peninsula; time has carved beautiful caves along the island's precipitous coastline. Just beyond Punta Campanella are islands known to Homer as the home of the Sirens.

THE BAY FROM MERGELLINA

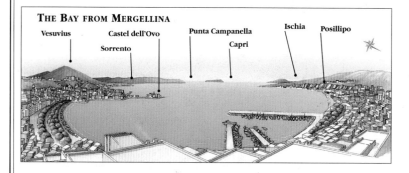

Vesuvius   **Castel dell'Ovo**   **Punta Campanella**   **Ischia**   **Posillipo**

Sorrento   **Capri**

The port of Naples, once a disembarkation point for transatlantic ships, is now the center of intense ship, ferry, and hydrofoil traffic for tourists along the coast and to the islands of Capri, Ischia, and Procida. The Angioino wharf is also important commercially.

The fertility of the soil in Naples was proverbial in ancient times. To this day you can still find unexpected pockets of terrace cultivation in built-up areas.

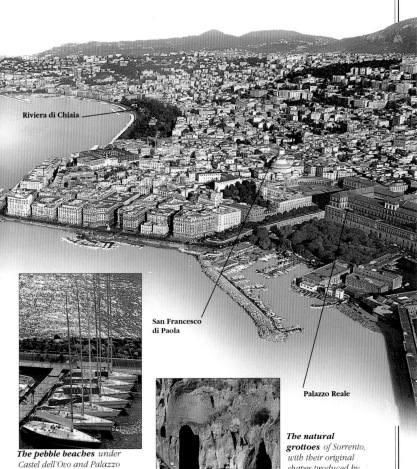

Riviera di Chiaia

San Francesco di Paola

Palazzo Reale

The pebble beaches under Castel dell'Ovo and Palazzo Reale serve as small marinas for all kinds of boats, especially leisure craft.

The natural grottoes of Sorrento, with their original shapes produced by water erosion, are a characteristic feature of the southern stretch of the bay.

The Architecture of Naples

O NE FEATURE of the architecture of Naples is the way in which traces of various epochs and styles can be seen in one short section of a street, from Roman foundations and remains to the turn-of-the-century galleria made of iron and glass. Little remainsof Naples' Greek heritage, yet in the heart of the city you can still discern the regular grid layout adopted in 5th-century BC Neapolis: the three main streets going east–west – present-day Via Anticaglia *(see p84)*, Via Tribunali *(see pp76–7)*, and Via San Biagio dei Librai – and the north–south roads that intersect them at right angles. Along the waterfront (Lungomare) and the Riviera di Chiaia, more modern buildings can be found, elegant palazzi alternating with villas and splendid luxury hotels.

The ancient grid layout of Neapolis (red lines) over a plan of the modern city

VIA FORIA

Caserma Garibaldi

VIA DUOMO

1956–7

RIVIERA DI CHIAIA

The wide, elegant Riviera di Chiaia, flanked by fine buildings, mostly dating from the 18th and 19th centuries

1940–41

LUNGOMARE

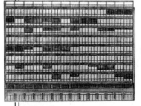

1955–6

College of Business Administration, 1934

Hotel Royal, 1956

A Multilayered City

San Lorenzo Maggiore *(see p80)* is one example of a layered building. Remains of the ancient city are visible under the monastery. The church itself is also the result of a series of reconstructions; the Angevin basilica, built over the ruins of a 6th-century church, was completely rebuilt in the 1700s and then restored to its original medieval state in the last century. The 18th-century facade still has the original 14th-century wooden doorway.

Greco-Roman remains

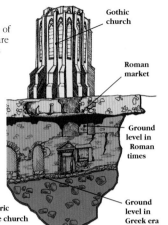

Gothic church

Roman market

Ground level in Roman times

Ground level in Greek era

The historic layers of the church

The Galleria Principe di Napoli, built in 1883, the oldest galleria in Naples

San Giuseppe a Chiaia, dating from 1666–73

The Neo-Classical Villa Pignatelli, 1826, designed by Pietro Valente, now a museum *(see p118)*

Hotel Continental

Hotel Vesuvio (reconstruction), 1948

Santa Lucia, 1902

Writers and Artists in Naples

Portrait of Virgil

THE BEAUTY OF THE BAY OF NAPLES and the fascination with Vesuvius have inspired writers and painters for hundreds of years. The Greeks wove stories around the landscape, seeing in it a variety of mythological creatures; volcanic activity was regarded as the work of the gods. The poet Virgil so loved Naples that he spent his last years there while writing the *Georgics* and the *Aeneid*. The city's rich classical inheritance again attracted travelers with the advent of the Grand Tour, over 17 centuries later, when no young man could be considered well educated without a visit to Italy.

"Virgil's tomb" *(see p119)*

FROM CLASSICAL WRITERS TO THE RENAISSANCE

BEFORE THE eruption of Vesuvius in AD 79, the volcano had been quiet for 1,200 years, but the inhabitants were nonetheless aware of the living nature of the land. In Greek myth, the Olympian gods had buried defeated giants in the Phlegraean Fields; the ground was said to stir if they moved. Pliny the Elder, author of the *Naturalis Historia*, lost his life at Pompeii in AD 79; his insatiable curiosity tempted him to go closer to the volcano, and he was suffocated by the fumes. His nephew Pliny the Younger was an eyewitness.

The Renaissance brought a revival of interest in Greek and Latin culture. In the 14th century the great lyric poet and scholar Petrarch was one of many writers, artists, and architects attracted to the court of Robert of Anjou. Boccaccio and Giotto were also at the court at this time. Torquato Tasso, a native of Sorrento, worked on his epic poetry at the monastery of Monteoliveto at the end of the 1500s.

Petrarch

TRAVELERS AND THE GRAND TOUR

THE GRAND TOUR first became a custom in the 16th century and had become an English fashion by the 18th century. Young aristocrats were expected to study Europe's classical past to complete their education. The route took in the main classical sites and focused on Rome and Naples as the highlights of the trip. Sir William Hamilton, envoy to Naples from 1764, entertained Grand Tour travelers at the embassy. An archaeologist and collector as well as a diplomat, his collections now form part of the classical antiquities section at the

British Museum in London. (Sir William's wife, Emma, was another source of attraction at the embassy; she became notorious as the mistress of Nelson.)

In 1775 Goethe visited the city with the painter Tischbein and was overwhelmed. He later wrote: "One may write or paint as much as one likes, but this place, the shore, the bay, Vesuvius, the citadels, the villas, everything, defies description."

Tischbein, *Goethe in the Country* **(Museo di San Martino)**

Goethe was not the only visitor to produce a book *(Italian Journey)* from his travels. Classical Italy inspired numerous diaries and descriptions, and guidebook writing began to flourish. When excavations began at Herculaneum in 1711 and at Pompeii in 1733, this only added to the enormous appeal of this part of Southern Italy.

Catel, *Death of Tasso* **(San Martino Museum)**

ROMANTIC NAPLES

THE 1800s brought writers and artists from all over Europe to Naples. The French writer Stendhal, who regarded Italy as his adopted country, left Naples in 1817 swearing he would never be able to forget Toledo and the Teatro San Carlo, the glories of the "most beautiful city in the universe." In 1812, another French writer, Alphonse de Lamartine, recalled his experiences of Naples in the *Gulf of Baia* and in *Graziella*, which featured a girl from Procida.

In the field of classical music, Rossini's *Othello* was performed at the Teatro San Carlo, the composer being forced to work at breakneck speed by his opera impresario friend Barbaja. Two of Rossini's operas had their world premieres in Naples. *Mosè in Egitto* (1818) was written for the opera singer Isabella Colbran, **Gioacchino** later to be Rossini's **Rossini** wife. *La Donna del Lago* (1819) was based on Sir Walter Scott's romantic poem *The Lady of the Lake*; the role of Ellen was written for Colbran. Scott's work was also the inspiration for Donizetti's *Lucia di Lammermoor*, first performed at the Teatro San Carlo in 1835.

Under Bourbon rule, Naples became a grand and very sophisticated place for those who could afford luxury. In 1828 the American author James Fenimore Cooper was so taken by the city that he managed to find good qualities even in its negative aspects. In his description of the area around Castel Nuovo, he declares: "This was the area of the *lazzaroni*; and it is no easy task to find lovelier or happier vagabonds than the ones here."

The Teatro San Carlo *(see p53)*, which began its great tradition in the romantic era with world premieres of Rossini and Donizetti operas

Foreign artists were drawn to the city by its beauty. In 1816 the Dutch landscape painter Anton Pitloo set up a private art academy, influencing a group of young local artists who later founded the Posillipo school of landscape painting. In 1825 Sylvester Scedrin, another landscape painter, came from St. Petersburg to work here. Charles Dickens paid a long visit to Italy in 1844, which resulted in a book, *Pictures from Italy*. He also distilled his experiences into lively anecdotes for the benefit of the readers of the *Daily News*. The end of Bourbon rule and the cholera epidemic of 1884 brought about a decline in the appeal of Naples. Visitors could not fail to be enchanted by Naples and the bay, but by degrees the city became only a stopping point for visitors heading for Pompeii or the temples of Paestum.

symbol of the destructive power of nature. He had a love/hate relationship with Naples, liking some aspects but mistrustful of the Neapolitans: "Scoundrels and buffoons, both noblemen and plebeians, all of them thieves and wretched barons most worthy of the Spanish and the gallows."

More recently, the Neapolitan writer Matilde Serao depicted the hectic life of Naples in *Il Paese di Cuccagna* (1891), a vividly written account of the hopes and passions inspired by the lottery. Fellow Neapolitan author Curzio Malaparte looks at the city in *La Pelle* (1948): "Naples is the most mysterious city in Europe. It is the only city of the ancient world that has not perished. …It is not a city: it is a world – the ancient pre-Christian world – which has survived intact on the surface of the modern world."

TO THE TWENTIETH CENTURY

THE ROMANTIC POET Leopardi (1798–1837) spent the last years of his life in Naples. In his poem *La Ginestra*, he makes the "destroyer Vesuvius" the

Portrait of Giacomo Leopardi

Naples and the Arts

Silent movie stars of 1914

NAPLES WAS FAMOUS in the 19th century for its spectacular operas and the emotional power of its popular songs. In more recent times, Neapolitan performers such as Eduardo De Filippo, Totò, and Sophia Loren, have all gained worldwide acclaim. The city is not content to dwell on past glories. The arts scene is very much alive, with creative experiments ranging from modern variations on the melodramatic *sceneggiata* to the new films of Mario Martone, and from the traditional melodies of Roberto Murolo to rock and rap.

Eduardo De Filippo and Totò

A scene from *The Gold of Naples*

MOVIES

ONE OF THE FIRST film companies in Italy, Lombardo Film, was founded in the early 1900s in the Vomero district of Naples. However, the first major film to be produced in Naples was probably *Assunta Spina* (1915), based on a novel by Salvatore di Giacomo. In its most memorable scene, the heroine, played by Francesca Bertini, has her face slashed while walking in the Mergellina quarter. Many of the silent films made in this period were based on stories of everyday life, often acted by locals

More familiar are the movies made in the 1950s, many featuring famous songs or plots based on the traditional melodrama of the *sceneggiata*. Most of these were fairly lightweight, but they did include the occasional masterpiece, such as Eduardo De

Filippo's *Napoli Milionaria* (1950). Two other notable exceptions were *Un Turco Napoletano* (1953) starring the great comic actor Totò, and De Sica's *The Gold of Naples* (1954) with Sophia Loren. Ten years later, the director De Sica and Sophia Loren collaborated once again in *Marriage Italian Style*, an adaptation of one of Eduardo De Filippo's best-loved stage plays, *Filumena Marturano*. For her services to Italian film for more than five decades, Sophia Loren was dubbed Knight of the Italian Republic in March 1997.

Many of Italy's greatest film directors have been inspired to communicate their personal impressions of Naples. The portrait of the city in Roberto Rossellini's *Viaggio in Italia* (1953) is unsentimental. In Francesco Rosi's *Mani sulla Città*, the Neapolitan director attacks the corrupt

links between the city's politicians and developers. This marked an awareness of social reality in the 1960s. This movie won first prize at the 1963 Venice Film Festival. Opposing views of Naples can be seen in Nanni Loy's mysterious *Mi manda Picone* (1983) and Ettore Scola's sunny, life-enhancing *Maccheroni* (1985). Then

Loren and Mastroianni in *Marriage Italian Style* (1964)

there are the movies of the late actor/director Massimo Troisi. The young man in *Ricomincio da Tre* finds it impossible to live a normal life away from Naples; he is always made to feel an "emigrant." Notable recent movies include Mario Martone's *L'Amore Molesto*, in which the city, for all its faults, still exerts a powerful pull on those who want to leave, and Antonio Capuano's *Pianese Nunzio, 14 Anni a Maggio*, shown at the 1996 Venice Film Festival.

Massimo Troisi on the set of *Ricomincio da Tre* (1980)

OPERA AND THEATER

ENTERTAINMENT in Naples has always catered to a broad range of tastes. The opera season at the San Carlo Theater *(see p35, p53)* is very popular, but the theater has a wider appeal, thanks to the great tradition of plays in Neapolitan dialect and the comic talents of native actors such as Eduardo Scarpetta (1853–1924), Totò (1898–1967), and Eduardo De Filippo (1900–84). De Filippo combined the roles of actor, manager, and play-wright. His brilliant comedies, which usually revolve around

THE SCENEGGIATA

The *sceneggiata*, or popular Neapolitan melodrama, dates from the end of the 19th century With the simplest of plots and characters crudely drawn in black and white, it was a grotesque mixture of tragedy and farce; audiences cheered the hero and booed the villain. Music played an important part in the show, and there was always a rousing title song, the *pezzo forte*. The genre was revived

Mario Merola

in the 1970s. The modern version is more sophisticated but has perhaps lost a little of the original flavor. Today, the leading exponent of the *sceneggiata* is Mario Merola.

Eduardo De Filippo on stage

the apparently petty con-cerns of family life, were performed by his famous family troupe.

The works of the actor and playwright Raffaele Viviani (1888–1950) also portray daily Neapolitan life with irony as well as affection, often with the use of local dialect.

Experimental theater has been active in Naples since the establishment of the "Falso Movimento" in 1979. Its founders are now involved in the Teatri Uniti, staging avant-garde plays at the Teatro Nuovo and the Galleria Toledo, where the leading actors are Enzo Moscato and Tonino Taiuti.

NEAPOLITAN SONGS

FOR MANY, the spirit of Naples is embodied by the sound of Neapolitan songs, overflowing with powerful expressions of love, longing, and melancholy, and filled with images of the sun and the sea. The songs' romantic melodies have always had a profound influence on the development of Italian music and are familiar the world over through the recordings made by Enrico Caruso and other great tenors.

Naturally, the best-known songs are the classics, first and foremost O Sole Mio, composed in 1898 and still as popular as ever.

Present-day masters of the tradition include Sergio Bruni, famous for his song *Carmela*, and Roberto Murolo, who is known respectfully as the "singers' singer." Their work is true to the spirit of Neapolitan songs but is fresh and original rather than mere pastiche.

Other less well-known traditional forms include the *macchietta* (a comic song routine) and *tammorriate* (dances accompanied by songs). These both enjoyed a revival in the 1970s. There is also an extensive repertoire of so-called "modern-traditional" songs. These are virtually unknown outside Naples but are extremely popular with the locals and sometimes

Roberto Murolo

sung by famous performers such as Nino D'Angelo.

Some composers graft Neapolitan song onto other musical forms such as jazz, blues, rock, and even rap. Among the more successful experiments of this kind are Eugenio Bennato's "pop" songs, the delicate melodies of Eduardo De Crescenzo, and the poetic accounts of everyday life by Pino Daniele, who has achieved fame outside Naples as well. The Almamegretta group *(see p197)* set their songs in Neapolitan dialect to typical British electronic music.

Pino Daniele

Symbols of the City

NAPLES IS A CITY that defies rational explanation, yet visitors have always found a wealth of sights and sounds that sum up aspects of its character. Some are positive: the beauty of the bay, the romantic melodies of Neapolitan songs, the craftsmanship of the church decorations. Others are quite the opposite. Northern Europeans (and Northern Italians) are often shocked by the contrast between the city's general air of *dolce far niente* and its widespread poverty and superstition. All of these things have become clichés, making it even harder to distinguish the true nature of Naples.

The pazzariello and his band

Street life: colorful stalls in a city market

FIRST IMPRESSIONS

NAPLES HAS ALWAYS been famous for the vivacity of its alleyways, streets, and squares. The zest for life in the Toledo district amazed foreign visitors such as Goethe and Stendhal *(see pp34–5)*. The *lazzaroni* (ruffians) lounging around on street corners made such a strong impression on foreign visitors to Naples in the 18th and 19th centuries that they became synonymous with the city. Ferdinand I, King of the Two Sicilies from 1759 to 1825, was even nicknamed the *Re Lazzarone* (King of the Ruffians).

Old water-seller's marble stand

Today, many people are struck by the ubiquitous street peddlers. There have been many attempts to regulate their activities, but most have come to nothing.

THE WATER-SELLER

THE NEAPOLITAN water-seller *(l'acquaiolo)* was once a very common sight on the streets of the city, offering refreshing drinks to passersby on torrid summer afternoons. The water often came from the sulfurous springs of Chiatamone, which used to rise near the church of Santa Lucia *(see p116).* It was kept cool in clay jugs, known as *mummere*. If you paid extra, you could have lemon or orange juice added to make a *spremuta*. In some parts of the old city you can still spot a *banco dell'acqua*, or water stand, with its solid marble counter and decorative citrus fruit. Most have been modernized by the addition of stainless steel, and they now sell cans of Coca-Cola as well as traditional drinks.

THE PAZZARIELLO

ON RARE OCCASIONS you may still come across a curious figure dressed in an old-fashioned military uniform, wielding a long ceremonial baton with a gold pommel at one end and leading a small marching band. The amusing and immensely popular figure of the *pazzariello* was originally a town crier, but his duties were later extended to include leading parades on local feast days and advertising goods for sale in a new shop. The *pazzariello* was immortalized by Totò in Vittorio De Sica's film *The Gold of Naples (see p36).*

THE SCUGNIZZO

THE STEREOTYPE of the cheeky, but basically good, street urchin plays a major part in the folklore of the city. Living by his wits, ready to run errands for anyone who would give him money or food, he made an indelible impression on the American troops based in Naples during World War II. The true *scugnizzo* no longer really exists. Yet one can perhaps sense his streetwise spirit in the many small boys who now zip around the city on mopeds.

A scugnizzo

PULCINELLA

THE CHARACTER of Pulcinella, stupid, yet at the same time cunning, dogged by chronic bad luck and always hungry, is the stock comic figure of a Neapolitan. One can never be quite sure, as the philosopher Benedetto Croce remarked, whether he represents a faithful portrait, a caricature, or an ideal to which Neapolitans aspire. Either as a puppet (he was the model for the English Mr. Punch) or in the theater, Pulcinella has always made people laugh. With his crazy schemes, wild gramaces, and the comic effects of his permanently empty stomach, he per-sonifies the city's age-old scourge of famine.

The character of Pulcinella, as we know him today, seems to have first appeared in about 1600, but he may well have had a Classical ancestor in the equally hungry Macchus, a character from the ancient farces of Atella, a town northeast of Naples.

Pulcinella

The greatest interpreters of the role within living memory were naturally the two actors who most fully represented the spirit of Naples – Eduardo De Filippo and Totò (see pp36–7). Their performances were especially poignant in the period of famine during and after World War II.

THE CHRISTMAS CRECHE

NOBODY KNOWS when the custom of representing the nativity of Christ in a sculpted tableau began. One of the earliest examples is the 13th-century sculpture by Arnolfo di Cambio at the Basilica of Santa Maria Maggiore in Rome, but the tradition may well be much older. In Naples it became such an important feature of the Christmas celebrations that people came to think

Detail of the creche scene at the Museo di San Martino (see p111)

of the creche (il presepe) as a Neapolitan institution. The traditional local craftsmen, who, in many cases, have produced magnificent works of art (see p111), do not limit themselves to the central figures of the Nativity grouped around the baby Jesus in the manger. The scene expands to become a miniature representation of the whole of Naples, with all its characteristic sights and personalities. Look at the figures in a modern creche scene and you may spot Pulcinella, Totò or even the current mayor of Naples, Antonio Bassolino.

THE LOTTERY

THE DRAWING of the lottery, in which a blindfolded child extracts the winning numbers, has remained unchanged, but the lottery is not quite the force it once was. Founded by Ferdinand I

in 1774, il lotto can be said, without exaggeration, to have ruled the lives of many 19th-century Neapolitans. It is still very popular; La Smorfia, a book that claims to interpret dreams and events to help you choose the winning numbers, has been reprinted many times (see p71).

PIZZA AND PASTA

Ingredients for the topping of a pizza Margherita

THE GASTRONOMIC symbols of Naples, pizza and pasta, were not always the city's staple foods. Before the population explosion of the 1600s, the poor lived mainly on cabbage and other vegetables. These were then replaced as the staple food by wheat flour, which was less perishable, and the Neapolitans acquired the nickname "macaroni eaters."

Pizza, in its present form, dates from the end of the 18th century. It may not have been a Neapolitan invention, but it was Naples that gave the world the napoletana and the Margherita (see p180), its two most enduring varieties.

Period print showing the traditional lottery-drawing ceremony

NAPLES THROUGH THE YEAR

THERE IS NO SINGLE ideal season for visiting Naples; the temperate climate means a pleasant stay at any time of year. However, every season has its particular attractions. In May, an increased number of churches and monuments are open to the public; while July and August are perfect for the beach. The miracle of the city's patron saint, San Gennaro, is celebrated in May and September. In December, local craftsmen create traditional Christmas scenes. In the outlying areas, old traditions, with processions at sea and feasts celebrated in historical costume, are still vital to local life.

SPRING

THE MILD SPRING climate is perfect for enjoying drinks at an outdoor café, walking around the town center, or visiting the surrounding countryside, which is relatively uncrowded during this season compared with summertime. At Easter it may be warm enough to swim in the sea, although traditionally May 1 marks the beginning of the swimming season. The months of March and April can be unsettled, and a brief spell of fine weather may be interrupted by a cold snap or even hailstorms. According to a local proverb, the weather experienced in Naples on April 4 will continue for the following 40 days.

San Giuseppe's day *zeppole*

MARCH

Feast of San Giuseppe (March 19). A festival is held in Via Medina, with *zeppole* (doughnuts) in every bar, bakery, and home. At one time the festival marked the change from winter clothes to the new spring wardrobe.

EASTER

In many outlying districts and in some quarters of Naples there are **Good Friday** processions. One of the most

Madonna dell'Arco, Easter Monday

interesting takes place on the island of Procida. The procession of priests and parishioners leaves at dawn from the top of Terra Murata and ends up at Marina Grande.

Easter Monday, or "Pasquetta," is the day for outings, when the whole family goes for a meal in a trattoria. For the more traditional, a ceremony is held at the sanctuary of Madonna dell'Arco, near Sant'Anastasia, 15 km (9 miles) east of the city. Barefooted men, *fuijenti*, ask for alms, and a statue of the Madonna is carried on flower-laden carts into the countryside. Here the occasion turns into a lively "pagan" feast.

Trotting races at the Agnano racetrack

APRIL

The Agnano racetrack hosts trotting races for the **Gran Premio della Lotteria di Agnano** in April. Dog races are held all year round at the Cinodromo.

MAY

One of the two annual celebrations of the miracle of **San Gennaro** *(see p83)* takes place on the first Sunday in May. The procession starts off at the cathedral (*duomo*), with the statue of San Gennaro, the patron saint of Naples, being carried from the church. The procession is known locally as the *Inghirlandata* (garlanding) because it was traditionally accompanied by flowered decorations, and the faithful

The *Inghirlandata* ceremony

would throw rose petals over the statue of the saint.

During May visitors can make the most of the **Maggio dei Monumenti**, when buildings and churches that are normally closed are open to the public. The program, also known as *Napoli Porte Aperte*, was started in 1992 by the Fondazione Napoli '99. Since 1995 it has been sponsored by the Naples city council to encourage the "rediscovery" of historic Naples. May is also the month of the **Vela Longa** regatta, open to any type of sailboat.

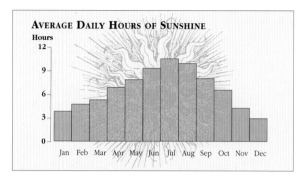

AVERAGE DAILY HOURS OF SUNSHINE

Hours

Jan Feb Mar Apr May Jun Jul Aug Sep Oct Nov Dec

Sunshine Hours
*Naples is famous for
its light. The longest
days fall in June,
when the midday
heat can be intense.
In autumn the sun
can still be quite hot,
particularly in the
middle of the day.*

The Vela Longa regatta is held every May

SUMMER

THIS SEASON can be quite
muggy, especially in July,
when the temperature sometimes exceeds 40°C (104°F).
However, after mid-August
the heat is sometimes interrupted by a brief, heavy, and
often violent thunderstorm,
known all along the coast as
the *tropea*.

Summer nights in the city
can be spent at the **Estate a
Napoli** festival, which, from
late July to September,
features various performance
art events and movies. The
week of the Assumption, or
Ferragosto (Aug 15), is ideal
for those who prefer a semi-
deserted, if hot, city.

Outside Naples, interesting
cultural events are held at the
Pompeii amphitheater *(see
p144)*, and the Vesuvian villas
(see p136) also host various
events. For music lovers,
there are the **Estate Musicale
Sorrentina** at Sorrento and
the well-known **Festival
Internazionale**, which takes
place at Ravello *(see p198)*.

JUNE

The feast of **San Giovanni**
(Jun 24), linked to the summer
solstice, was once celebrated
with magicians and feasting,
and night swimming. Out in
the countryside people still
gather walnuts to make the
traditional walnut liqueur
called *nocino*, which will be
ready by late autumn.

From late June to mid-July,
the Mostra d'Oltremare *(see
p25)* features the **Fiera della
Casa**, when furniture, interior
furnishings, and local handicrafts are on sale or simply
on display. The *fiera* gives
you the chance to join the
busy crowds and makes a
change from sightseeing.

JULY

Piazza Mercato *(see p73)*
plays host to the feast of the
Madonna del Carmine (Jul
16), an ancient tradition. The
Madonna Bruna is kept inside
the church of Santa Maria del
Carmine: according to legend
she miraculously saved the
bell tower from a fire.

Fireworks are used to reenact
the miracle wrought by the
Madonna; the ceremony ends
with the so-called "burning"
of the bell tower.

Sant'Anna is celebrated in
Ischia on July 26 with a night
procession of illuminated
boats and a fireworks display.

AUGUST

August is the traditional
vacation month in Italy, and
you may find many of the
city restaurants closed until
September. Throughout the
region, the traditional "fast"
held on the Eve of the
Assumption (the night of
August 14-15) is helped
along by huge servings of
watermelon, eaten on the
beach in the moonlight. At
Positano, a ceremony in
period costume celebrates
the landing of the Saracens.

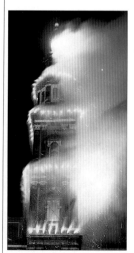

Feast of the Madonna del Carmine

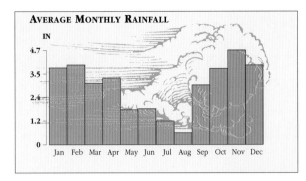

AVERAGE MONTHLY RAINFALL

IN											
Jan	Feb	Mar	Apr	May	Jun	Jul	Aug	Sep	Oct	Nov	Dec

(scale: 0, 1.2, 2.4, 3.5, 4.7)

Rainfall
The wettest months of the year are November and February. The rainfall does not last for long, but it comes in brief, violent downpours. The driest month is August, but this can also be interrupted by heavy thunderstorms near the end of the month.

AUTUMN

AUTUMN IN NAPLES is quite mild; September and October are perfect for outings and long hikes in the countryside. The sea is warm enough for swimming well into October and even in early November. Nature lovers and amateur photographers will enjoy the splendid soft autumn light and clear days. There are popular local feast days, known as *sagre*, in nearby towns, such as the famous wine festivals *(sagra del vino)* that coincide with the harvesting of the grapes.

Naples itself also comes back to life after the quiet and empty summer months. From September onward soccer fans can spend Sunday afternoons in the stadium, following the Neapolitans' favorite sport.

SEPTEMBER

The **Madonna di Piedigrotta** feast is held in the first half of the month. The ancient cave next to the sanctuary *(see p118)*, which has been closed for many years, was once the place for popular rituals. Today, the festival has once again become fashionable. According to an old proverb, the date of the festival of Piedigrotta marks the beginning of the rainy season.

An increasingly popular festival is the **Settembrata Anacaprese**. Throughout the month of September, shows, games, and gastronomic contests are held in Anacapri, Capri's second largest town.

The Piedigrotta feast in a 1930s photograph

The 19th marks another celebration of the miracle of the blood of **San Gennaro** in Naples' duomo. For centuries this ceremony, in which the congealed blood of the saint becomes liquid, has attracted scholars, tourists, local worshipers, and city authorities. Some aspects of the ritual, such as the violent supplications uttered in dialect, are today considered to be too pagan and are no longer practiced.

OCTOBER

The **Classical music season** begins at the Teatro San Carlo.

NOVEMBER

On **All Souls' Day** (Nov 2), also called the Day of the Dead, families take flowers to the graves of their loved ones. This was traditionally followed by a family meal at a trattoria outside town. This is the time of year when confectioners make the delicious *torrone dei morti*, or almond nougat.

Aerial view of the San Paolo soccer stadium

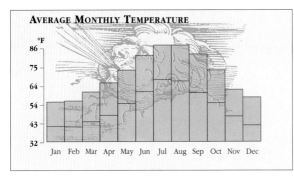

AVERAGE MONTHLY TEMPERATURE

°F
86
75
64
54
43
32
Jan Feb Mar Apr May Jun Jul Aug Sep Oct Nov Dec

Temperature
This chart gives the average minimum and maximum temperatures for each month. July and August are the hottest months, February the coldest. During the winter, relatively cold days may alternate with a spell of very mild and sunny days.

WINTER

THE MONTH OF DECEMBER and the holiday season may sometimes be accompanied by little snow. However, neither December and January are especially cold, and the days can be bright and sunny. February sometimes brings rain and cold. Although the rainfall is not persistent, heavy showers may occur. The "land of the sun" is not warm all year, as many think, and the few cold days can be quite uncomfortable.

DECEMBER

The day of the **Immacolata** (Immaculate Conception, Dec 8) opens the Christmas holiday season. People prepare the *presepe* (Nativity scene) in their homes with moss and statuettes of figures of Mary, the ox and donkey, the Wise Men, and Jesus in the creche The Cardinal and Mayor of the city lay wreaths on the Guglia dell'Immacolata *(see p65)*.
   Christmas is celebrated with dinner and presents on Christmas Eve followed by midnight mass. The streets are illuminated, and the stalls on Via San Gregorio Armeno have creche figures on display *(see p39)*. A few days before New Year's Day the fireworks start to appear, and the traditional bagpipers add color to the street scene.

A bagpipe player, a tradition at Christmas

JANUARY

New Year's Eve is celebrated with an impressive display of fireworks. For an enjoyable midnight outdoors, go and join the merrymaking in the central Piazza del Plebiscito.
   Traditionally the year begins with **Sant'Antuono** (Sant' Antonio Abate, Jan 17) and in the old center *cippi*, or old things, are thrown in bonfires.
   On **Epiphany** (Jan 6) the Befana witch arrives in Piazza del Plebiscito. This is a feast for children and sweets and "gifts from the Befana" are sold, particularly in Via Foria. Naughty children are brought (sweet) "lumps of coal."

FEBRUARY

Masked festivities for **Shrove Tuesday** and **Carnival** are accompanied by lasagna dishes. The **Galassia Gutenberg** book and multimedia fair opens, and the **Mostra d'Oltremare** offers exhibits, lectures, and cultural events.

Pulcinella, the protagonist of the Naples Carnival

PUBLIC HOLIDAYS

New Year's Day (Jan 1)
Epiphany (Jan 6)
Easter Sunday and Monday
Liberation Day (Apr 25)
Labor Day (May 1)
Ferragosto (Aug 15)
All Saints' Day (Nov 1)
Immaculate Conception (Dec 8)
Christmas Day (Dec 25)
Santo Stefano (Dec 26)

A Christmas feast in a square illuminated with fairy lights

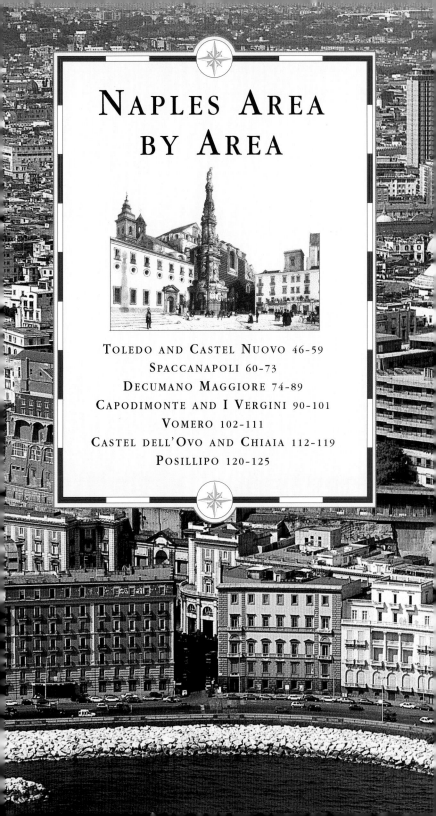

NAPLES AREA BY AREA

TOLEDO AND CASTEL NUOVO

CASTEL NUOVO CASTS its impressive shadow on an area that is both the commercial and administrative center of modern Naples and the heart of the old capital. This zone extends as far as the harbor, the boarding point for ferry trips. Centuries of history are concentrated in the area – from the ancient archaeological ruins on the hill of Pizzofalcone to 19th-century buildings such as the Galleria Umberto I. Near the royal palace and

Cannonballs at Castel Nuovo

fortress of Castel Nuovo, opposite the basilica of San Francesco di Paola, is the majestic Palazzo Reale, a palace built by the Spanish viceroys. Running north from here is a long and famous 16th-century road, Via Toledo, the main artery of Naples. It is still better known by this name (after the man who built it, Viceroy Don Pedro of Toledo) than its newer, official name, Via Roma. Lining the thoroughfare are elegant buildings, stately churches, and shops.

SIGHTS AT A GLANCE

Historic Buildings
Castel Nuovo pp54–5 **8**
Palazzo delle Poste e Telegrafi **14**
Palazzo Reale pp50–51 **1**
Palazzo Serra di Cassano **19**

Churches
Santa Brigida **12**
San Ferdinando **4**
San Francesco di Paola **2**
San Giacomo degli Spagnoli **11**
Santa Maria degli Angeli **17**
Santa Maria Egiziaca a Pizzofalcone **18**
Santa Maria Incoronata **10**
Nunziatella **20**

Historic Streets and Squares
Galleria Umberto I **6**
Piazza Giovanni Bovio **15**
Quartieri Spagnoli **13**
Via Chiaia **16**
Via Toledo **5**

Historic Theaters
Teatro Mercadante **9**
Teatro San Carlo **7**

Museums
Museo dell'Appartamento Reale *(see Palazzo Reale)*
Museo Artistico Industriale **21**
Museo Civico *(see Castel Nuovo)*

Historic Landmarks
Caffè Gambrinus **3**

GETTING THERE
Piazza del Plebiscito is closed to traffic, but a number of city buses run nearby. Route R2 comes from the main train station (Napoli Centrale), while R3 and C4 come from Mergellina train station. From Vomero, take route R1 or the Centrale funicular. Bus 109 is on the same route as Capodimonte and the Museo Archeologico. Route C80 comes from the airport.

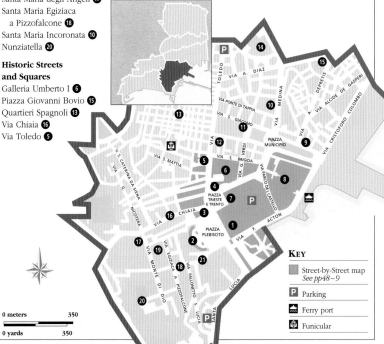

KEY

(gray)	Street-by-Street map *See pp48–9*
P	Parking
(ferry)	Ferry port
(funicular)	Funicular

0 meters 350
0 yards 350

◁ **The Scalone d'Onore in Palazzo Reale**

Street-by-Street: Toledo and Castel Nuovo

NAPLES IS A CITY of contrasting moods: the quiet solemnity of Piazza del Plebiscito, a symbol of the city's rebirth, is very different from the animation – you might even call it confusion – of the surrounding streets. It is a pleasure to mingle with the crowd in Via Toledo, drop in at the Caffè Gambrinus or Galleria Umberto I, pause in the shade of the historic church of San Francesco di Paola, or visit the museums at Palazzo Reale and Castel Nuovo. In addition to the rich history and art treasures in this area, Via Toledo is good for shopping.

Galleria Umberto I
The iron and glass dome was built in the late 1800s by Boubée **6**

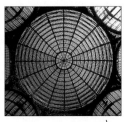

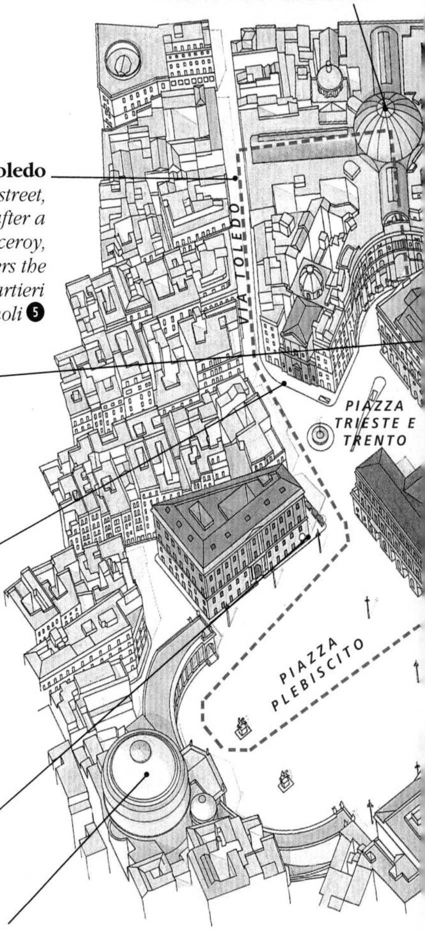

Via Toledo
This street, named after a Spanish viceroy, borders the Quartieri Spagnoli **5**

Teatro San Carlo
Richly decorated in gilded stucco, the theatrer seats 3,000, and the acoustics are excellent **7**

PIAZZA
TRIESTE E
TRENTO

San Ferdinando
Each year on Good Friday there is a performance of Pergolesi's Stabat Mater *for the confraternity that has been based here since 1837* **4**

PIAZZA
PLEBISCITO

Caffè Gambrinus
Gabriele d'Annunzio wrote the lyrics to the Neapolitan song "A vucchella" in this café **3**

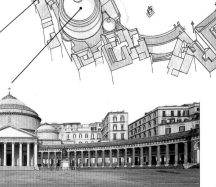

★ **San Francesco di Paola**
This Neo-Classical church was designed by Lugano architect Pietro Bianchi in 1817 **2**

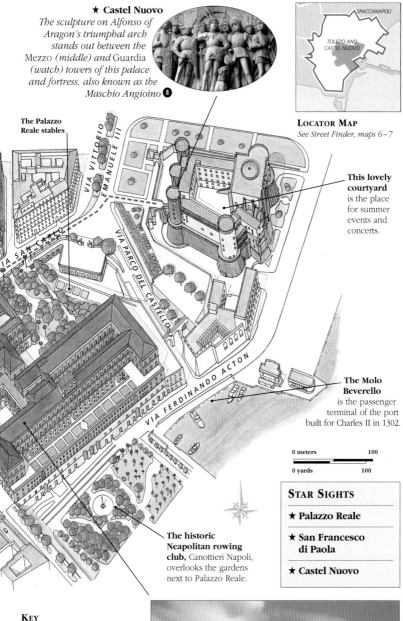

★ Castel Nuovo
The sculpture on Alfonso of Aragon's triumphal arch stands out between the Mezzo *(middle) and* Guardia *(watch) towers of this palace and fortress, also known as the* Maschio Angioino 8

LOCATOR MAP
See Street Finder, maps 6–7

SPACCANAPOLI

TOLEDO AND CASTEL NUOVO

The Palazzo Reale stables

VIA VITTORIO EMANUELE III

VIA SAN CARLO

VIA PARCO DEL CASTELLO

VIA FERDINANDO ACTON

This lovely courtyard is the place for summer events and concerts.

The Molo Beverello is the passenger terminal of the port built for Charles II in 1302.

0 meters	100
0 yards	100

STAR SIGHTS

★ **Palazzo Reale**

★ **San Francesco di Paola**

★ **Castel Nuovo**

The historic Neapolitan rowing club, Canottieri Napoli, overlooks the gardens next to Palazzo Reale.

KEY

----- Suggested route

★ Palazzo Reale
This palace was begun in 1600 for a visit by Philip III of Spain, which never took place 1

Palazzo Reale ❶

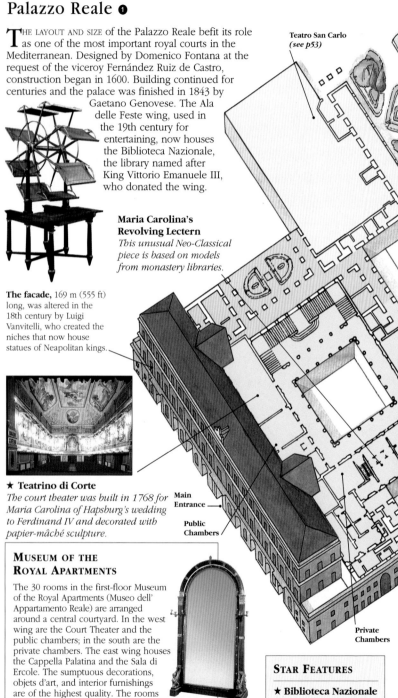

T HE LAYOUT AND SIZE of the Palazzo Reale befit its role
as one of the most important royal courts in the
Mediterranean. Designed by Domenico Fontana at the
request of the viceroy Fernández Ruiz de Castro,
construction began in 1600. Building continued for
centuries and the palace was finished in 1843 by
Gaetano Genovese. The Ala
delle Feste wing, used in
the 19th century for
entertaining, now houses
the Biblioteca Nazionale,
the library named after
King Vittorio Emanuele III,
who donated the wing.

Teatro San Carlo
(see p53)

**Maria Carolina's
Revolving Lectern**
*This unusual Neo-Classical
piece is based on models
from monastery libraries.*

The facade, 169 m (555 ft)
long, was altered in the
18th century by Luigi
Vanvitelli, who created the
niches that now house
statues of Neapolitan kings.

★ Teatrino di Corte
*The court theater was built in 1768 for
Maria Carolina of Hapsburg's wedding
to Ferdinand IV and decorated with
papier-mâché sculpture.*

**Main
Entrance**

**Public
Chambers**

**Private
Chambers**

MUSEUM OF THE
ROYAL APARTMENTS

The 30 rooms in the first-floor Museum
of the Royal Apartments (Museo dell'
Appartamento Reale) are arranged
around a central courtyard. In the west
wing are the Court Theater and the
public chambers; in the south are the
private chambers. The east wing houses
the Cappella Palatina and the Sala di
Ercole. The sumptuous decorations,
objets d'art, and interior furnishings
are of the highest quality. The rooms
in the private chambers house 16th-
to 19th-century paintings.

**A mirror in
the Museo**

STAR FEATURES

★ **Biblioteca Nazionale**

★ **Teatrino di Corte**

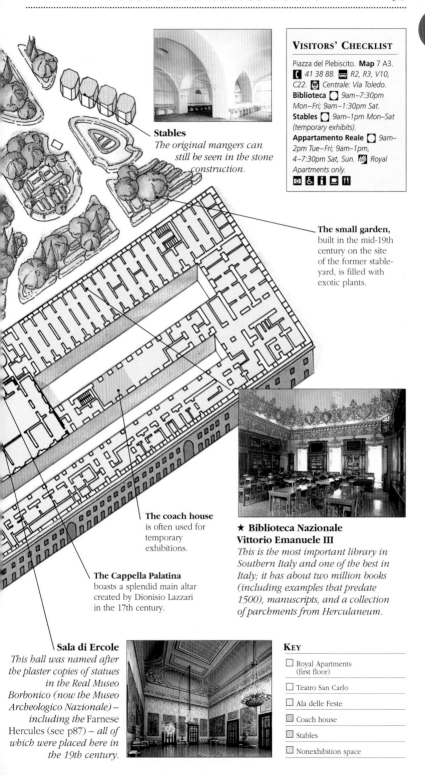

Stables
The original mangers can still be seen in the stone construction.

VISITORS' CHECKLIST

Piazza del Plebiscito. **Map** 7 A3.
C 41 38 88. **R2, R3, V10,
C22.** Centrale: Via Toledo.
Biblioteca 9am–7:30pm
Mon–Fri; 9am–1:30pm Sat.
Stables 9am–1pm Mon–Sat
(temporary exhibits).
Appartamento Reale 9am–
2pm Tue–Fri; 9am–1pm,
4–7:30pm Sat, Sun. Royal
Apartments only.

The small garden,
built in the mid-19th
century on the site
of the former stable-
yard, is filled with
exotic plants.

The coach house
is often used for
temporary
exhibitions.

The Cappella Palatina
boasts a splendid main altar
created by Dionisio Lazzari
in the 17th century.

★ **Biblioteca Nazionale
Vittorio Emanuele III**
*This is the most important library in
Southern Italy and one of the best in
Italy; it has about two million books
(including examples that predate
1500), manuscripts, and a collection
of parchments from Herculaneum.*

Sala di Ercole
*This hall was named after
the plaster copies of statues
in the Real Museo
Borbonico (now the Museo
Archeologico Nazionale) –
including the Farnese
Hercules (see p87) – all of
which were placed here in
the 19th century.*

KEY

☐ Royal Apartments
(first floor)

☐ Teatro San Carlo

☐ Ala delle Feste

☐ Coach house

☐ Stables

☐ Nonexhibition space

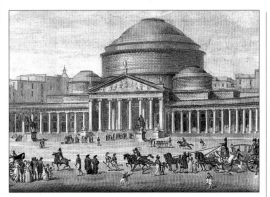

19th-century print of a riding competition at San Francesco di Paola

San Francesco di Paola ❷

Piazza del Plebiscito. **Map** 7 A3.
📞 764 51 33. 🚌 R2, R3, V10, C22.
🚇 Centrale: Via Toledo. ⏰ 7:30–11am, 3:30–6pm Mon–Sat, 8am–1pm Sun. 🚻 📷

JOACHIM MURAT, Napoleon's brother-in-law, ruled the city of Naples from 1808 to 1815. Dissatisfied with the chaotic jumble of buildings opposite the Palazzo Reale, he decided to rebuild the whole area. The Largo di Palazzo, now called the Piazza del Plebiscito, was meant to play a major role in city life and was used for festivities, ceremonies, and military parades.

The first buildings to go up were the palace built for the Prince of Salerno, and the palazzo that is now the home of the Prefecture. Both were laid out symmetrically. Murat did not see the final results of his scheme, he saw only Leopoldo Laperuta's design for the Doric colonnade and the initial construction work before the French were driven out of Naples.

In 1815 Ferdinand of Bourbon was reinstated to the throne and, having fulfilled his vow of reconquering the Kingdom of Naples, completed the project begun by Murat. He commissioned

Statue of Charles III by Canova

the architect Pietro Bianchi to design the central royal basilica, which was dedicated to San Francesco di Paola. Inspired by the Pantheon in Rome, the church has a circular plan with radiating chapels and a large cupola 53 m (174 ft) high and 34 m (112 ft) wide, complete with rosettes.

The sculpture and paintings inside the church are almost all Neo-Classical except for the high altar, which was rebuilt in 1835 with semi-precious stones, multi-colored marble, and lapis lazuli taken from a 17th-century altar in the church of Santi Apostoli (see p96). The cool, formal interior can have a rather chilling effect on visitors. According to architectural historian Renato De Fusco: "Despite the large size of the interior and the rich marble, stucco, and garlanding decoration, the overall impression is not that of Neo-Classical rigor, but rather a lack of harmony between man and the setting, a funereal coldness compared to the exterior." The sobering effect is soon dispelled by emerging into the lovely Piazza del Plebiscito, which is pedestrian street. The two equestrian statues of Charles III and Ferdinand I are the work of Antonio Canova and Antonio Calì.

Caffè Gambrinus ❸

Piazza Trieste e Trento. **Map** 7 A3.
📞 41 75 82. 🚌 R2, R3, V10, C22.
🚇 Centrale: Via Toledo. ⏰ 8am–midnight Wed–Mon. ⏺ One week in Aug. 📷

THE CAFÉ dates from 1860; its walls decorated by the leading Neapolitan painters of the time. It soon became the haunt of politicians, artists, and writers, including Guy de Maupassant and Oscar Wilde, as well as the local composers Roberto Murolo and Giovanni Bovio. When the literary café also became popular with opponents of the Fascist regime, the prefect closed it down, initiating a long period of decline and neglect. Fortunately, its lavish Belle Epoque decor has been restored, and this historic landmark is once again a favorite. Neapolitans drop in for coffee and cakes, or for iced tea and ice cream.

Interior of the historic Caffè Gambrinus

San Ferdinando ❹

Piazza Trieste e Trento 5. **Map** 7 A3.
📞 *40 05 43.* 🚌 *R2, R3, V10, C22.*
🚇 *Centrale: Via Toledo.* ⏱ *8am–noon, 5–7pm Mon–Sat; 9:30am–1pm Sun.* ⛪

THIS CHURCH was founded in 1622 as San Francesco Saverio. In 1769 Ferdinand I dedicated it to his namesake saint. The Baroque interior contains frescoes by Paolo De Matteis and sculptures by Vaccaro as well as the tomb of Lucia Migliaccio, the Duchess of Floridia. Ferdinand gave her his estate on the Vomero hill, which became Villa La Floridiana *(see p106).* Until 1919 the square was called Piazza San Ferdinando.

Gay Odin shop in Via Toledo

Via Toledo ❺

Map 3 A5, 7 A1 (9 B4). 🚌 *R1, R2, R3, V10.* 🚇 *Centrale: Via Toledo.*

IN THE 1600s travelers were struck by the lively crowds in the most famous street in Naples and by its amazing length. Via Toledo owes its name to the Spanish viceroy Don Pedro de Toledo, who commissioned its construction alongside the Aragonese city walls in 1536. Fine buildings alternate with many shops and churches.

Shopping in Via Toledo caters to all tastes and budgets. Neapolitans like to stop at Gay Odin to sample the exquisite homemade chocolates and at Pintauro's for the excellent *sfogliatelle* millefeuille pastry *(see p181).*

The marble floor of the Galleria Umberto I

Galleria Umberto I ❻

Via San Carlo, Via Verdi, Via Santa Brigida, Via Toledo. **Map** 7 A2. 🚌 *R2, R3, V10, C22.* 🚇 *Centrale: Via Toledo.*

THE GALLERIA was built as part of the Urban Renewal plan, drawn up after the cholera epidemic that struck the city in 1884 *(see pp24–5).* The impressive iron and glass roof and elegant patterned marble floor fill the large open space with light. The arcade soon became the favorite haunt of local composers and musicians. From the galleria it was possible to gain entry to the Salone Margherita, which until 1912 was a famous *café chantant* and considered the heart of cabaret entertainment in Naples. Patrons paid two lire for admission.

Teatro San Carlo ❼

Via San Carlo 101–3. **Map** 7 A3.
📞 *797 21 11.* 🚌 *R2, R3, V10, C22.*
🚇 *Centrale: Via Toledo.* ⏱ *15 Sep–30 Jun: 2–4pm Mon, Sat, Sun; 1–25 Jul: 10am–noon Mon, Tue, Thu, Sat, Sun.* 📷 *except during rehearsals, Via San Carlo 98f,* **Season** *Oct–Jun. See* **Entertainment in Naples** *p196, p199.*

THIS IS ONE OF the oldest remaining opera houses in the world. Designed by Giovanni Antonio Medrano for the Bourbon King Charles I, it was built in a few months and officially opened on 4 November 4, 1737, 40 years before La Scala in Milan, on the king's saint's day. It soon became one of the most important opera houses in Europe, known for its magnificent architecture and excellent productions. For many years, a performance at the San Carlo was considered the high point in the career of a singer or composer.

A fire in 1816 severely damaged the interior, which was immediately rebuilt by Antonio Niccolini, the architect who a few years earlier had modified the facade by adding the foyer and balcony. The focal point of the magnificent auditorium, with its six tiers of boxes, is the royal box, surmounted by the crown of the Kingdom of the Two Sicilies.

Many great musical figures, including Gioacchino Rossini and Gaetano Donizetti, were at one time artistic directors here. The world premieres of Donizetti's *Lucia di Lammermoor* and Rossini's *Mosè* were performed here. Founded in 1812, the San Carlo ballet school vies with La Scala for the title of the oldest ballet school in Italy.

The Teatro San Carlo façade, remodeled by Niccolini in 1810

Castel Nuovo ❽

THE CASTLE WAS called *nuovo* (new) to distinguish it from two earlier ones, dell'Ovo and Capuano *(see pp116 and 81)*, which were too small to hold the entire Angevin court. Charles I of Anjou began construction in 1279, but the Cappella Palatina is the only remaining part of the original building. Alfonso V of Aragon (who later became Alfonso I, King of Naples and Sicily) began to rebuild it completely in 1443, the year that marked his triumphant entry into Naples. To celebrate this event, Alfonso later ordered the construction of the superb Arco di Trionfo, one of the most significant expressions of early Renaissance culture in Southern Italy. The castle, with its five impressive cylindrical towers, is designed on a trapezoidal plan facing onto a beautiful central courtyard. From here you can gain access to the most famous chamber in the castle, the Sala dei Baroni (Barons' Hall), now used by the town council. Since 1990 a small but fine art collection, the Museo Civico, has occupied three floors of the west wing.

The Renaissance doorway of the Cappella Palatina

Cappella Palatina

This is the only surviving part of the 13th-century building. An elegant Renaissance doorway leads to the chapel, which is dedicated to St. Barbara. The portal itself is crowned with an elaborate rose window typical of the Catalan style of its creators. The portal is adorned with a Madonna executed by Francesco Laurana (c.1425–1502) in 1474.

The walls inside the chapel were once decorated with frescoes by Giotto and his workshop; today, only small fragments on the splays of the lofty Gothic windows remain.

Sala dei Baroni

Next to the chapel, the Barons' Hall, which is reached by means of an outer stairway, owes its name to the grim events that took place there in 1486. Then, the great barons who had plotted a conspiracy against Ferdinand I of Aragon, were arrested and subsequently executed.

The imposing Castel Nuovo, with its stunning Renaissance triumphal arch

TIMELINE

1279 Charles I of Anjou begins construction of Castel Nuovo	**1443** Alfonso V's total rebuilding plan	**1443–68** Building of Arco di Trionfo	**1547** Popular revolt against the Inquisition		**1647** Signing of pact between the viceroy and Masaniello after popular uprising		
1200	1300	1400	1500	1600	1700	1800	
	1329 Giotto and his assistants paint the Cappella Palatina frescoes	**1486** The Barons' conspiracy	**1509–37** Reconstruction of the defense system with new battlements and moats			*The* Barricades at San Ferdinando during the 1848 uprisings *(detail of a painting in the Museo Civico)*	

Sala dei Baroni: the splendid Spanish Gothic vault

This elegant, yet grand and austere hall, 26 m (85 ft) wide and 28 m (92 ft) high, was built by the Spanish craftsman Guglielmo Sagrera, who was summoned to Naples for this purpose in 1446. It is now the main meeting room of the town council. Its principal features are the magnificent Catalan-inspired ribbed vault with intersecting ribs in the shape of a huge star, the monumental fireplace, and the large rectangular "cross windows."

19th-century Neapolitan painting, Museo Civico

Museo Civico

A large part of the west wing of Castel Nuovo and part of the Cappella Palatina are occupied by the Museo Civico (civic museum). Before visiting the museum, do not miss the opportunity to take in the splendid panoramic views of the Bay of Naples and Mount Vesuvius from the upper floors of the castle.

The museum houses paintings, sculptures, and objets d'art that come from the castle itself, from neighboring churches, and other Neapolitan monuments. These works date from the 14th to the 19th century, but by far the largest section consists of 19th-century Neapolitan paintings. Some of these – such as Vincenzo

Caprile's *Vecchia Napoli* (Old Naples), depicting the famous Zizze fountain in its original state – offer views of a city that no longer exists.

Arco di Trionfo

The combination of white marble against the gray volcanic stone of Castel Nuovo is immediately striking to the visitor, as is the contrast between the ornamental reliefs and the severe geometric form of the towers. The structure, with its two superimposed arches, takes its inspiration from ancient Roman architecture.

The monumental gateway of the *Arco di Trionfo* (Triumphal Arch) was built in 1443 in honor of Alfonso V of Aragon. The bas-relief depicting the *Trionfo di Alfonso* (Triumph of Alfonso) lies above the lower section, while the upper arch, which was once intended to house a statue of the sovereign, now holds allegorical figures representing the Four Virtues (looking from left to right, Temperance, Justice, Fortitude, and Magnanimity). On the tympanum, supporting two large symbolic statues of rivers, stands a figure

VISITORS' CHECKLIST

Largo Castello. **Map** 7 B2.
795 20 03. R2, R3, 109, 149, 105, C55. Centrale: Via Toledo. 9am–7pm Mon–Sat. see attendants for assistance.

Upper section of Arco di Trionfo

of the archangel St. Michael. A number of Italian artists contributed to the final building of the arch. The most significant among them was Francesco Laurana, who also worked on the Cappella Palatina and sculpted the statues of Justice and the bas-relief of Alfonso I on his chariot. Another noteworthy artist was Laurana's pupil and assistant, Domenico Gagini.

Castel Nuovo in a painting by Antonio Joli

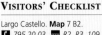

Teatro Mercadante **9**

Piazza Municipio 74. **Map** 7 B2.
(552 42 14. AT, C4, R2, R3.
Centrale: Via Toledo. See **Enter-tainment in Naples**, p196, p199.

BUILT IN 1778 to a design by Francesco Securo, this theatrer was originally known as *"del Fondo"* because money for its construction came from a fund created by the sale of confiscated Jesuit property. The three-tier facade, with eight caryatids supporting the cornice, was added in 1892. The theater opened in 1779 with *L'Infedeltà Fedele* by Cimarosa, a leading Neapolitan composer.

Late 19th-century façade of the Teatro Mercadante

Santa Maria Incoronata **10**

Via dell'Incoronata. **Map** 7 B2.
R2, R3, V10, C22. Centrale: Via Toledo. 9am–12:45pm Mon–Sat.

IT IS IMMEDIATELY obvious that this church is at a lower level than Via Medina. The reason goes back to the 16th century, when Charles V built the new moats for Castel Nuovo. Earth had been dug out to make room for the ditches, and when it was dumped nearby it partially buried this small mid-14th century church. Santa Maria Incoronata was originally built for Jeanne I of Anjou to celebrate her coronation and also to house a fragment of Jesus's crown of thorns. The two fresco cycles in the first bay of the main nave are the work of a pupil of Giotto's, Roberto Oderisi.

Detail of the portico of Santa Maria Incoronata

San Giacomo degli Spagnoli **11**

Piazza Municipio. **Map** 7 B2.
(552 37 59. R2, R3, V10, C22, C4, C80. Centrale: Via Toledo.
7:30–11:15am Mon–Sat.

PART OF THE NEARBY 19th-century Palazzo San Giacomo (now the town hall), the church of San Giacomo dominates Piazza Municipio. In 1540 Don Pedro Alvarez de Toledo, the vice-roy responsible for the present appearance of the city center, built the church and adjoining hospital for the Spanish community. This was the church of the local aristocracy and although rebuilt in 1741, it still belongs to the Real Hermandad de Nobles Hespanoles de Santiago, a confraternity founded more than four centuries ago.

San Giacomo contains tombs of Spanish nobles, including that of Don Pedro and his wife Maria. They were never buried in their sumptuous tomb however: Don Pedro died in Florence and was buried there in the cathedral.

The marble tomb of Don Pedro Alvarez de Toledo in San Giacomo degli Spagnoli

Santa Brigida **12**

Via Santa Brigida 72. **Map** 7 A2.
(552 37 93. R2, R3, V10, C22.
Centrale: Via Toledo. 7:30am–12:30pm, 5:30–7pm daily.

THE CURIOUS aspect of this 17th-century church is the dome, which could not be more than 9 m (30 ft) high because it would have obstructed artillery fire from Castel Nuovo. However, the fresco of a vivid sky created by Luca Giordano (1632–1705) on the cupola makes the most of boldly conceived perspective and creates a feeling of immense space.

The artist, nicknamed Luca Fapresto (Luca the Swift) because he worked so rapidly, painted the dome in exchange for his tomb, which can be found in the left transept.

Quartieri Spagnoli **13**

Map 7 A1. R2, R3. Centrale: Via Toledo.

THE SPANISH QUARTER is one of the city's working class dis-tricts; densely populated and rather run-down so tourists should take care when visiting the area.. Built in the 17th century to the west of Via Toledo to house Spanish troops, its origins live on in the name, but today it is difficult to appreciate the original grid layout. Alleys are festooned with laundry, shielding the streets from the light.

Despite the state of neglect, there is still some fine archi-tecture such as the church of Montecalvario (founded in

A stall laden with fish in the atmospheric 17th-century Quartieri Spagnoli district

1560), which gives its name to one of the area's districts, and Santa Maria della Concezione, a Baroque masterpiece by Domenico Antonio Vaccaro.

The great Italian poet Leopardi once lived at No. 24 Via Santa Maria Ognibene, and the local playwright Eduardo De Filippo *(see p36)* used the area as a setting for his plays.

Entrance to the Palazzo delle Poste e Telegrafi

Palazzo delle Poste e Telegrafi ⑭

Piazza Matteotti 3. **Map** 7 B1 (9 B5). 551 19 47. R1, C55. 7am–7:20pm Mon–Sat.

THE POST OFFICE building was designed in 1933 by Giuseppe Vaccaro as part of an Urban Renewal and Development plan that resulted in the demolition of the San Giuseppe quarter. The monumental, bombastic style of the civic architecture of this period (also found in the

police headquarters, the tax office, and the provincial administration building) is typical of buildings constructed during the Fascist era. The Post Office combines these emphatic features with other innovative elements of European Modern Movement.

The curvilinear facade and broad staircase make this one of the most interesting examples of 20th-century Neapolitan architecture. In striking contrast to the Post Office is the nearby cloister of Monteoliveto *(see p64)*, sadly now very dilapidated.

Piazza Giovanni Bovio ⑮

Map 7 B1 (9 C5). R1, C55.

NEAPOLITANS call this square Piazza della Borsa, after the building that dominates it, which used to be the Stock Exchange *(Borsa)*. Built in 1895 when taste was eclectic, the old exchange is reminiscent of 16th-

century buildings in the Veneto. It is now the home of the Chamber of Commerce. Incorporated into the left side of this building is the small church of Sant'Aspreno al Porto, originally medieval but totally rebuilt in the 1600s.

The square marks the beginning of Corso Umberto I, also known as the *Rettifilo*. This grand avenue was built after slum clearance around the harbor, to connect the city center and the central train station, giving a new look to early 20th-century Naples *(see pp26–7)*. Like a splendid traffic island, the 17th-century Fountain of Neptune towers over the middle of the square. Frequently altered, the fountain was moved several times before finding its final home in Piazza Bovio in 1898. It was the work of three artists: the statue of Neptune was sculpted by Michelangelo Naccherino, the balusters and lions were by Cosimo Fanzago, and the monsters at the base by Pietro Bernini.

The Fountain of Neptune

Via Chiaia **⑯**

Map 7 A3. ▦ *AT, C4.*

IN NEAPOLITAN DIALECT, *chiaia* means "beach," and in fact this street was opened up in the 16th century to connect Largo di Palazzo (now Piazza del Plebiscito) with the coast. Together with Via Toledo *(see p53)* and Via dei Mille *(see p113)*, this is one of the best shopping streets in Naples. While browsing, it is worth stopping to see the Ponte di Chiaia, a 17th-century gateway restored in the 1800s. Nearby is Palazzo Cellamare, built in the 16th century and enlarged in the 18th century, when it became known for the magnificent banquets and receptions held there. The impressive portal was designed by Ferdinando Fuga. Near the Ponte, take the elevator to Piazza Santa Maria degli Angeli and the Pizzofalcone hill.

Via Chiaia and Ponte di Chiaia

The portal of the church of Santa Maria degli Angeli

Santa Maria degli Angeli **⑰**

Piazza Santa Maria degli Angeli.
Map 3 C2. ▐ *764 49 74.* ▦ *AT.*
◷ *7:30am–noon, 5–7pm daily.*
🚻 📷

CONSTRUCTION of this church began in the 17th century on land donated to the devout Theatine religious order by Donna Costanza del Carretto Dira, the Princess of Melfi. The building was designed by the Theatine cleric Francesco Grimaldi, and it is clearly visible from any point overlooking the city. The three-nave

interior is so well designed that Francesco Milizia, the author of an 18th-century guide to Naples, said that it "is perhaps the most well-proportioned church in the city."

The frescoes on the vaults, which depict episodes from the life of the Virgin Mary in vivid and luminous color, are the work of Giovan Battista Beinaschi (1638–88).

Santa Maria Egiziaca a Pizzofalcone **⑱**

Via Egiziaca 30. **Map** 7 A3.
▐ *764 51 99.* ▦ *AT.* ◷ *9:30am–1pm, 5–7pm daily.* 🚻 📷

THE PORTAL on Via Egiziaca opens out onto the area in front of this Baroque church.

Its construction began in 1661 at the request of the cloistered order of nuns who lived nearby in the Sant'Agostino convent. The building's design was entrusted to Cosimo Fanzago (1593–1678), a Lombard architect and sculptor who became one of the most prestigious creators of the local Baroque style. Its octagonal plan was greatly admired by contemporaries of Fanzago. The paintings in the main chapels are by Paolo De Matteis (1662–1728), and the sculptures are by Nicola Fumo. The high altar is in pure Rococo style.

Palazzo Serra di Cassano **⑲**

Via Monte di Dio 14–15.
Map 6 F2. ▐ *764 26 52.* ▦ *AT.*
◷ *7:30am–7:30pm Mon–Fri; 7:30am–noon Sat.* 📷

THE MAIN DOORWAY to Prince Aloisio Serra di Cassano's palace is no longer the main entrance to one of the most beautiful examples of 18th-century Neapolitan civic architecture. To express his grief over the execution of his son Gennaro – one of the leaders of the 1799 revolution in Naples – the prince ordered the original entrance (at No.

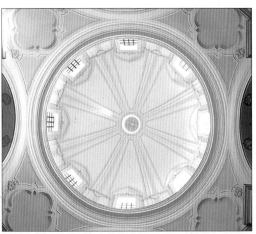

Interior of the cupola of Santa Maria Egiziaca a Pizzofalcone

The impressive double staircase in Palazzo Serra di Cassano

67 Via Egiziaca) to be closed that same year. The originality of this building, which was designed by one of the leading architects of the time, Ferdinando Sanfelice (1675–1748), lies in the majestic staircase with its double flight of steps. Set in the entrance hall that opens on to the courtyard, it is decorated with white marble that contrasts with the building's gray volcanic stone.

The *piano nobile* (upper floor) of the palazzo is now the home of the Istituto Italiano per gli Studi Filosofici, a leading international cultural institution.

Nunziatella 🄮

Via Generale Parisi. **Map** 7 A4.
🕿 764 15 20. 🚌 AT. 🛈 ask
for the military college chaplain
(cappellano). 🚻

THE FACADES of the church and former convent of the Nunziatella, which has been occupied since 1787 by the military college of the same name, converge at a right angle to form a beautiful little square. At the beginning of the 18th century, the Jesuits at the Nunziatella asked architect Ferdinando Sanfelice – who was working on the nearby Palazzo Serra di Cassano at the time – to build the church and restore the convent, which dates from the 16th century.

Entering the little church, the first thing to strike the visitor is the harmonious balance Sanfelice established between the architectural space and the pictorial and sculptural decorative elements. The most important frescoes were painted by Neapolitan artist Francesco de Mura (1696–1782); in the apse is the *Adoration of the Magi*, the *Assumption of the Virgin* is on the ceiling, and on the inside of the facade is *Rest during the Flight to Egypt*. The altar, the work of Giuseppe Sanmartino (1720–93), is one of the most important examples of Neapolitan Baroque art.

Museo Artistico Industriale 🄯

Piazzetta Demetrio Salazar 6. **Map** 7 A3. 🕿 764 74 71. 🕑 9am–1:30pm Mon–Sat. 🛈 make inquiries at Art Institute. 🚻

FOUNDED IN 1878 by Gaetano Filangieri, who also founded the Filangieri Civic Museum *(see p70)*, and Demetrio Salazar,

Scroll decoration on the Nunziatella façade

this was the school where young artists were educated following past examples. The most important works of art are the ceramics. Among these are two large ceramic tile panels designed by the important 19th-century Neapolitan artists Domenico Morelli and Filippo Palizzi.

Façade of the Museo Artistico with its decorative tiles

THE BIRTHPLACE OF PARTHENOPE

Ancient ruins on Pizzofalcone

In the 7th century BC, Greek colonists from Rhodes founded the first urban settlement in Naples on the hill of Pizzofalcone: Parthenope was renamed Palaepolis (old city) three centuries later when Neapolis (new city) was founded to the east. The old city was later abandoned, and by the Middle Ages the area had reverted to farmland. However, the site of ancient Naples was revived in the 16th century, when it became a residential neighborhood favored by aristocrats and important officials, who were attracted by the beauty of the site and its proximity to the Royal Palace. In the 18th century Via Monte di Dio was one of the most important residential streets in Naples, and to this day it retains some of its original character.

SPACCANAPOLI

THE STRAIGHT STREET called Spaccanapoli (Split Naples) corresponds to the lower *decumanus,* one of the three main thoroughfares in Greco-Roman Naples; the other two are the present-day Via Anticaglia *(see p84)* and Via dei Tribunali *(see pp76–7).* At the end of the 13th century, after the construction of Castel Nuovo *(see pp54–5),* the administrative hub of the city began to shift toward the waterfront. Commercial activity developed in the Piazza

Bust-reliquary of San Bartolomeo, Santa Chiara

Mercato zone, while in the old center there was a concentration of churches and convents, notably Santa Chiara. The city expanded around the newly built Via Toledo *(see p53)* during the era of the Spanish viceroyalty, and the Piazza del Gesù Nuovo area became the junction point between the old and the modern cities. Development in the 19th century, including the opening up of Corso Umberto I, led to the demolition of the city's medieval fabric.

SIGHTS AT A GLANCE

Historic Buildings
Archivio di Stato **17**
Monte di Pietà **14**
Palazzo Carafa Santangelo **13**
Palazzo Filomarino **7**

Churches
Cappella Sansevero **10**
Gesù Nuovo **3**
Gesù Vecchio **20**
Sant'Angelo a Nilo **11**
Sant'Anna dei Lombardi **2**
Santissima Annunziata **23**
Santa Chiara pp66–7 **5**
San Domenico Maggiore **9**
Sant'Eligio Maggiore **25**
San Giorgio Maggiore **15**
San Giovanni dei Pappacoda **22**
Santi Marcellino e Festo **19**
Santa Maria del Carmine **24**
Santa Maria La Nova **1**
Santa Marta **6**
Santi Severino e Sossio **18**

Historic Streets and Squares
Corso Umberto I **21**
Piazza San Domenico Maggiore **8**

Spires and Statues
Guglia dell'Immacolata **4**
Statue of the Nile **12**

Museums
Museo Civico Filangieri **16**

GETTING THERE
Spaccanapoli is partly closed to traffic. The circle bus lines R1 (from Vomero), R2 (from the central train station) and R3 (from the Mergellina station) stop in Via Toledo, a short walk away from the district. Piazza Mercato can be reached by trams 1 and 4. You can also get to Spaccanapoli by subway (Montesanto station) and, from Vomero, via the Centrale and Montesanto funiculars.

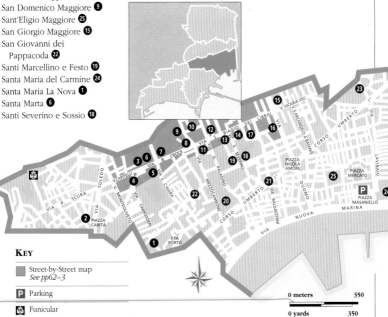

KEY

Street-by-Street map *See pp62–3*

P Parking

Funicular

0 meters 350
0 yards 350

◁ **View of Spaccanapoli, once a major thoroughfare in ancient Naples**

Street-by-Street: Spaccanapoli

THE LONG STREET commonly known as Spaccanapoli is divided into seven sections bearing different names. Because of its rich array of churches, squares, and historic buildings it has been called an "open-air museum," like nearby Via dei Tribunali. It is also one of the livliest and most atmospheric places in Naples, with shops, crafts, and cafés. Piazza San Domenico, near the university, is always crowded with young people. Those with a sweet tooth can enjoy the excellent pastries at the Scaturchio pasticceria.

Piazza San Domenico
An unusual siren with two tails is sculpted on the base of the spire ❽

San Domenico Maggiore
This church was built in 1283 by Charles I of Anjou ❾

★ Gesù Nuovo
The rusticated facade of the church was once part of Palazzo Sanseverino ❸

Sant'Angelo a Nilo
The interior houses the tomb of Cardinal Brancaccio, sculpted by Donatello and Michelozzo ⓫

Palazzo Filomarino
The philosopher Benedetto Croce died here in 1952 ❼

Guglia dell'Immacolata
Erected in the 1700s, this spire was named after the statue of the Virgin at its pinnacle ❹

Santa Marta
This small church dates from the 15th century ❻

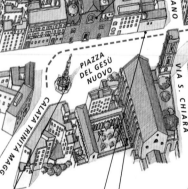

★ Santa Chiara
Robert of Anjou was responsible for building this church. The tiled cloister was designed by Domenico Antonio Vaccaro in 1742 ❺

★ Cappella Sansevero
This moving Veiled Christ *is the only work of art by a Neapolitan artist (Giuseppe Sanmartino) in the di Sangro family chapel* ⑩

LOCATOR MAP
See Street Finder, maps 4, 5, 7

Statue of the Nile
This statue, erected in honor of the Egyptian god Nile, gives its name to the square in which it stands ⑫

Ospedale delle Bambole,
the dolls' hospital, is a unique place where dolls and puppets are repaired.

Palazzo Marigliano

San Nicola a Nilo

VIA NILO

VIA S. BIAGIO DEI LIBRAI

VIA PALADINO

VIA GRANDE ARCHIVIO

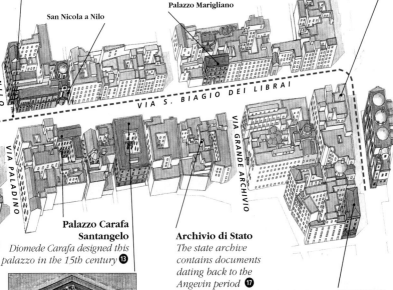

Palazzo Carafa Santangelo
Diomede Carafa designed this palazzo in the 15th century ⑬

Archivio di Stato
The state archive contains documents dating back to the Angevin period ⑰

Museo Civico Filangieri
Prince Filangieri's art collection in elegant Palazzo Como includes detailed mosaic floor tiles like these ⑯

Monte di Pietà
This majestic building and the adjoining chapel were designed by Giovan Battista Cavagna ⑭

KEY

- - - - - Suggested route

0 meters   100

0 yards   100

STAR SIGHTS
★ Gesù Nuovo
★ Santa Chiara
★ Cappella Sansevero

Santa Maria La Nova ❶

Largo Santa Maria La Nova 1.
Map 7 B1 (9 C5). 552 32 98.
R3. Centrale: Via Toledo.
7:30am–12:30pm, 4:30–6pm
Mon–Sat; 8:30am–1pm Sun.

IN ORDER TO MAKE ROOM for Castel Nuovo (see pp54–5) a Franciscan church devoted to the Virgin Mary had to be demolished. In exchange, Charles I of Anjou gave the friars a nearby plot of land and had a new church built at his own expense, Santa Maria La Nova.
Inside, the richly decorated wooden ceiling was painted by the leading artists of the time (Santafede, Curia, Imparato, and Corenzio), creating a stunning gallery of 16th- and 17th-century Neapolitan painting. In the fourth chapel on the right is Giovanni da Nola's altarpiece of Sant'Eustachio. Other chapels contain works by Caracciolo, Teodoro d'Errico, and Santacroce. In the former monastery, now the seat of the provincial government, there are two cloisters: the

smaller one (No. 44) has Renaissance frescoes and marble tombs, and the other (No. 43) contains a garden. Nearby, at 11 Piazza Tommaso Monticelli, is the 15th-century facade of Palazzo Penna.

Sant'Anna dei Lombardi ❷

Piazza Monteoliveto 3. **Map** 7 A1
(9 B5). 551 33 33. R3.
Centrale: Via Toledo. 8:30am–12:30pm Tue–Thu, Sat.

FOUNDED IN 1411 as Santa Maria di Monteoliveto, this was the favorite church of the Aragonese kings, who summoned the leading artists of the time to decorate it. Its name changed when it was assigned to the Confraternity of Lombards (to whom it still belongs), whose church had collapsed in the 1805 earthquake. The roof was damaged during World War II and has not been restored, but the interior contains some fine examples of Renaissance sculpture.

Cappella Piccolomini, altarpiece decoration

The marble altarpiece in the Cappella Piccolomini, by Antonio Rossellino (1475), has dancing angels on the top, the work of Benedetto da Majano. The latter also executed the altarpiece in the Terranova chapel (1489). The Tolosa chapel was decorated by the della Robbia workshop in Florence. To the right of the presbytery is Guido Mazzoni's *Lamentation over the Dead Christ* (1492), an amazingly realistic tableau of eight life-size terra-cotta figures surrounding Christ. Their grief-stricken faces are said to be modeled on those of the Aragonese kings.
At No. 3 Via Monteoliveto is the 16th-century Palazzo Gravina, now occupied by the College of Architecture.

Detail of the reliquary in Gesù Nuovo

Gesù Nuovo ❸

Piazza del Gesù Nuovo. **Map** 3 B5
(9 B4). 44 05 11. R3. M
Montesanto. 6:30am–12:45pm,
4:15–7:30pm Mon–Sat;
6:30am–1:30pm Sun.

THE FACADE, COVERED IN diamond-point rustication, was once part of 15th-century Palazzo Sanseverino. It was retained by the Jesuits when they bought the building and in 1584 transformed it into the large church seen today. The 17th-century doorway incorporates the original Renaissance entrance to the palazzo. The Baroque interior is richly decorated with multicolored marbles and ornate artworks including statues, a reliquary, and vivid frescoes. In the chapel of St. Ignatius of

The smaller cloister in the former monastery of Santa Maria La Nova

Loyola, founder of the Society of Jesus (left-hand transept), are two of Cosimo Fanzago's finest works: the dramatic sculptures of *David* and *Jeremiah*. The cupola, frescoed by Lanfranco, collapsed in the 1688 earthquake; the only survivors were the corbels showing the four Evangelists in flight. Above the main entrance is Francesco Solimena's huge fresco, *Expulsion of Heliodorus from the Temple* (1725). The statue of the Virgin, on a lapis lazuli globe above the altar, dates from the mid-19th century. The second chapel on the right houses the remains of San Giuseppe Moscati, canonized in 1987.

Guglia dell'Immacolata ❹

Piazza del Gesù Nuovo. **Map** 3 B5 (9 B4). R3. M Montesanto.

THE JESUITS commissioned this gigantic, ornate marble spire as a symbol of devotion to the Virgin Mary and also as a tangible sign of the power of their Society. The monument, modeled on ancient Egyptian obelisks, was begun in 1743 to a design by Giuseppe Genuino. The complex stone ornamentation depicting the Jesuit saints and stories of Mary, was sculpted by Francesco Pagano and Matteo Bottigliero and is regarded as a key work in 18th-century Neapolitan sculpture. The statue of the Madonna is the center of festivities on the Feast of Immaculate Conception.

Guglia dell'Immacolata

Facade of Gesù Nuovo

Santa Chiara ❺

See pp66–7.

Santa Marta ❻

Via San Sebastiano 42. **Map** 3 B5 (9 B3). 726 04 95. R3. M Montesanto. 8:30am–noon Sun.

THIS SMALL CHURCH was founded by Margherita di Durazzo in the 15th century and became the headquarters of one of the city's most important confraternities, whose members included kings, viceroys, and high-ranking officials. The church stands opposite the bell tower of Santa Chiara *(see pp66–7)*. The doorway still retains its original depressed arch structure. On the high altar is a painting by Andrea and Nicola Vaccaro (1670), depicting St. Martha, to whom the church is dedicated. The *Codice di Santa Marta (Codex of St Martha)*, with its valuable miniatures, came from this church and is now kept in the Archivio di Stato, or state archive *(see p70)*. You can get to the underground cemetery from the room next to the sacristy.

Palazzo Filomarino ❼

Via Benedetto Croce 12. **Map** 3 B5 (9 C5). 551 71 59 (Istituto Italiano di Studi Storici). R3. M Montesanto. **Library** 9am–noon Mon, Wed, Fri.

THIS IS THE first of many noble buildings you will see in the Spaccanapoli and Decumano Maggiore areas. These mansions and palaces are often in a sad state of preservation yet have retained an air of splendor and stateliness, and even now traces of the lives of the generations of aristocrats who built and lived in them. The original Palazzo Filomarino dates back to the 14th century, but the building was substantially altered in the 16th century. It then underwent restoration in the following century after being damaged during Masaniello's uprising *(see p73)*. The 18th-century doorway is the work of the architect Sanfelice. Philosopher Benedetto Croce, a leading figure in Italian culture and politics in the first half of this century *(see p24)*, lived in this palazzo in the latter part of his life. The Italian Institute of Historical Studies, founded by Croce, takes up the whole of the first floor with its 40,000-volume library. At No. 45 on the same street is the impressive Baroque doorway of Palazzo Carafa della Spina.

The library of philosopher Benedetto Croce on the first floor of Palazzo Filomarino

Santa Chiara ⑤

IN 1310 ROBERT OF ANJOU laid the first stone of the convent and church that the Angevin rulers later chose as the site for their tombs. Santa Chiara was where the kingdom's assemblies were held as well as ceremonies, such as the one celebrating the miracle of San Gennaro's blood *(see p40)*. In the mid-1700s, the church's Gothic lines were obscured by the addition of elaborate Baroque ornamentation. After the church was destroyed by fire in 1943, restoration work tried to recover as much as possible of the original; the present interior is simple and austere, typical of a Franciscan church. Near the apse are the fine sculpture groups of the royal Angevin tombs; a beautiful wooden 14th-century crucifix executed by an unknown artist is on the altar. The lovely cloisters are an oasis of calm and a convenient meeting place for Neapolitans.

★ Poor Clares' Choir
Built by Leonardo Di Vito, this choir is one of the best examples of Neapolitan Gothic. It was frescoed by Giotto and his assistants, but only fragments of the original have remained intact.

The bell tower still has its original base, with Gothic inscriptions describing the founding of the church.

Marble floor by Vaccaro

The rose window tracery consists of six marble circles.

The main gateway is a 14th-century portal with a large jutting vault.

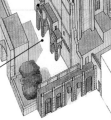

Projecting Porch
This massive structure in piperno stone stands out against the yellow tufa facade. On the marble portal is the coat-of-arms of Queen Sancia of Majorca, the wife of Robert of Anjou.

Tertiaries' Cloister

TIMELINE

1340 Santa Chiara consecrated and declared a royal church	**1742** Building of the tiled cloister		**1943** Aug 4: fire caused by bomb destroys church	**1995** Museo dell'Opera opens to the public

Detail of the cloister

1300	1700	1900

1310 Robert of Anjou lays the first stone

1343 Giovanni and Pacio Bertini sculpt tomb of Robert of Anjou

1769 Church totally rebuilt in Baroque style

1953 Aug 4: restored church reopens for worship

Royal Tombs
The tombs of Charles of Calabria (shown here) and his wife, Mary of Valois, are by Tino da Camaino (c.1285–1337). In the center of the rear wall is the tomb of Robert of Anjou, one of Italy's greatest medieval funerary monuments.

VISITORS' CHECKLIST

Via Benedetto Croce. **Map** 3 B5.
📞 552 62 80. 🚌 R3. 🚇
Ⓜ Montesanto. ⬜ **Church**
7am–12:30pm, 4–7pm; **Cloister**
8:30am–12:30pm, 3:30–6:30pm
Mon–Sat; 9:30am–1pm Sun;
Museum 9:30am–1pm, 3:30–
5:30pm Mon–Sat; 9:30am–1pm
Sun. 🏛 museum only. 📷 ♿

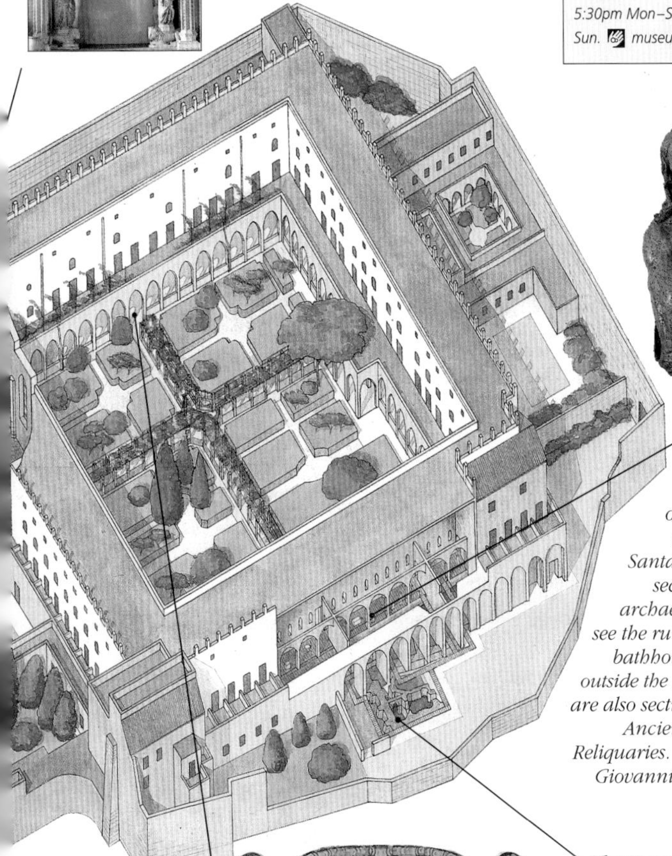

★ **Museo dell'Opera**
This museum houses objects, ornaments, and sculptures from Santa Chiara. In the section devoted to archaeology, you can see the ruins of a Roman bathhouse that extend outside the museum. There are also sections on History, Ancient Marbles and Reliquaries. This last boasts Giovanni da Nola's Ecce Homo *(1519).*

The Roman baths, which once marked the city's western limit, lie between the first two rooms of the Museo dell'Opera and the outer courtyard.

The tomb of Philip of Bourbon, the son of Charles III who died in 1777, is found in the last chapel on the right. Designed by Ferdinando Fuga, it is one of the few 18th-century works that survived the fire in 1943.

★ **Tiled Cloister**
The simple arches of the 14th-century cloister frame the garden redesigned by Domenico Antonio Vaccaro in 1742. The 72 octagonal pillars are punctuated by seats at intervals, and every surface is decorated with majolica tiles painted by Donato and Giuseppe Massa.

STAR FEATURES

★ Royal Tombs

★ Poor Clares' Choir

★ Tiled Cloister

★ Museo dell'Opera

Guglia di San Domenico

Piazza San Domenico Maggiore ❽

Map 3 B5 (9 C3).
🚌 R3. Ⓜ 🚋 Montesanto.

THIS PIAZZA was the result of a rare Renaissance town-planning project in Naples. In the 1500s the area, once crossed by the Greek city walls, was still being used for kitchen gardens. Rebuilding by the Aragonese rulers transformed the zone into a setting appropriate for the church of San Domenico, which had been chosen to house the royal tombs. They also wanted to improve the area around the statue of the Nile, the aristocratic residential district. The top of the piazza is dominated by the apse of San Domenico; next to this, at the end of a tall stairway, is the lovely 14th-century portal of the church of Sant'Arcangelo a Morfisa. Imposing buildings line the other sides of the square. Opposite the church (at No. 17) is the 17th-century Palazzo Sangro di Casacalenda; to the left (No. 3) is Palazzo Petrucci with its 15th-century portal; to the right (Nos. 12 and 9) are Palazzo Corigliano and Palazzo Sangro di Sansevero. In the center stands the Guglia di San Domenico, built in gratitude for release from the 1656 plague .The spire was designed by Cosimo Fanzago and finished in 1737 by Domenico Antonio Vaccaro.

San Domenico Maggiore ❾

Piazza San Domenico Maggiore 8/a.
Map 3 B5 (9 C3). 🕻 557 32 04.
🚌 R3. Ⓜ 🚋 Montesanto.
🕐 7:30am–noon (9am–1pm Sun), 4:30–7pm. 🏛

IN 1238 CHARLES I OF ANJOU ordered the construction of a new church and monastery for the powerful Dominican order. The Gothic three-nave building was built onto the medieval church of Sant'-Arcangelo a Morfisa, whose 14th-century doorway still remains. The appearance of the present-day church is the result of radical restoration and reconstruction. In 1506 a fire almost totally destroyed the basilica. In 1850–53 Federico Travaglini rebuilt the interior in Neo-Gothic style, removing much of the original spirit of this monument. However, in the second chapel on the right there are 14th-century frescoes ascribed to Pietro Cavallini, a pupil of Giotto. The tombs of 45 rulers and

Corradini's *Modesty* in the Cappella Sansevero

Fresco by Francesco Solimena in the sacristy of San Domenico Maggiore

dignitaries at the Aragonese court are arranged along a balcony in the sacristy. The ceiling fresco was painted by Francesco Solimena in 1706.

Cappella Sansevero ❿

Via Francesco de Sanctis 19.
Map 3 B5 (9 C3). 🕻 551 84 70.
🚌 R3. Ⓜ 🚋 Montesanto.
🕐 10am–5pm; 10am–1pm Tue & Sun. 🦺 🚫 ♿

THE LAVISH decoration in the small family chapel was planned by Raimondo di Sangro, Prince of Sansevero, in the second half of the 18th century. In each sculpture group a member of the powerful family is represented by an allegorical figure. Antonio Corradini's *Modesty* (to the left of the altar) is set on the tomb of the prince's mother. On the tomb of his father, said to be a dissolute man who later repented his ways, is Francesco Queirolo's *Deception* (to the right of the altar). The focal point of the chapel is the extraordinary *Veiled Christ*, the masterpiece of Neapolitan sculptor Giuseppe Sanmartino (1720–93). Sculpted from a single block of marble, the recumbent figure of Christ lies draped with the thinnest of translucent veils. In the chapel crypt, two "anatomical machines," perhaps creations of the mysterious Raimondo di Sangro himself, are on display. The stories about the famous prince – inventor, alchemist, lover of science and the occult, and Masonic Grand Master – have engendered legends depicting him as a demon or a sorcerer.

Sant'Angelo a Nilo ⓫

Piazzetta Nilo. **Map** 3 B5 (9 C3).
551 62 27. R3. M
Montesanto. 8am–1pm.

BUILT IN THE late 1300s by Cardinal Brancaccio next to his family palace, this church was drastically remodeled four centuries later by Arcangelo Guglielminelli. The interior houses the earliest Renaissance work in Naples: the cardinal's funerary monument, sculpted in Pisa by Donatello and Michelozzo in 1426–7 and sent to Naples by ship. On the front of the sarcophagus, in the bas-relief representing the *Assumption of the Virgin*, Donatello created one of the first examples of his revolutionary "stiacciato" technique – the relief receding gradually from foreground to background to give the illusion of depth. From the church you can visit the courtyard of Palazzo Brancaccio where, thanks to the family's patronage, the first public library in Naples was founded in 1690.

Statue of the Nile ⓬

Largo Corpo di Napoli. **Map** 3 B5.
R3. M Montesanto.

AN 18TH-CENTURY inscription informs the reader that the Alexandrian merchants who worked in this area of the Greco-Roman city had this statue sculpted in honor of the Egyptian god Nile. The statue disappeared after the merchants left Naples; although it was found in the 1400s, the head was missing. At that time the recumbent putti next to the god, symbols of the many tributaries of the river god, were interpreted as babies at their mother's breast, so that the sculpture was

The frescoed ceiling in the Monte di Pietà chapel

called "the Body of Naples," the mother-city suckling her children. The statue (and the square where it stands) has kept this name despite the addition of a bearded head in the 17th century.

Palazzo Carafa Santangelo ⓭

Via San Biagio dei Librai 121. **Map** 3 C5 (10 D3). R3. M Montesanto. 7am–1pm, 4–7pm Mon–Sat.

THIS IMPORTANT example of Neapolitan Renaissance architecture is known as *Palazzo della Capa di Cavallo* because of the terra-cotta copy of a horse's head (now in the courtyard). This was a gift from Lorenzo de' Medici to his friend Diomede Carafa in 1471 to embellish his new palace. The original sculpture, a Roman bronze, has been in the Museo Archeologico *(see pp86–9)* since 1809.

Statue of the Egyptian god Nile, known as the "Body of Naples"

The marble portal, similar to that of Palazzo Petrucci in Piazza San Domenico *(see p68)*, and the facade with its shallow rustication are examples of the new Renaissance style. In late 15th-century Naples this look merged with the late Gothic style, as can be seen in the form of the arches and pilasters and in the inlay in the wooden doors with the Carafa family coats of arms. Opposite the palace is the animated Baroque facade of the church of San Nicola a Nilo, which is also the site of a second-hand dealer's shop.

Monte di Pietà ⓮

Via San Biagio dei Librai 114.
Map 3 C5 (10 D3). 551 70 74.
R3. M Montesanto.
9am–2pm Sat.

THIS MAJESTIC BUILDING (and the adjoining church) was built in the late 1500s for the charitable institute set up to grant loans to people in debt to moneylenders. The Cappella della Pietà at the end of the courtyard has a late Renaissance façade with sculptures by Pietro Bernini (at the sides of the entrance) and Michelangelo Naccherino (on the tympanum). The church interior was frescoed by Belisario Corenzio and the young Battistello in the early 1600s. Today this is the main office of the Banco di Napoli.

San Giorgio Maggiore **⓯**

Via Duomo 237/a. **Map** 3 C5 (10 E3).
[*28 79 32.* **▦** *R2.* **◯** *8am–noon,
5–7:30pm Mon–Sat; 8:30am–1:30pm
Sun.* **[**

One of the cloisters in the Archivio di Stato

SAN GIORGIO MAGGIORE,
originally an early Christian
basilica, is one of the city's
oldest churches. It was
completely rebuilt in the mid-
1600s to a design by Cosimo
Fanzago. The only surviving
part of the original church is
the semicircular apse with
Corinthian columns at the
entrance of the 17th-century
church, originally built facing
a different direction. The
right-hand nave of the rebuilt
church was demolished in
the late 19th century to make
room for the extended Via
Duomo. The frescoes in the
third chapel are by Francesco
Solimena. Before visiting the
church, pause for a moment
at Palazzo Marigliano (at No.
39 Via Duomo). Although
rundown, it is one of the
most important examples of
16th-century Neapolitan civic
architecture.

Museo Civico Filangieri **⓰**

Via Duomo 288. **Map** 3 C5 (10 E3).
[*20 31 75.* **▦** *R2.* **◯** *9am–7pm
Mon–Sat; 9am–2pm Sun.* **▦** **∅**

THE BUILDING now occupied
by the Civic Museum was
built in the late 15th century
as the Como family residence
in the Florentine Renaissance
style. It became a monastery
in the late 1500s, was
demolished during work on
Via Duomo (1879), and then
was faithfully rebuilt 20 m (66
ft) from its original site. In
1882 Prince Gaetano
Filangieri established his fine
art collection there and
donated it to the city in 1888.
Much of the collection was
scattered during World War II
and was reassembled through
private donations. Today it
consists of different types of
objects from varied sources,
including weapons, furniture,
paintings, medallions,
porcelain, coins, and
costumes. The spiral staircase
leads from the ground floor
to the Sala Agata (named after
the founder's mother), which
leads to the prince's library by
an elevated passageway.

Archivio di Stato **⓱**

Piazzetta Grande Archivio 5.
Map 3 C5 (10 E3). **[** *20 44 91.*
▦ *R2.* **◯** *9am–6pm Mon–Fri;
9am–1pm Sat.*

IN 1835 FERDINAND II decided
to use the former
Benedictine monastery of
Santi Severino e Sossio to
house the enormous quantity
of documents relating to the
administration of the kingdom
that had accumulated since
the Angevin period. The old
monastery, built in the 9th
century and enlarged in 1494,
was remodeled to allow for
its new function.
    The huge complex has four
cloisters and a number of
rooms containing numerous
works of art. One cloister is
known as the *Chiostro del
platano*, named after an
ancient plane tree (removed
in 1959 because it was dying),
which, according to tradition,
had been planted by St.
Benedict himself. The mid-
16th century frescoes
depicting the life of the saint
are the work of Antonio
Solario, known as Lo Zingaro
or "gypsy.". The State Archive
contains over a million files,
registers, documents, and
parchments, and is one of the
most important in Europe.
    By the entrance to the
former monastery is the 17th-
century Fontana della Selleria.

The Sala Agata in the Museo Civico Filangieri, Palazzo Como

Santi Severino e Sossio ⑱

Via Bartolomeo Capasso 22.
Map 3 C5 (10 D4). 📞 26 09 03.
🚌 R2. ⏰ 8–10am Mon–Sat;
9am–12:30pm Sun. 🚻

Marco Pino, *Adoration of the Magi*

FOUNDED IN THE 9th century together with the adjoining monastery (which became the Royal Archives in 1835), this church was rebuilt from the late 1400s on, and finished in 1571. The facade is the result of restoration done after the 1731 earthquake. Inside, there are some excellent works of art. Among the paintings are beautiful canvases by the Sienese painter Marco Pino (first, third, and sixth chapels on the right). The sculptures include the tomb of Andrea Bonifacio (who died at the age of six), a masterpiece by the Spanish sculptor Bartolomeo Ordoñez, in the vestibule of the sacristy. From here you can go downstairs to the lower church, which is undecorated.

Santi Marcellino e Festo ⑲

Largo San Marcellino 10. **Map** 3 C5
(10 D4). 📞 551 61 77. 🚌 R2. ⏰
8am–8pm Mon–Fri; 8am–2pm Sat.

THE TWO ADJACENT monasteries of Santi Marcellino e Pietro and Santi Festo e Desiderio date from the 8th century. In the mid-15th century they were

---

A NUMBER FOR EVERY OCCASION

At noon every Saturday, life stands still for a few minutes in the streets and alleyways of Old Naples in anticipation of an important event – the lottery drawing. In the hall of the lottery office (Ufficio Lotto e Lotterie) at No. 17 Via del Grande Archivio, a crowd will be waiting impatiently for the result. Devised in Genoa in the 16th century, the lottery was legalized the following century and grew rapidly in popularity in the 1800s. Neapolitans were immediately hooked. As Matilde Serao wrote in the late 19th century: "Even Neapolitans who can't read know *La Smorfia* by heart

The lottery in a 19th-century print

and immediately apply it to any dream or real-life event whatsoever." *La Smorfia* is a guide to the significance of numbers and is the lottery "bible." It can be found in any Lotto office. There are about 60,000 entries in alphabetical order, and each entry has a corresponding number. The book was first published in the 19th century and is regularly updated in order to offer readers interpretations of even the most modern events and dreams. For example, should you dream of owning a computer, you will find that the number to choose is 45.

---

combined to create a single large complex. The church, built the following century, is adorned with refined 18th-century marble inlay. Unfortunately, at present it is in a state of almost total abandon and has been closed to the public for many years. The spacious cloister with piperno stone arches has a lovely garden in the center;

from the south-facing side there is a splendid panoramic view of the Bay of Naples. By royal decree, the complex became the property of the University of Naples in 1907. The building next to the church is occupied by the Museum of Paleontology, which has a fine painted majolica floor and over 50,000 artifacts on display.

The airy cloister of the San Marcellino monastery

Gesù Vecchio ⑳

Via Giovanni Paladino 39. **Map** 3 C5
(10 D4). **Library** 551 70 25;
Anthropology Museum 552 78
07; **Zoology Museum** 552 70
89; **Mineralogy Museum Library**
552 77 37. R2.
9am–6:45pm Mon–Fri.
Museums 9am–2pm Mon–Fri;
10am–1pm Sat–Sun. museums.

THE HOME OF the University
of Naples since 1777, this
late 16th-century building was
the first Jesuit college in the
city. In the late 19th century,
thanks to the Urban Renewal
plan (see pp24–5), the
university expanded with the
addition of a large factory
building looking out over
Corso Umberto I. One
remaining part of the original
college is the lovely Cortile
delle Statue (courtyard of
statues). Here you can visit
the upstairs rooms, occupied
by the university library since
1808 and home to 850,000
volumes. In 1801 the large
hall that was once the Jesuits'
library was turned over to the
Mineralogy Museum, the most
important in Italy and one of
the most famous in the world.
Other sections house the
Anthropology Museum and
the Zoology Museum,
founded in 1811 by Joachim
Murat, then ruler of Naples.
   Returning to Via Paladino,
notice the sumptuous
Baroque interior of the
college church (at No. 38),
begun in 1564; this space
contains works by Solimena
and Fanzago. Other rooms
next to the sacristy house life-
size crèche figures and
Nativity scenes.

Corso Umberto I ㉑

Map 4 D5 & 7 C1 (10 E4). R2.

THIS WIDE straight street,
known to Neapolitans as
the Rettifilo, connects the
central train station (Stazione
Centrale) with the city center
and Piazza Giovanni Bovio
(see p57). It was built in the
late 19th century as part of
the Urban Renewal plan (see
pp24–5). The most important
building is the University of
Naples, with its impressive
Neo-Renaissance facade.

**Piazza Giovanni Bovio, at one end
of Corso Umberto I**

Cappella Pappacoda ㉒

Largo San Giovanni Maggiore. **Map** 7
B1 (9 C4). 552 69 48 (Istituto
Universitario Orientale). R2.
apply at the Istituto or during
temporary exhibitions.

IN THE EARLY 15th century
Artusio Pappacoda, Grand
Seneschal and councillor in
the Angevin court, founded
this small church. The original

Portal of Cappella Pappacoda

late Gothic doorway, like
marble embroidery on the
austere tufa facade, is the
work of Antonio Baboccio
(1351–1435), a sculptor,
architect, and goldsmith who
also sculpted the main portal
of the cathedral (see pp82–3).
The campanile is particularly
interesting because of the
color contrast created by the
different materials – marble,
tufa, and piperno. The church
is now deconsecrated and
is used as the Aula Magna
(Great Hall) by the nearby
Istituto Universitario Orientale
(Oriental Institute).

Santissima Annunziata ㉓

Via dell'Annunziata 35. **Map** 4 D4
(10 F3). 20 74 55. R2.
8–12am, 4:30–7pm Mon–Sat;
8am–1pm Sun.

THE SANTA CASA dell'-
Annunziata was a
charitable institution that
existed as long ago as the

The facade of the university in Corso Umberto I after expansion of the site

early 1300s to offer help to abandoned children. The church was destroyed by fire in 1757 and rebuilt by Luigi and Carlo Vanvitelli, who designed the cupola and light-filled, one-nave interior with 44 Corinthian columns and three chapels on each side. Among the parts untouched by the fire is the sacristy, with frescoes by Corenzio (1605) and 16th-century inlaid wooden cabinets. To the left of the church, an impressive marble doorway leads to the former orphanage, which is now used as a hospital.

Painting of the *Madonna Bruna* in Santa Maria del Carmine

Santa Maria del Carmine ㉔

Piazza del Carmine. **Map** 4 E5.
『 20 11 96. 🚋 1, 2.
🕐 6:30am–12:30pm, 5–7:30pm Mon–Sat; 6:30am–1:30pm Sun. ✝

NEAPOLITANS are devoted to this church because of its many works of art, in particular the *Madonna Bruna*, a 14th-century painting kept behind the altar. This famous effigy, the object of deeply felt veneration, is celebrated annually on July 16 at the feast of the Madonna del Carmine *(see p41)*, during which the miracle of the Madonna is reenacted.

Except for the cross dome in the presbytery, little remains of the original Angevin construction. Instead the church displays typical 18th-century architectural forms

PIAZZA MERCATO

Due to their location near the harbor, the churches of Sant'Eligio and Santa Maria del Carmine and the area around them became the focal point of commercial life in late 13th-century Angevin Naples. The lively market quarter around Piazza Mercato in the heart of Naples was also the setting for significant events in the city's history. In 1268, Corradino, the last Hohenstaufen king of Naples, was beheaded at the tender age of 16 in front of the Carmine church, and the new Angevin rulers decreed

View of Piazza Mercato, with Santa Maria del Carmine

that in the future all executions were to be carried out in the square. In 1647 the uprising against the Spanish headed by Tommaso Aniello d'Amalfi, known as Masaniello *(see pp20–21)*, began here. Ten years later the square was used for the graves of those who had died during the plague epidemic. But the most dramatic events occurred in 1799, when the short-lived, glorious Parthenopean Republic was crushed, and its leaders were executed in Piazza Mercato.

both inside and out. The interior was decorated by Tagliacozzi Canale; the ceiling, destroyed in World War II, has been completely rebuilt in keeping with the original. To the left of the nave is the tomb of Corradino, Duke of Swabia, who was beheaded in 1268 in Piazza Mercato, opposite the church *(see above)*. The medieval wooden crucifix, placed in a tabernacle under the triumphal arch, is also the object of devout worship. There are frescoes and canvases by Solimena in the wings of the transept. The 75-m (246-ft) campanile, completed by Fra Nuvolo in 1631, is the tallest in Naples.

Sant'Eligio Maggiore ㉕

Largo Sant'Eligio. **Map** 4 D5 (10 F4).
『 553 84 29. 🚋 1, 2.
🕐 7:30am–12:30pm Mon–Sat; 7:30am–1:30pm Sun. ✝

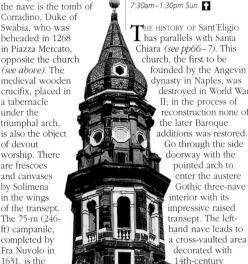

The campanile of Santa Maria del Carmine (1631)

THE HISTORY OF Sant'Eligio has parallels with Santa Chiara *(see pp66–7)*. This church, the first to be founded by the Angevin dynasty in Naples, was destroyed in World War II; in the process of reconstruction none of the later Baroque additions was restored. Go through the side doorway with the pointed arch to enter the austere Gothic three-nave interior with its impressive raised transept. The left-hand nave leads to a cross-vaulted area decorated with 14th-century frescoes by artists of the Giotto school.

DECUMANO MAGGIORE

I N THE HEART of Greco-Roman Naples, part of the ancient grid plan with three parallel east-west roads (Roman *decumani*), intersected at right angles by the north-south *cardines*, is present-day Via dei Tribunali. It was once called Decumano Maggiore (or Massimo) because it was so vital a part of the city structure. In the late 13th and early 14th centuries the area was significant for its Gothic

One of the lions at the duomo entrance

religious architecture. Today, the churches of San Lorenzo, San Pietro a Maiella, and especially the duomo (cathedral), reveal this past. The Duomo is a wonderful blend of art and architectural styles from the 4th to 19th centuries. Outside the city walls, past 18th-century Piazza Dante, lies the Museo Archeologico Nazionale, home of one of the world's richest classical archaeological collections.

SIGHTS AT A GLANCE

Historic Buildings
Accademia di Belle Arti ⓴
Castel Capuano
  and Porta Capuana ⓮
Palazzo Spinelli di Laurino ❺
Pio Monte della Misericordia ⓭

Churches
Cappella Pontano ❸
Duomo pp82–3 ⓫
Gerolamini ❿
Santa Caterina a Formiello ⓯
San Gregorio Armeno ❾
San Lorenzo Maggiore ❽
Santa Maria delle Anime
  del Purgatorio ad Arco ❻
Santa Maria di
  Donnaregina Nuova ⓱
Santa Maria di
  Donnaregina Vecchia ⓰
Santa Maria Maggiore
  della Pietrasanta ❹
San Paolo Maggiore ❼
San Pietro a Maiella ❷

Historic Streets and Squares
Piazza Bellini ❶
Piazza Dante ㉑
Via Anticaglia ⓲

Spires
Guglia di San Gennaro ⓬

Museums
*Museo Archeologico
  Nazionale pp86–9* ⓲

GETTING THERE
Via dei Tribunali allows limited traffic and no buses cross it. The circular routes R1 (from Vomero), R2 (from the Centrale train station), and R3 (from the Mergellina train station) stop in Via Toledo, Via Diaz and Via Monteoliveto. The R2 bus runs along Corso Umberto I, which crosses Via Duomo at Piazza Nicola Amore. R1 passes by the Museo Archeologico Nazionale. You can also take the subway (Montesanto station) and, from Vomero, the Montesanto funicular. The Metro also goes to the Museo Nazionale (Piazza Cavour station).

KEY
Street-by-Street map
See pp76–7

P Parking

M Metro station

◁ **Interior of the Duomo, with its Mannerist paintings set into the carved, gilded wooden ceiling**

Street-by-Street: Via dei Tribunali

Via dei Tribunali was named after Castel Capuano, visible in the distance at the end of this long avenue, when it became the home of the civil courts *(tribunali)* in the 1500s. One of the streets crossing the Decumano Maggiore is Via San Gregorio Armeno, among the loveliest streets in Old Naples, where art and handicrafts flourish. The craftsmen in San Gregorio Armeno still carve shepherds and other figures for the traditional Neapolitan nativity scenes *(see p39)*, just as they did four centuries ago – to the delight of visitors and Neapolitans alike.

San Paolo Maggiore
The sacristy was frescoed by Solimena in 1689– 90 ⑦

Piazza Bellini
This is one of the liveliest spots in the center ①

Sant'Antonio a Port'Alba Monastery

Croce di Lucca

Palazzo Firrao

Santa Maria delle Anime del Purgatorio ad Arco
Funerary motifs adorn the area in front of the church and its interior ⑥

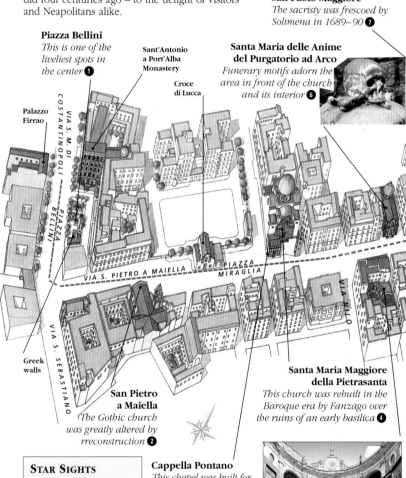

VIA S. M. DI COSTANTINOPOLI
PIAZZA BELLINI
VIA S. PIETRO A MAIELLA
PIAZZA MIRAGLIA
VIA NILO
VIA S. SEBASTIANO

Greek walls

San Pietro a Maiella
The Gothic church was greatly altered by reconstruction ②

Santa Maria Maggiore della Pietrasanta
This church was rebuilt in the Baroque era by Fanzago over the ruins of an early basilica ④

STAR SIGHTS

★ San Lorenzo Maggiore

★ San Gregorio Armeno

★ Duomo

Cappella Pontano
This chapel was built for the humanist Pontano ③

Palazzo Spinelli
Created in the 1700s by merging two 16th-century palaces, Palazzo Spinelli has an original oval courtyard with stuccoes ⑤

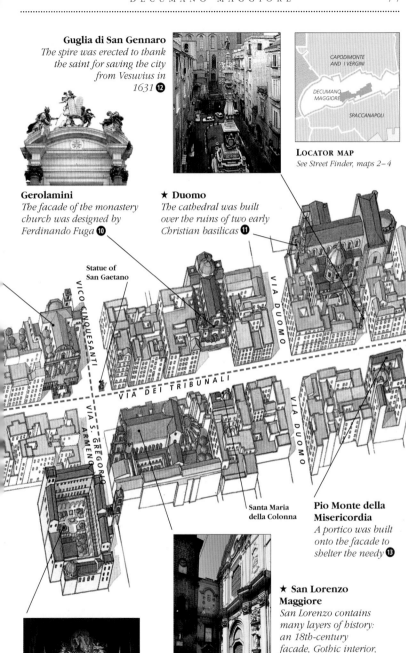

Guglia di San Gennaro
The spire was erected to thank the saint for saving the city from Vesuvius in 1631 ⑫

LOCATOR MAP
See Street Finder, maps 2–4

Gerolamini
The facade of the monastery church was designed by Ferdinando Fuga ⑩

★ Duomo
The cathedral was built over the ruins of two early Christian basilicas ⑪

Statue of San Gaetano

VICO CINQUESANTI

VIA DUOMO

VIA DEI TRIBUNALI

VIA S. GREGORIO ARMENO

VIA DUOMO

Santa Maria della Colonna

Pio Monte della Misericordia
A portico was built onto the facade to shelter the needy ⑬

★ San Lorenzo Maggiore
San Lorenzo contains many layers of history: an 18th-century facade, Gothic interior, and ancient ruins under the cloister ⑧

★ San Gregorio Armeno
The lavish decoration of this monastery is immediately apparent in the vestibule ⑨

KEY

- - - - - Suggested route

0 meters   100

0 yards   100

Piazza Bellini **❶**

Map 3 B5. 🚌 *R3.*
Ⓜ 🚃 *Montesanto.*

THIS SQUARE, at the southern end of Via Santa Maria di Costantinopoli, is one of the liveliest and most interesting places in Old Naples. The area now occupied by the piazza and street lay outside the city proper until the mid-16th century, when the viceroy Pedro de Toledo extended the city walls. The remains of part of the ancient Greek walls of Neapolis were uncovered in the piazza after excavations carried out in 1954. The walls are visible in the middle of the square, at the foot of the monument to the composer Vincenzo Bellini. Overlooking the square is the monastery of Sant'Antonio a Port'Alba, which incorporates the 15th-century Palazzo Conca. On the opposite side is Palazzo Firrao (No. 99 Via Santa Maria di Costantinopoli), an important example of 17th-century Neapolitan civic architecture. The facade is adorned with busts of the Spanish royal family.

San Pietro a Maiella **❷**

Via San Pietro a Maiella 4. **Map** 3 B5.
🎫 *45 90 08.* 🚌 *R3.* Ⓜ 🚃 *Montesanto.* 🕐 *7am–noon, 5–7:30pm Mon–Sat; 8:30am–1pm Sun.* �︎

THE FOUNDER OF this church, the nobleman Pipino da Barletta, dedicated it to Pietro da Morrone, the hermit friar from Maiella who became Pope Celestine V in 1294. The original Gothic architecture, modified by numerous additions over the centuries, was restored over a 40-year period (from 1888 to 1927). The restoration uncovered some 14th-century frescoes in two of the chapels. The removal of the Baroque decoration also revealed splendid gilded

An outdoor café in Piazza Bellini

wooden ceilings in the nave and transept with paintings by Mattia Preti (1656–61), considered as among the supreme examples of 17th-century Neapolitan painting.

Since 1826 the monastery (at No. 35) annexed to the church has been occupied by one of Italy's major music conservatories. The courtyard is well worth visiting.

Cappella Pontano **❸**

Via Tribunali *(no street number, opposite No. 376).* **Map** 3 B4. 🚌 *R3.* Ⓜ 🚃 *Montesanto.* 🕐 *9am–2pm Mon–Sat.*

THE FAMOUS HUMANIST Giovanni Pontano, secretary to King Ferdinand of Aragon, commissioned this small, elegant chapel in 1492. Based on a design for a pagan temple, the harmonious proportions make it one of the most significant works produced in Renaissance Naples. The chapel contains a frescoed triptych by Francesco Cicino da Caiazzo – restored in 1792 – and a 15th-century floor of colored tiles that is remarkably well preserved. The numerous engraved Latin inscriptions were written by Giovanni Pontano himself.

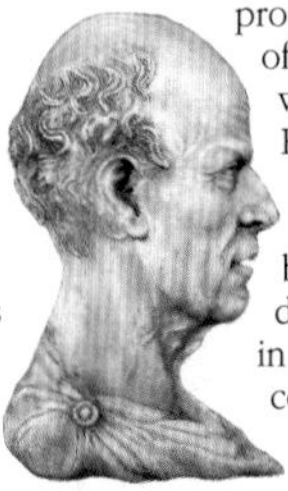

Bust of Giovanni Pontano

Santa Maria Maggiore della Pietrasanta **❹**

Via Tribunali *(opposite No. 376).*
Map 3 B5. 🚌 *R3.* Ⓜ 🚃 *Montesanto.* 🕐 *9am–2pm Mon–Sat.*

The interior of Santa Maria Maggiore della Pietrasanta

THE CHURCH WAS named after a holy stone *(pietrasanta)* with an inscribed cross that was kept here until recently and was popular with worshipers. This majestic, centrally planned church was built by Cosimo Fanzago over the ruins of an early Christian basilica. Traces of the original church have been discovered in the crypt. The campanile *(see p18)* also belonged to the basilica. Dating from the 10th–11th centuries, it is the sole example of early medieval architecture in Naples. Many fragments of even older buildings, from the Roman age on, were inserted into the lower part of the campanile. In the Middle Ages the road was lower and passed under the bell-tower arch.

Palazzo Spinelli di Laurino **⑤**

Via Tribunali 362. **Map** 3 B5.
C *45 93 12.* R3. **M** Montesanto. ☐ *8am–7pm Mon–Sat.*

IN THE 18TH CENTURY, the architect Ferdinando Sanfelice carried out radical changes to this 16th-century palazzo. He also created the unusual oval courtyard and the building beyond, where the chatter from the crowded Via dei Tribunali could be clearly heard by the dukes of Laurino. The double-flight monumental staircase is another of Sanfelice's designs. Similar examples can be seen in the Palazzo Serra di Cassano *(see p58)*, Palazzo dello Spagnolo, and Palazzo Sanfelice *(see p94).*

Santa Maria delle Anime del Purgatorio ad Arco **⑥**

Map 3 B4. Via Tribunali 39. R3. **M** Montesanto. **Church** ☐ *9am–2pm Mon–Sat.* **Cemetery** ☐ *11:30am–12:30pm Mon–Sat.*

THIS CHURCH STILL belongs to the confraternity of the same name founded in 1604 to collect alms to pay for the masses for the souls of the dead. Evidence of the importance attached to worship of the dead in 17th-century Naples is shown by the many skulls, bones, and other funerary motifs on the small stone columns in front of the facade, on the facade itself, and in the interior. The church has a single nave and lavish Baroque decoration. In the apse area there is a disturbing relief with a winged skull by Cosimo Fanzago, who also designed the church. Left of the entrance, steps lead to the underground cemetery. Here, secular services are

Interior of the church of Purgatorio ad Arco

dedicated to the worship of the dead, a practice frowned on by the Catholic church.

San Paolo Maggiore **⑦**

Piazza San Gaetano. **Map** 3 C4.
C *45 40 48.* R3. **M** Montesanto. ☐ *9am–2pm Mon–Sat; 11am–noon Sun.*

IN GRECO-ROMAN NAPLES, present-day Piazza San Gaetano was the site of the Greek *Agora* and later, of the Roman Forum. The Romans built a Temple of the Dioscuri here that was converted into a Christian basilica in the 8th century. This ancient church was then remodeled from 1583 to 1603 by Francesco Grimaldi. The new church, with a three-nave Latin cross

plan, also incorporated the pronaos of the pagan temple. Only two Corinthian columns of the temple survived the 1688 earthquake.

In the richly decorated interior there are fine frescoes by Massimo Stanzione on the vault over the central nave. Unfortunately, they were damaged by water seepage and bombardment during World War II. The Cappella Firrao, on the left side of the apse, has many 17th-century tombs, sculptures, and frescoes. The marvelous paintings in the sacristy are by Francesco Solimena (1689–90). A stairway leads down to the crypt (also accessible from outside the church).

Facade of San Paolo Maggiore

UNDERNEATH THE CITY

Underneath Naples there is another world to be explored, just as fascinating as the city above. Since its early days the city has been built out of material quarried from the ground – the local yellow tufa is excellent for building. Over the years, caves and tunnels were left in this way, and became catacombs, aqueducts, passageways, and escape and shelter areas during

Entrance to underground Naples

World War II bombing raids. The caves were extended to their current size during Spanish rule *(see pp20–21)*, when it was forbidden to import raw material for building houses and palazzi. Today you can descend into the bowels of Naples: on the left-hand side of San Paolo Maggiore is one of the entrances to *Napoli Sotterranea (see p203).*

San Lorenzo Maggiore ❽

Via dei Tribunali 316. **Map** 3 C4
(10 D3). 🚋 29 05 80. 🚌 R3.
Ⓜ 🚇 Montesanto. **Church** ◐
8–noon, 4–7pm. **Excavations** ◐
10am–1pm Mon–Sat. 🚻

T HE CONSTRUCTION of one of
Naples's oldest and richest
monumental complexes was
begun in 1265, for Charles I
of Anjou, on the site of a 6th-
century church (see p33). The
facade was totally rebuilt by
Sanfelice in 1742, but the
large 14th-century portal and
original wooden doors are
intact. The single-nave Gothic
interior has an apse, designed
by French architects, with
nine chapels placed around
the ambulatory. Here is the
tomb of Catherine of Austria,
a fine sculpture by Tino da
Camaino (c.1323) and, in the
sixth chapel from the right,
frescoes by a Neapolitan
pupil of Giotto. It was in
this church that the writer
Boccaccio first saw the girl
he celebrated in his writings
as Fiammetta.
To the right of San Lorenzo
is the monastery, where you
can visit the cloister, the
chapterhouse, and the
refectory that was the
assembly hall of the royal
Parliament from 1442 on. The
cloister allows access to
the excavation site that has
revealed important remains
of the Greco-Roman city.
These include a *macellum*
(market) and a vast area
below this where you can see

The Baroque interior of the church of San Gregorio Armeno

the building that housed the
aerarium (public treasury)
and a street of workshops.

San Gregorio Armeno ❾

Convent: Piazzetta San Gregorio
Armeno 1; **Church**: Via San Gregorio
Armeno 44. **Map** 3 C5 (10 D3).
🚋 552 01 86. 🚌 R3. Ⓜ 🚇 Montesanto. ◐ 9:30–noon daily. **Church**
◐ 8am–1pm Tue. 🚻

T HIS IS ONE OF the most
important religious sites in
Naples. San Gregorio was
founded in the 8th century by
a group of nuns who had fled
Byzantium with the relics of
St. Gregory in order to escape
religious persecution. The
monastery was rebuilt in the
1500s and enlarged the
following century. The lovely
campanile was erected in
1716 on a footbridge that

connected two parts of the
complex. The decoration of
the sumptuous Baroque
interior – a "room of Paradise
on Earth," as Carlo Celano
wrote in his guide to Naples –
was designed in the mid-18th
century by Niccolò Tagliacozzi Canale. Notable works
include the late 16th-century
wooden ceiling, the two
organs and, above the
entrance, Luca Giordano's
frescoes of *The Embarkation,
Journey and Arrival of the
Armenian Nuns with the
Relics of St. Gregory*
(1671–84).
There is a fountain in the
cloister with a 1733 statue of
Christ and the Samaritan (see
p21). From here you can visit
the Cappella della Madonna
dell'Idria, decorated by Paolo
De Matteis in 1712.

Gerolamini ❿

Church: Piazza Gerolamini 107;
Cloisters, Library & Gallery: Via
Duomo 142; **Cappella dell'Assunta**:
Via Duomo 144. **Map** 3 C4 (10 D2).
Library 🚋 29 44 44. **Oratorio
dell'Assunta** 🚋 44 91 39. 🚌 R3.
Ⓜ 🚇 Montesanto. **Church,
Cloisters & Gallery** ◐ 9:30am–1pm
Mon–Sat. **Library** ◐ 10:30am daily
except Sat (11:15am). 📷 📕

T HE MONASTERY of the
Gerolamini was founded
in the late 16th century by the
Oratorio di San Filippo Neri
congregation, also called "dei
Gerolamini" because they
came from San Girolamo alla
Carità in Rome. The church

Cloister of San Lorenzo Maggiore

The cloister in the Gerolamini

was built in the Tuscan Renaissance style; the interior was rebuilt in the early 1600s, and the facade was modified by Ferdinando Fuga in 1780. Luca Giordano, Pietro da Cortona, and Guido Reni, among others, decorated the splendid Baroque interior.

Alongside the church there are two cloisters. The first, designed by Giovanni Dosio, shares features with the cloister he created at the Certosa di San Martino *(see pp108–11).* There are fine paintings in the Quadreria (art gallery). The 60,000-volume library has 18th-century furnishings and decoration.

Duomo ⓫

See pp82–3.

Guglia di San Gennaro ⓬

Piazza Riario Sforza. **Map** 3 C4 (10 D2). R2. **M** *Cavour.*

THIS SCULPTED marble spire is dedicated to San Gennaro, the patron saint of Naples, for having protected the city during the 1631 eruption of Vesuvius. The *guglia*, the oldest of the three spires in Naples, was designed by Cosimo Fanzago in 1636, the same artist who later worked on the Guglia di San Domenico *(see p68).* The bronze statue at the top of the spire was sculpted by Tommaso Montani. Behind the spire in the

Guglia di San Gennaro

small square you can glimpse the stairway of the side entrance to the Duomo *(see pp82–3)* and, higher up, the dome of the Cappella del Tesoro di San Gennaro (Chapel of the Treasury of San Gennaro).

Pio Monte della Misericordia ⓭

Via Tribunali 253. **Map** 3 C4.
44 69 73. R2. **M** *Cavour.*
Church 9:30am–1:30pm Mon–Sat. **Art gallery** 9am–1pm Thu–Sat. by appt.

The Seven Acts of Mercy, a masterpiece by Caravaggio

PIO MONTE is one of the most important charitable institutions in Naples. It was founded in 1601 to aid the poor and ill and to free the Christian slaves in the Ottoman Empire. The entire complex was designed by Francesco Antonio Picchiatti in the second half of the 17th century. After passing through the five-arch loggia (where pilgrims could stay) decorated with sculptures by Andrea Falcone (1666–71), you enter the church. Your eye is immediately drawn to the extraordinary altarpiece, *The Seven Acts of Mercy*, a masterpiece by Caravaggio (1571–1610), one of Italy's greatest artists. The art gallery on the first floor of the building houses the

fine Pio Monte collection. Pio Monte is still active as a charitable institution today.

Castel Capuano and Porta Capuana ⓮

Piazza Enrico De Nicola and Via Concezio Muzy. **Map** 4 D4 (10 F2).
223 71 11. R2. **M** *Cavour.*
Cappella Sommaria 8–9am Thu.

A PALACE AND FORTRESS built by the Normans in 1165 to defend the nearby city gateway, Castel Capuano remained a royal residence for the Angevin and Aragonese rulers even after the construction of Castel Nuovo *(see pp54–5).* In 1540 Don Pedro de Toledo turned the castle into law courts, a function it maintains to this day. On the first floor is the huge frescoed Court of Appeal, which leads to the splendid Renaissance Cappella della Sommaria, decorated by the Spanish painter Pietro Roviale.

A short distance away from the courts stands the gateway of Porta Capuana. Although much older in origin, its present appearance is the result of late 15th-century reconstruction by Giuliano da Maiano. The two towers, named Honor and Virtue, enclose the marble arch, repeating the pattern established in the Arco di Trionfo in Castel Nuovo.

The marble arch of Porta Capuana, rebuilt in the 1400s

Duomo ⓫

T HIS GREAT CATHEDRAL was built for Charles I of Anjou between 1294 and 1323. The church incorporated older Christian buildings and has been altered substantially over the

The bust of San Gennaro

centuries. The left-hand nave leads to the early medieval basilica of Santa Restituta, radically changed in the 17th century, and the San Giovanni in Fonte baptistry. The Cappella Minutolo has retained its original Gothic structure and decoration; the mosaic pavement and 13th-century frescoes are by Montano d'Arezzo. The Crypt of the Succorpo was built under the apse in the 1500s to house the relics of San Gennaro, until then in the Montevergine sanctuary. In the early 1600s the Cappella del Tesoro di San Gennaro was erected after the 1527 plague epidemic ended.

★ Baptistry
This is the oldest baptistry in the Western world, built around AD 550. The mosaics date from the same period.

★ Santa Restituta
The structure of the early Christian basilica was changed in the Angevin period (when it became a side chapel in the new cathedral), and its decoration was replaced in the late 1600s. In the last chapel on the left is the beautiful mosaic Madonna and Saints Gennaro and Restituta, executed by Lello da Orvieto in 1322.

The archaeological area, which can be entered from the left-hand nave, reveals layers of buildings from three successive periods: Greek, Roman, and early Middle Ages.

The three portals were the work of Antonio Baboccio da Piperno (1407); the middle one still bears two 14th-century lions and Tino da Camaino's *Virgin and Child* in the lunette.

TIMELINE

c.450 The Santa Restituta and Santa Stefania basilicas built	**1300** Duomo built on the site of the two basilicas	**1497** Work begins on crypt to house relics of San Gennaro		**1876** The façade is rebuilt in Neo-Gothic style	**1969** Digs begin in archaeological area
400	**1300**	**1500**	**1600**		**1900**
	c.550 The San Giovanni in Fonte baptistry added to Santa Restituta	**1349** An earthquake destroys the façade of the Duomo	**1608–37** Cappella del Tesoro di San Gennaro erected	**1621** Old ceiling replaced by present-day one in gilded wood	

Over 100 ancient columns are used as facing for the nave pillars.

The Crypt of the Succorpo, with three naves, was decorated with Renaissance statues by Tommaso Malvito and assistants.

VISITORS' CHECKLIST

Via Duomo 147. **Map** 3 C4 (10 E2). **Church** ⟨C⟩ 44 90 97. 🚌 R2. Ⓜ Cavour. **Church** ☐ 8am–1pm, 5–7:30pm daily; **Cappella del Tesoro di San Gennaro** ☐ 8am–noon daily; **Santa Restituta, Archaeological area, Baptistry** ☐ 9am–noon, 4:30–7pm Mon–Sat; 9am–noon Sun. 🎟

Font
The basin is made of Egyptian basalt. There are Greek sculptures and a 14th-century episcopal throne in the right-hand nave.

Cappella Minutolo

MIRACLE OF THE BLOOD

Every first Sunday in May and on September 19 *(see pp40–42)* the blood of San Gennaro, kept in two phials in the duomo, turns to liquid. This ritual dates from the late 1300s; in Naples this is the equivalent of an oracle: if the miracle does not occur, catastrophes are imminent.

Guglia di San Gennaro *(see p81)*

★ **Cappella del Tesoro di San Gennaro**
The dome with its depiction of Paradise was frescoed by Lanfranco in 1641–3. The most precious object in the chapel is the reliquary bust of San Gennaro, a masterpiece of Gothic craftsmanship in gold.

STAR FEATURES

★ Cappella del Tesoro di San Gennaro

★ Baptistry

★ Santa Restituta

The monumental facade of Santa Maria di Donnaregina Nuova

Santa Caterina a Formiello **⓯**

Piazza Enrico De Nicola. **Map** 4 D4 (10 F1). **C** 44 42 97. ▦ R2. **M** Cavour. **○** 8:30am–12:30pm, 4:30–8pm Mon–Sat; 8:30am–1:30pm Sun.

THE DOME OF Santa Caterina a Formiello dominates the surrounding area. The church was called *formiello* because it was built next to *formali*, the ancient city aqueducts. The 16th-century building has delightful Baroque decoration in the interior. Luigi Garzi and Guglielmo Borremans executed the frescoes (1695–1709). The marble tombs of the Spinelli family are in the apse area.

Santa Maria di Donnaregina Vecchia **⓰**

Vico Donnaregina 25. **Map** 3 C4 (10 D1). **C** 29 91 01. ▦ R2. **M** Cavour. **○** 9am–noon Sat.

THE MONASTERY and the church of Santa Maria di Donnaregina Vecchia were founded in the 8th century and then totally rebuilt in 1293, at the request of Marie of Hungary, wife of Charles II of Anjou. The interior of the church, with one nave that ends in a pentagonal apse, was built on two levels in order to create a separate area for the nuns' enclosure. The lower part boasts an elegant marble tomb of the queen who founded the complex, sculpted by Tino da Camaino in 1325–6. In the upper section – which can be reached via a stairway

Detail of the 13th-century fresco cycle in Donnaregina Vecchia

to the right of the entrance – is the largest 14th-century cycle of frescoes in Naples painted by Roman artists and local pupils of Giotto from 1332 to 1335 *(see p19)*.

Santa Maria di Donnaregina Nuova **⓱**

Largo Donnaregina 7. **Map** 3 C4 (10 D1). **C** 29 91 01. ▦ R2. **M** Cavour. **●** for restoration.

IN THE EARLY 1600s the Poor Clares in the Santa Maria Donnaregina convent decided to build a new church, incorporating part of the old church in the new construction. The two churches, connected by the apse areas, were separated during restoration work in 1928–34. The original 14th-century features were rediscovered and the plan of the 17th-century construction was modified. The single-nave interior is richly decorated in multicolored marble with floral motifs, and there are fine frescoes by Francesco Solimena (1657–1747) in the nuns' choir.

Via Anticaglia **⓲**

Map 3 C4 (10 D2). **C** 779 41 11. ▦ R2. **M** Cavour.

THE THIRD, northernmost *decumanus* (east–west major road) in Greco-Roman Naples today has four official sections (Via Sapienza, Via Pisanelli, Via Anticaglia, and

The elegant interior of the pharmacy in the Ospedale degli Incurabili

Foro Carolino, present-day Piazza Dante, the 18th-century palace and hemicycle designed by Luigi Vanvitelli

Via Santi Apostoli), as does Spaccanapoli, the lower *decumanus (see p61)*.

The name "Anticaglia," meaning ruins, derives from the remains of the brick walls of a Roman building in this stretch of the street. These walls connected the ancient theater, on the left as you go toward Via Santa Maria di Costantinopoli, and the bath-house on the opposite side of the street. The theater, where Emperor Nero is known to have acted, had a seating capacity of about 8,000. Nearby was the *odeion*, or ancient roofed theater, used for concerts and poetry readings.

On the corner of Via Duomo and the third *decumanus*, there is a fine marble and piperno double stairway – from here you can visit the atrium of the church of San Giuseppe dei Ruffi, which was added in the early 18th century. Once past the Roman ruins, a right-hand turn at Via Armanni takes you to the Ospedale degli Incurabili. Inside is the unusual *Farmacia* (pharmacy) with about 400 brightly colored majolica vases on shelves of inlaid wood – a virtual art gallery of Neapolitan ceramics. However, visits are allowed only during the month of May for the "Maggio dei Monumenti" *(see p40)*.

Museo Archeologico Nazionale ⓳

See pp86–9.

Accademia di Belle Arti ⓴

Via Vincenzo Bellini 36. **Map** 3 B4 (9 B2). **[** 564 05 57. 🚊 *R1, R3.* **Ⓜ** *Montesanto.* ◯ *9am–5pm Mon–Sat.*

ARCHITECT Enrico Alvino transformed the 18th-century convent of San Giovanni delle Monache into the Academy of Fine Arts in the 1840s. The Neo-Renaissance style reflects the prevailing fashion of the time. A broad staircase with plaster casts of ancient sculptures leads to the first floor, which still bears traces of the convent cloister. There is an important collection of modern painting, especially works by 19th-century Neapolitan and southern Italian artists.

The Accademia di Belle Arti staircase

Piazza Dante ㉑

Map 3 A5 (9 B3).

THE NAMES given to this square over the centuries sum up its history. Up to the 1700s it lay outside the city walls and was used as a marketplace, hence the name Largo del Mercatello. In the second half of the 18th

18th-century print of Largo del Mercatello

century the square took on its present form and was called Foro Carolino, after King Charles III, who commissioned the new layout. The semicircular facade with its colossal columns was designed by Luigi Vanvitelli as a setting for the king's statue, which was intended for the central niche but was never sculpted. The 26 figures on the cornice are allegories of the sovereign's qualities. Following the unification of Italy, a statue of Dante was placed in the middle of the square and renamed Piazza Dante. To the left of the piazza is Port'Alba, the gateway built in 1625 to connect the city with outlying districts.

Museo Archeologico Nazionale ⑲

THIS BUILDING houses one of the world's most important archaeological museums. It started life in the late 1500s as the home of the royal cavalry and was rebuilt in the early 17th century as the seat of Naples university. In 1777, when Ferdinand IV transferred the university to the monastery of Gesù Vecchio *(see p72)*, the building was adapted to house the Real Museo Borbonico and library. In 1860 it became public property. Restoration and reorganization of exhibits still continue in the museum.

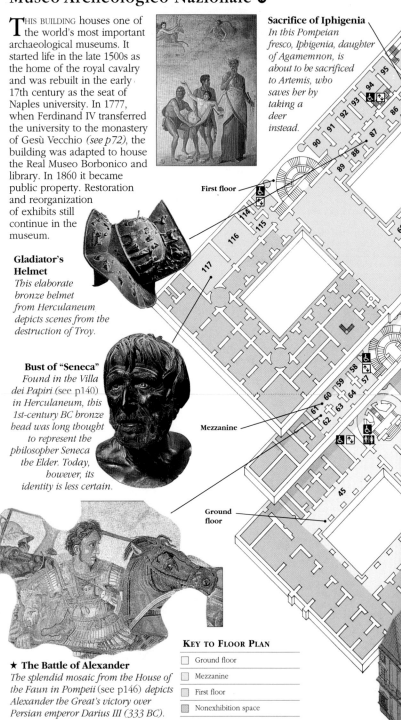

Sacrifice of Iphigenia
In this Pompeian fresco, Iphigenia, daughter of Agamemnon, is about to be sacrificed to Artemis, who saves her by taking a deer instead.

First floor

Gladiator's Helmet
This elaborate bronze helmet from Herculaneum depicts scenes from the destruction of Troy.

Bust of "Seneca"
Found in the Villa dei Papiri (see p140) in Herculaneum, this 1st-century BC bronze head was long thought to represent the philosopher Seneca the Elder. Today, however, its identity is less certain.

Mezzanine

Ground floor

★ **The Battle of Alexander**
The splendid mosaic from the House of the Faun in Pompeii (see p146) depicts Alexander the Great's victory over Persian emperor Darius III (333 BC).

KEY TO FLOOR PLAN

☐	Ground floor
☐	Mezzanine
☐	First floor
☐	Nonexhibition space

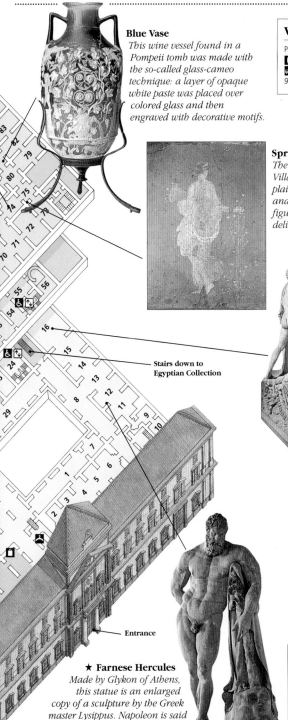

Blue Vase
This wine vessel found in a Pompeii tomb was made with the so-called glass-cameo technique: a layer of opaque white paste was placed over colored glass and then engraved with decorative motifs.

Spring Fresco
The fresco removed from the Villa Stabia in the Varano plain is a masterpiece of grace and elegance; the female figure rendered with soft, delicate colors.

Stairs down to
Egyptian Collection

★ **Farnese Bull**
Excavated in the Baths of Caracalla in Rome, this is the largest sculptural group (c.200 BC) to have survived from antiquity. The best-known piece in the Farnese Collection, it shows the punishment of Dirce who, having ill-treated Antiope, was tied to an enraged bull by Antiope's sons.

Entrance

★ **Farnese Hercules**
Made by Glykon of Athens, this statue is an enlarged copy of a sculpture by the Greek master Lysippus. Napoleon is said to have regretted leaving it behind when he removed his booty from Italy in 1797.

STAR FEATURES

★ **Farnese Hercules**

★ **Farnese Bull**

★ **The Battle of Alexander**

Exploring the Museo Archeologico

Wild goat from Edessa

THE REAL MUSEO BORBONICO, as the museum was known, held the Farnese Collection of paintings, ancient artifacts and books, and archaeological finds from sites in Campania and Southern Italy. In 1925 the books moved to the Palazzo Reale *(see pp50–51)* and in 1957 the Farnese Collection paintings returned to Capodimonte *(see pp98–101)*. The remaining material consisted of ancient finds, and the museum became the Archaeological Museum.

The impressive Farnese Collection and sculpture from Herculaneum, Pompeii and other Campanian cities can be seen on the ground floor. Pompeiian mosaics, on the mezzanine level, and domestic items, weapons and murals, on the first floor, show daily life in the ancient cities. A lower ground floor level houses the Egyptian Collection. The arrangement tries to display the exhibits in context, but be prepared for areas to be closed.

SCULPTURE

THE FINE collection of Greco-Roman sculpture consists mostly of works found in excavations around Vesuvius and the Phlegraean Fields, as well as the treasures from the Farnese Collection. The sculptures – most of which are the only existing Roman copies of lost Greek originals – are displayed on the ground floor. Among the numerous fine works are the statues of *Harmodios and Aristogeiton*, or the "tyrannicides," young Athenians who killed the 6th-century BC tyrant, Hipparchos, and the bronze and alabaster *Artemis of Ephesos*, whose many breasts symbolize fertility. The *Doryphoros* carrying a spear is a copy of a famous Greek original, as is the impressive *Farnese Hercules*. The *Farnese Atlas*, holding up the world, is a Hellenistic statue. The huge *Dioscuri* statues, discovered in the Roman baths of Baia *(see p133)*, and the harmonious *Farnese Flora* are copies by Roman sculptors.

Cameo with Dionysus and satyr

INCISED GEMS

THIS PRECIOUS collection, begun by Cosimo de' Medici, contains Greek, Roman and Renaissance gems. The highlight is the veined sardonyx *Farnese Cup*, a large and beautiful cameo carved in Egypt around the 2nd and 1st centuries BC. Another stunning agate and sardonyx cameo shows the infant Dionysus playing with a satyr.

THE EGYPTIAN COLLECTION

VALUABLE works of Egyptian art from the Ancient Kingdom (2700–2200 BC) to the Roman age are exhibited here. The black basalt *Farnese Naophorous*

The Farnese Flora

Funerary stela of the scribe Huy

represents a kneeling official. These were the intermediaries between men and gods. The limestone funerary stela of Huy (1320–1200 BC) retains some of its original coloring.

As well as human and animal mummies, the Egyptian section includes Canopic vases, containers for the internal organs of the deceased with lids in the shape of animal heads. The collection of *shabti* comprises wood, stone, and faience statuettes representing workers for the deceased in the afterlife.

MOSAICS

THE MAJORITY of the mosaics on display in the museum come from Pompeii, Stabiae, Herculaneum, and Boscoreale and date from the 2nd century BC to AD 79. The realistic images, such as the female portraits from Pompeii, are particularly fascinating.

Mosaic of a female from Pompeii

Among the many pavement mosaics made of tiny tesserae and often derived from Greek paintings, is *La Fattucchiera* (the Sorceress). This interesting example of the Hellenistic tradition depicts a scene from *Synaristoi*, a comedy by the Greek playwright Aristophanes. Another masterpiece is the *Battle of Alexander* found at Pompeii. This large, detailed mosaic was based on a Hellenistic painting and depicts Alexander the Great leading his cavalry against Darius III, the Persian Emperor, seen fleeing in his chariot.

Some rooms in the museum have reconstructions of large mosaic paved floors.

observatory. A large sundial *(meridiana)*, decorated with the signs of the zodiac, was created for the spacious hall that had originally been destined to be the Bourbon library (Biblioteca Borbonica).

The idea of the observatory, however, was discarded when experts realized that the location of the building meant that it was impossible to have a total view of the sky. A few years later the observatory was built elsewhere *(see p97)*. As originally planned, the Salone della Meridiana was opened to the public in 1804 as a library.

There are also numerous fragments of frescoes that depict landscapes, portraits, and mythological scenes and characters, such as the *Sacrifice of Iphigenia*. These show the variety and quality of Roman painting from this period.

TEMPLE OF ISIS

THE PAINTINGS, sculptures and furnishings from the Temple of Isis in Pompeii are presented in order to re-create the sanctuary as it appeared to the first archaeologists in 1764. *The Portrait of Io at Canopos* was uncovered on November 18 of the same year in the presence of King Ferdinand IV. It shows the nymph Io being welcomed to Egypt by Isis. The marble head of the goddess, to whom the temple was dedicated, dates from the 1st century AD.

Head of Isis

VILLA DEI PAPIRI

THIS VILLA in Herculaneum *(see p140)*, still partly buried today, was an art gallery in its own right. The rich array of artworks found here during the excavations in 1750–61 are exceptional: this ancient private collection has been handed down to us intact. A map of the villa shows where every object was found.

Among the pieces on display are life-size statues and small sculptures in marble and bronze, such as the *Dancing Faun*, which greeted visitors in the atrium of the villa. Most of the pieces were inspired by Greek figurative art. A vast library of around 1,700 papyrus scrolls was also found in the villa. An apparatus used to unroll the charred scrolls is on display. The original scrolls are now kept in the Biblioteca Nazionale *(see p51)*.

Statue of a faun, Villa dei Papiri

FRESCOES

MOST OF THE frescoes in the collection were removed from buildings in cities buried by the eruptions of Vesuvius and assembled here from the mid-1700s onward. The most important came from the Basilica in Herculaneum (such as the painting of *Achilles and Chiron*). Others were taken from the Villa di Fannio Sinistore at Boscoreale, where one wall was decorated with illusionistic architectural perspective, and from the extensive landed property of Julia Felix in Pompeii *(see p147)*. The frieze from her house, with a still life of apples and grapes and scenes from the forum, gives a fascinating glimpse of everyday life in a 1st-century AD city.

THE MODEL OF POMPEII

Model of Pompeii

PAPER, CORK, AND WOOD were all used in the making of this extensive scale model of the Pompeii excavations. The archaeologist Giuseppe Fiorelli had the original idea and the model was constructed in various stages between 1861 to 1879. The extraordinarily exact reproduction of every detail found in the ruins (including paintings and mosaics done in watercolor), make this an extremely important historical document. In some cases, when detailed records of Pompeiian decoration are needed, this model is the only useful source that remains.

SALONE DELLA MERIDIANA

WHEN THE BUILDING was being reorganized and fitted out as a museum in the late 18th century, the architects had the idea of adding an

The famous fresco *Achilles and Chiron* from Herculaneum

CAPODIMONTE AND I VERGINI

ALTHOUGH THE SPANISH viceroys had forbidden construction outside the city walls, from the 17th century onward suburban development continued. In the early 19th century, building began in the northern suburbs. The avenue leading to the Capodimonte palace, now the home of one of Europe's most important museums, was created as an extension of Via Toledo. The

Porcelain at Capodimonte

square next to the Museo Archeologico was redesigned and the Via Foria was widened. There, the Botanic Garden and, from 1751, the huge Albergo dei Poveri were built. The old Sanità, Vergini, and Fontanelle districts have retained the character of a lively working quarter. On the streets leading to the early Christian cemeteries, tenements alternate with historic churches and buildings.

SIGHTS AT A GLANCE

Churches and Cemeteries
Cimitero delle Fontanelle ❻
Santi Apostoli ❽
San Gennaro Catacombs ❿
San Giovanni a Carbonara ❼
Santa Maria degli Angeli
 alle Croci ❾
Santa Maria della Sanità and
 San Gaudioso Catacombs ❺
San Severo and Catacombs ❹

Historic Buildings
Albergo dei Poveri ⓫
Osservatorio Astronomico ⓮
Palazzo Sanfelice ❸
Palazzo dello Spagnolo ❷

Historic Gate
Porta San Gennaro ❶

Museums and Galleries
Museo Nazionale and Park of Capodimonte pp98–101 ⓭

Parks and Gardens
Orto Botanico ❿

GETTING THERE
The Capodimonte museum and Catacombs of San Gennaro can be reached via bus routes 24 and 109, which start off at Piazza del Municipio. You can walk to the Vergini and Sanità districts from the Metro station at Piazza Cavour. Many buses run along Via Foria. Bus 105 serves the Fontanelle.

KEY

	Street-by-Street map *See pp92–3*
P	Parking
M	Metro station

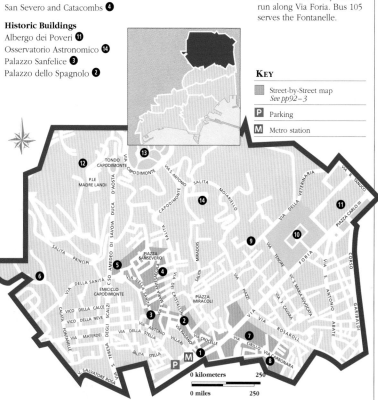

◁ Caravaggio's *Flagellation of Christ* (1610), on display in the Museo di Capodimonte

Street-by-Street: North of the Ancient Walls

THE AREA NORTH OF THE CITY WALLS was used for burials and worship of the dead since it was first inhabited. A visit to the catacombs (which were underground cemeteries and not hiding places), first created in the early Christian era, is an unforgettable experience. The area outside the walls was also used in the Middle Ages as a garbage dump. The district known today as Via San Giovanni a Carbonara was once called the Fosso Carbonario (literally, "coal ditch"), and this is how the street and the beautiful 14th-century church acquired their current names.

The church of Santa Maria dei Vergini, built in the 14th century, was badly damaged in World War II.

San Severo
This church was built over the burial site of St. Severus, Bishop of Naples from 364 to 410 ❹

★ Palazzo Sanfelice
This staircase in the smaller courtyard was the prototype for another one designed by Ferdinando Sanfelice in San Giovanni a Carbonara (see p96) ❸

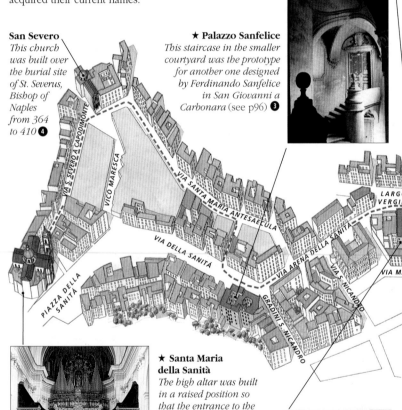

★ Santa Maria della Sanità
The high altar was built in a raised position so that the entrance to the San Gaudioso catacombs could be seen ❺

Palazzo dello Spagnolo
This monumental gateway is one entrance to the double-flight staircase, the highlight of this palazzo, which was designed by Sanfelice in 1738 ❷

KEY

- - - - - Suggested route

0 meters   50

0 yards   50

★ San Giovanni a Carbonara
The double-flight winding staircase here was designed by Ferdinando Sanfelice. The magnificent sculptures inside make this one of the most important churches in Naples **7**

LOCATOR MAP
See Street Finder, maps 2–4

The Padri della Missione Church was designed by Vanvitelli.

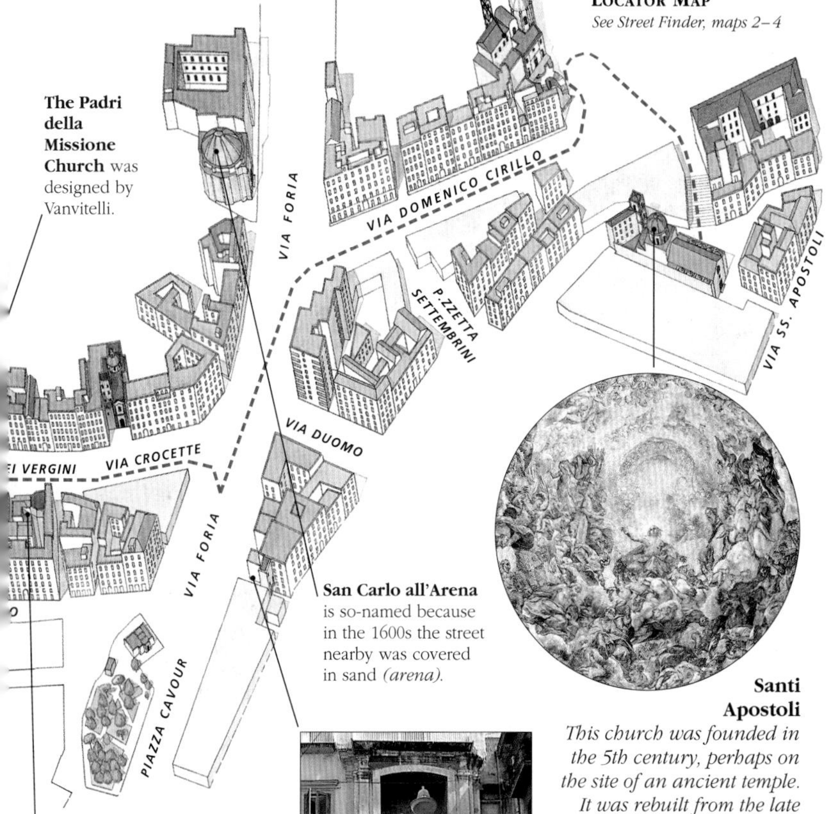

Santa Maria Succurre Miseris was founded in the 14th century and rebuilt in the 1700s by Ferdinando Sanfelice, using Baroque motifs throughout.

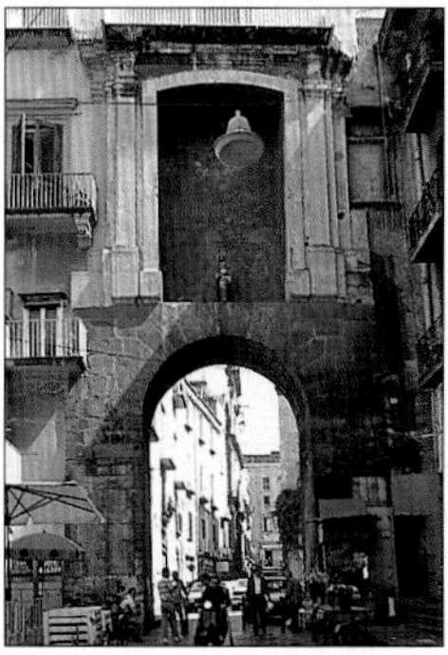

San Carlo all'Arena is so-named because in the 1600s the street nearby was covered in sand *(arena)*.

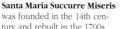

Porta San Gennaro
In the mid-15th century the city walls were extended, and this gateway was rebuilt in its present location **1**

Santi Apostoli
This church was founded in the 5th century, perhaps on the site of an ancient temple. It was rebuilt from the late 1500s to the mid-1600s. The Paradise *in the dome was painted by Giovanni Battista Beinaschi in 1680* **8**

STAR SIGHTS

★ Palazzo Sanfelice

★ Santa Maria della Sanità and San Gaudioso Catacombs

★ San Giovanni a Carbonara

Map labels: VIA FORIA · VIA DOMENICO CIRILLO · P.ZZETTA SETTEMBRINI · VIA SS. APOSTOLI · VIA DUOMO · EI VERGINI · VIA CROCETTE · VIA FORIA · PIAZZA CAVOUR

The double-flight staircase in Palazzo dello Spagnolo

in order to win the Neapolitans' favor. This theatrical aspect of his work can be clearly seen in the two palazzi he designed for the Sanità district.

Once through the majestic doorway of the Palazzo dello Spagnolo, you will notice a feature taken from the Palazzo Sanfelice: the magnificent double-flight external staircase. This type of staircase, which effectively separates the main courtyard from the smaller one, like stage scenery, is one of the most notable features of Neapolitan palaces.

Porta San Gennaro ❶

Map 3 C3. Ⓜ *Cavour.*

THIS GATEWAY was named after San Gennaro, the patron saint of Naples, because it marked the beginning of the street that leads to the catacombs where he was buried *(see p97)*. After the plague epidemic of 1656, Mattia Preti painted a fresco on each city gate as an *ex voto* from those who survived. Porta San Gennaro is the only one that still has traces – albeit quite faded – of the artist's work. On the inner facade is a bust of San Gaetano with a dedication and the date 1658.

Palazzo dello Spagnolo ❷

Via Vergini 19. **Map** 3 B3. Ⓜ *Cavour.* ◷ *7:30am–2pm, 3:30–8pm Mon–Fri; 7:30am–1pm Sat.*

BUILT IN 1738 by Ferdinando Sanfelice (1675–1748) for the Marquis Nicola Moscati, this building became the property of the Spanish nobleman Tommaso Atienza in the 19th century and was renamed the Palace of the Spaniard. In addition to his work as an architect, Sanfelice also designed temporary staging and scenery for outdoor feasts, organized by the court

Palazzo Sanfelice ❸

Via Sanità 2–4. **Map** 3 B3. Ⓜ *Cavour.* ◷ *8am–1pm, 3–7pm Mon–Fri; 8:30am–1pm Sat.*

FERDINANDO SANFELICE built this large palazzo for his own family in 1728, as can be seen in the inscription on the top of the right-hand doorway. It is one of the finest palazzi in Naples, and it was here that the famous Neapolitan architect first created the unusual external staircase he subsequently adopted, with some variations, in Palazzo dello Spagnolo ten years later. This type of strikingly original staircase became Sanfelice's trademark. His contemporaries

Painting by Giovan Battista Spinelli in San Severo

likened it to a large bird with outspread wings, and it became known as a stair *ad ali di falco* – a "falcon's wing" staircase.

The best way to grasp the beauty and practicality of the intriguing design is to walk up the steps; from the first landing you can see the garden behind. On the far side of the second courtyard (at No. 2 Via Sanità), which has unfortunately lost its original decoration, there is yet another elliptical staircase.

San Severo and Catacombs ❹

Piazza San Severo 81. **Map** 3 B2. Ⓒ *45 46 84.* Ⓜ *Cavour.* ◷ *9am–noon, 5–9pm Mon–Sat; 9am–noon Sun.* ⛪

Fresco of *San Pietro* in the catacombs of San Severo

SAN SEVERO was the Bishop of Naples from 364 to 410. This site was chosen for his tomb and, as was the usual practice among early Christians, a large underground cemetery grew up around it. The basilica over the catacombs was abandoned in the 9th century when the saint's relics were transferred to San Giorgio Maggiore *(see p70)*. The building was restored in the 16th century and again more comprehensively in the late 17th century. In the third chapel on the left is the entrance to the catacombs. In the same chapel there is a cell with three arched niches hewn out of the stone to house sarcophagi. The niches are decorated with frescoes that, despite their poor condition, are good examples of catacomb painting.

Central nave of Santa Maria della Sanità

Santa Maria della Sanità and San Gaudioso Catacombs ❺

Via Sanità 124. **Map** 3 A2. ☎ 544 13 05. Ⓜ Cavour. ⭘ 8am–noon, 5–6:30pm Mon–Sat; 8am–noon Sun. 👥 💺 **Catacombs** 💰 9:45 & 11:45am Sun (or by appt, min 10).

View of Santa Maria Sanità from the Ponte della Sanità

THE HEART of the working-class Sanità quarter is the basilica of Santa Maria. Confusingly, the church is also known as the church of San Vincenzo because it houses a much revered image of the popular saint, known locally as 'o munacone (the big monk). Designed by Fra Nuvolo, the church was built on a Greek cross plan in 1603–13, with 24 columns supporting one central dome and 12 lateral domes (a reference to Christ and the Apostles). The central tiled dome is overlooked by the 19th-century Ponte della Sanità, linking the city center to Capodimonte.

Inside, the main altar was raised to allow worshipers to see the space that serves as a kind of atrium for the underground cemetery. The entrance to the catacombs can be clearly seen.

Tradition has it that in 452, the African bishop Settimio Celio Gaudioso died in exile in Naples and was buried in the Sanità valley. The catacombs grew up around his tomb and were named after him. The many corridors still bear traces of frescoes and mosaics (4th–6th centuries AD). The catacombs remained in use for centuries. Evidence for this includes some rather gruesome early 17th-century tombs, each with a skeleton drawn on the wall and a skull set into the surface in a real-istic depiction of the deceased.

Cimitero delle Fontanelle ❻

Via Fontanelle 77. **Map** 3 A3. ☎ 544 77 46 (Church of Maria Santissima del Carmine). 🚌 105. Ⓜ Cavour. ⭘ for restoration.

A WALK ALONG Via Fontanelle through an area that is more like a country village than a city district leads to the church of Maria Santissima del Carmine, from which you can visit the Fontanelle cemetery (cimitero). The huge rock-hewn caverns on the hill of Materdei were already being used as the city ossuary when they were selected as the final resting place for the thousands of victims of the devastating 1836 cholera epidemic.

Some people may find the place disturbing, as did the tourist played by Ingrid Bergman in Rossellini's film Viaggio in Italia, which made the cemetery famous.

The ossuary of the Fontanelle Cemetery

San Giovanni a Carbonara **❼**

Via San G. a Carbonara 5. **Map** 3 C3.
[29 58 73. **◯** 9am–1pm Mon–Sat.

Cappella Caracciolo di Vico, San Giovanni a Carbonara

THE IMAGINATIVE double-flight staircase designed by Ferdinando Sanfelice in the early 1700s leads to the 14th-century Chapel of Santa Monica. Left of the chapel is the doorway to San Giovanni a Carbonara. Founded in 1343 by Augustinian monks, this church was restored and enlarged at the end of the century by King Ladislas to make it a worthy burial site for the Angevin rulers.

When the king died in 1414, his tomb, the work of anonymous Tuscan and Lombard sculptors *(see p18)*, was erected at the request of his sister, Joan II, who succeeded him to the throne. The grandiose funerary monument, with seated statues of Ladislas and Joan, dominates the single-nave interior. Through a small doorway beneath the monument is the circular Cappella Caracciolo del Sole, built in 1427 and paved with colored Tuscan tiles. Behind the altar is the tomb of Ser Gianni Caracciolo, Joan's lover and Grand Seneschal at the court, who died in 1432.

To the left of the presbytery is the harmonious Cappella Caracciolo di Vico, built in the Renaissance style in 1517 by Giovan Tommaso Malvito following a design by Bramante. Another work by Malvito is the richly decorated tomb of the Miroballo family opposite the entrance of the church.

Santi Apostoli **❽**

Largo Santi Apostoli 9. **Map** 3 C4.
[29 93 75. **Ⓜ** Cavour.
◯ 8–11:30am, 5:30–8pm Mon–Sat; 8:30am–1pm Sun.

TO REACH the church of Santi Apostoli you have to go along a short stretch of Via Pisanelli, which turns into Via Anticaglia *(see p84)*. The church was founded in the 5th century and rebuilt at the beginning of the 17th century by Francesco Grimaldi (1610) and, after 1627, by Giovanni Conforto. The church is best known for a wonderful fresco cycle by Giovanni Lanfranco (1638–46). This masterpiece influenced artistic development in Naples. The artist also frescoed the cupola of the Cappella del Tesoro di San Gennaro *(see pp82–3)*.

Santa Maria degli Angeli alle Croci **❾**

Via Veterinaria 2. **Map** 3 C2. **[** 44 07 56. **Ⓜ** Cavour. **◯** 7am–noon, 4:30–7:30pm (7am–2pm Sun). **Ⓟ**

THE NAME of this church refers to the Stations of the Cross, once marked by wooden crosses *(croci)* alongside the ascent to the church. Santa Maria was founded at the end of the 16th century by Franciscans and rebuilt in 1638 by Cosimo Fanzago. The facade is simply decorated with white and gray marble. This plain design was a daring

The white and gray marble facade of Santa Maria degli Angeli alle Croci

shift from the usually lavish architecture of Neapolitan Baroque. The interior of the church houses a magnificent marble pulpit sculpted by Cosimo Fanzago. The eagle supporting it symbolizes St. John the Evangelist. The extraordinary bas relief of the dead Christ on the altar was sculpted by Carlo Fanzago, Cosimo's son.

Cactus plants in the Orto Botanico

Orto Botanico **❿**

Via Foria 223. **Map** 4 D2. **[** 44 97 59. **Ⓜ** Cavour. **◯** 9am–2pm Mon–Fri by appt; Apr–Jun: Wed–Thu.

ESTABLISHED IN 1807 by Joseph Bonaparte, the "Royal Plant Garden" is one of the leading Italian botanical gardens, known for the high quality of its collections as well as its sheer size, covering (30 acres). It has a rich variety of tree and shrub specimens from all latitudes and examples of many known plant species as well as several glasshouses with varying climatic conditions. The temperate house is an early 19th-century Neo-Classical building. The collections of citrus trees, desert plants, and tree ferns are particularly interesting. You may not be a botanical enthusiast, but a walk along the wide paths of this green oasis, in the heart of Naples, can make a very pleasant break from the city.

Albergo dei Poveri ⓫

Piazza Carlo III. **Map** 4 E2.
C55. M Cavour.

THE ENORMOUS BUILDING you
see today is only one-fifth
of the large-scale complex
that King Charles III wanted
to build to provide a refuge
for "the poor of the entire
kingdom." Construction of the
"Hotel of the Poor" began in
1751 according to a design by
Ferdinando Fuga. Work
continued until 1829, but the
project was never finished. It
has been in a state of neglect
for many years (the 1980
earthquake further damaged
an already dilapidated
building) and restoration
plans have yet to begin.

San Gennaro Catacombs ⓬

Via Capodimonte 13. **Map** 3 A1.
741 10 71. 109, 24.
9:30, 10:15, 11, 11:45am.

THE ORIGINAL nucleus of this
large subterranean
cemetery may have been the
tomb of a pagan aristocrat
donated in the 2nd century to
the Christian community. The
catacombs began to grow in
importance in the 3rd century
after the acquisition of the
tomb of Sant'Agrippino, but it
was as the burial site of the
saint, bishop, and martyr
Gennaro, brought here in the

The Neo-Classical facade of the Osservatorio Astronomico

5th century, that the catacombs
became famous. The cemetery
also housed the tombs of
Neapolitan bishops up to the
11th century. The vast size
and two-level layout of this
holy site distinguish it from
other catacombs of the same
era and make it the most
important complex in Southern
Italy. Remains of precious
2nd- to 10th-century mosaics
and frescoes (including the
oldest known portrayal of San
Gennaro, dating from the 5th
century) adorn the walls of
the catacombs. Don't miss the
Bishops' Crypt on the upper
floor and the Sant'Agrippino
Oratory and baptistry on the
lower level. The basilica of
San Gennaro extra Moenia
was erected over the catacombs in the 5th century but
was greatly modified by subsequent rebuilding in the 11th
century and then again in 1932.

Museo Nazionale and Park of Capodimonte ⓭

See pp98–101.

Osservatorio Astronomico ⓮

Salita Moiariello 16. **Map** 3 B1.
29 32 66. 24. ◯ Mon–Fri
by appt. the museum.

SITUATED IN THE MIDDLE of a
large park on top of the
hill of Miradois, 150 m (490 ft)
above sea level, the observatory benefits from a splendid
vantage point with fine
panoramic views of the city
and the bay. Founded in 1819
by Ferdinand IV, this was the
first scientific facility of its
kind in Europe. The Bourbon
court had always been
interested in astronomic
studies, and it was Charles III
who established the first
university chair of astronomy
in Naples in 1735. The observatory was originally planned
for the Museo Archeologico,
and construction of a new
observatory began there in
1791 *(see p89)*, but the project
was discarded. A few years
later the elegant Neo-Classical
building that now houses the
observatory was built by the
Gasse brothers. Today part of
the observatory is occupied
by a museum with a fine
collection of clocks,
telescopes, and interesting old
scientific instruments.

Watercolor of the Catacombs of San Gennaro by Giacinto Gigante

Museo Nazionale and Park of Capodimonte ⓭

FROM THE BEGINNING Capodimonte was both a royal palace and a museum because Charles III wanted a home for the works of art he had inherited from his mother Elizabeth Farnese. Construction began in 1738 under architect Antonio Medrano, but the palace was completed a century later, despite the fact that a large part of the Farnese Collection had been on display there since 1759. The collection was dispersed after the French occupation in 1799 *(see p23)*, but was enlarged following the Bourbon restoration in 1815.

In 1860 Capodimonte became the property of the House of Savoy and was the residence of the Dukes of Aosta until 1947. The museum was opened to the public again in 1957.

In 1996, after restoration, the first floor was reopened, and in 1997 the Neapolitan and contemporary art collections were arranged on the second floor (not shown here).

Pietà
This painting by Annibale Carracci, which dates from around 1600, drew inspiration from Michelangelo and is one of the masterpieces of Carracci's monumental style.

Main Entrance

THE PARK OF CAPODIMONTE

Charles III was drawn to Capodimonte because of hunting, his favorite pastime, and he decided to build an important hunting lodge here. The first section of this large park (more than 300 acres), with many ancient trees, was laid out by Ferdinando Sanfelice in 1742 into five broad radiating roads, lined with holm oaks. The buildings used for various court activities can be found in the woods.

Ferdinand IV at Capodimonte by Antonio Joli

The rooms in the Royal Apartments on the first floor reveal the two-fold function as royal palace and museum that Capodimonte fulfilled from the outset.

KEY

- ▨ Farnese Gallery
- ▢ Borgia Collection
- ▢ De Ciccio porcelain collection
- ▢ Farnese and Bourbon Armory
- ▢ Maria Amalia's Porcelain Parlor
- ▢ Royal apartments
- ▨ Nonexhibition space

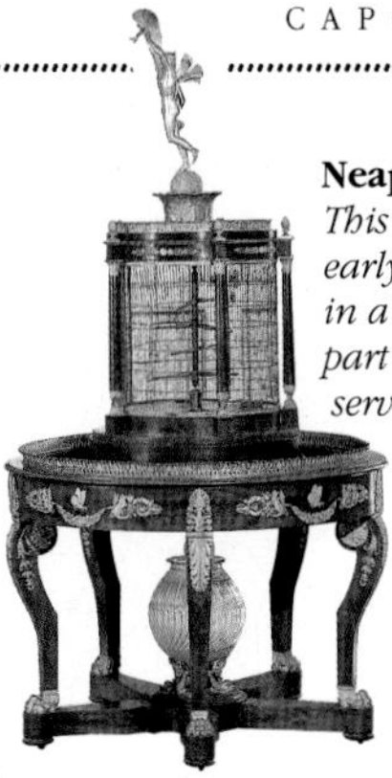

Neapolitan Craftsmanship
This is a multipurpose piece of early 19th-century furniture made in a Neapolitan factory: the lower part contains a glass bowl, which serves as an aquarium, and a table with a bird cage, which serves as a jardinière. The rotating figure of Fortune is perched on top.

Café

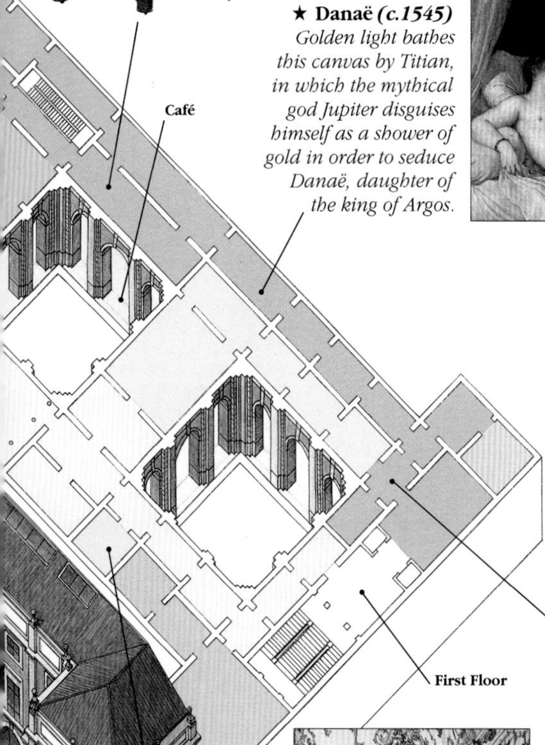

★ Danaë (c.1545)
Golden light bathes this canvas by Titian, in which the mythical god Jupiter disguises himself as a shower of gold in order to seduce Danaë, daughter of the king of Argos.

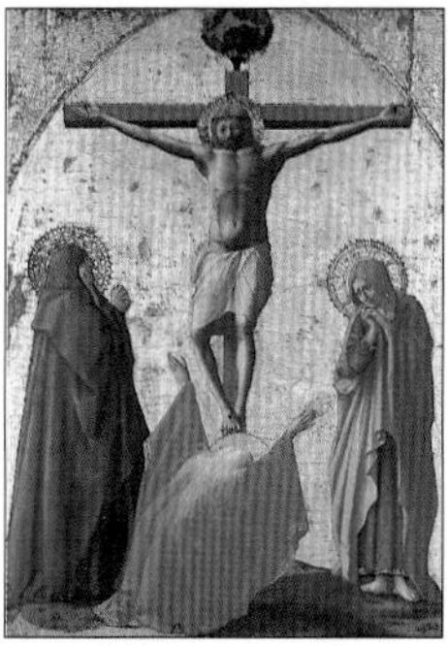

First Floor

★ Crucifixion (1426)
In this early Renaissance painting by Masaccio, the emotional intensity of faces and gestures emphasizes the drama. The panel was part of an altarpiece for a church in Pisa, now dismantled and scattered in various museums.

★ Maria Amalia's Porcelain Parlor
This room was built in 1757–9 for the Royal Palace at Portici (see p136); then dismantled and moved here in 1866. The walls and ceiling of the queen's parlor are tiled with nearly 3,000 pieces of finest Capodimonte porcelain.

STAR EXHIBITS

★ **Crucifixion by Masaccio**

★ **Danaë by Titian**

★ **Maria Amalia's Porcelain Parlor**

Exploring the Museo di Capodimonte

THE FARNESE COLLECTION, which is the core of the Art Gallery, features the major Italian and European schools of painting from the 15th to the 17th centuries. When the Real Museo (now the Museo Archeologico Nazionale, *see pp86–9*) was created in Palazzo degli Studi in the early 1800s, the paintings were transferred from Capodimonte. They were returned in 1957, along with other works purchased since the 19th century by the Bourbon rulers and the Italian government. Once the restoration and rearrangement of the collections is complete, 13th–19th century Neapolitan painting and sculpture will be displayed on the second floor. The 19th-century collection will be placed in the mezzanine; the reorganized first floor, will be devoted to the Farnese Collection and the Royal Apartments.

Antea (1531–35) by Parmigianino

PAINTING FROM THE 13TH TO THE 16TH CENTURIES

THE FARNESE COLLECTION did not focus on medieval works, so that paintings from this period are later purchases or come from churches in the Naples region. For example, the beautiful *Santa Maria de Flumine* (c.1290) came from a church of the same name in Amalfi. The most important 14th-century painting is the large altarpiece painted by Simone Martini in 1317 on the occasion of the canonization of St. Louis of Toulouse *(see pp18–19), St. Louis of Toulouse Crowning Robert of Anjou King of Naples*.

The 15th century is also represented by a superb canvas – Masaccio's *Crucifixion*, actually the upper part of a dismantled polyptych taken from the church of the Carmine in Pisa. The other panels are in Pisa, London, Berlin, and Malibu.

Transfiguration by Giovanni Bellini

Giovanni Bellini's masterpiece, *Transfiguration* (c.1480–85), has been considered one of the gems of the Farnese Collection since the 1600s. The *Tavola Strozzi* panel is an extraordinary "snapshot" of 15th-century Naples.

The focal point of the 16th-century paintings is the splendid Titians: *Portrait of Pope Paul III, Pope Paul III with His Grandchildren*, and *Danaë (see p99)*, which exemplify the Venetian genius's masterly use of color. Artists from the region of Emilia Romagna, the home of the Farnese family, are well represented. Major works are Correggio's masterpiece

Mystic Marriage of St. Catherine and the *Antea* by Parmigianino, a portrait of a young woman with elegant dress and a marten stole. An important group of canvases by the Carraccis includes Annibale Carracci's *Pietà*, inspired by the strong sculptural forms of Michelangelo, and his large allegorical work, *Hercules at the Crossroads*, in which the mythical hero has to choose between pleasure and virtue.

PAINTING FROM THE 17TH TO THE 20TH CENTURIES

AMONG THE 17TH-CENTURY works in the museum, Bartolomeo Schedoni's *Charity* (1611) is one of the most famous and is greatly admired for its expressive intensity. The myth of *Atalanta and Hippomenes* is depicted in Guido Reni's canvas, which the Bourbon rulers bought in 1802 because they lacked a major work by the Bolognese master.

The astounding *Flagellation of Christ* by Caravaggio *(see p74)* was painted in stages from 1607 to 1609–10 and hung in San Domenico Maggiore until its move to Capodimonte. It is regarded as the linchpin of all 17th-century Neapolitan painting, represented here by many leading artists such as Battistello Caracciolo, Luca Giordano, and Mattia Preti. No less amazing is Artemisia Gentileschi's painting of

The *Tavola Strozzi*, a representation of 15th-century Naples (detail)

Judith and Holofernes, a subject she made her own. The artist, who favored rather violent themes, was an exceptionally gifted painter and remarkably independent for a woman of her time.

Portrait of Ferdinand IV as a Youth was painted by the German artist Anton Raphael Mengs in 1760; the young king, whose luxurious clothes are rendered in great detail, was nine at the time. In addition, there are some fine landscapes by Ferdinand IV's court painter, Jakob-Philipp Hackert.

Capodimonte also has a large body of 19th-century Neapolitan paintings, including works by Anton Pitloo, the Dutch painter who settled in Naples *(see p35),* and Giacinto Gigante. Don't miss Gigante's famous painting of the Cappella del Tesoro in the duomo. Among the modern works, Andy Warhol's *Mount Vesuvius (see p26)* was painted in 1985 for an exhibition at the museum in the same year.

Francesco Solimena's *Study of a Young Man's Face* (1728)

Vatican. Perforations (which can still be seen) were made with a needle, and powder was sprinkled over the holes to transfer the lines to the wall where the fresco was to be painted.

Solimena's *Study of a Young Man's Face* is a charming study for a later painting. Another important cartoon is Raphael's *Moses before the Burning Bush,* a preparatory drawing for a detail of a fresco in the Stanza di Eliodoro in the Vatican.

THE DECORATIVE ARTS

THE MAJOR SECTION in the fine Decorative Arts collection is the armory, which has about 4,000 weapons and is one of the most important of its kind. Many of the objects here

come from the Naples Royal Arms Factory, founded in 1734 by Charles III. There are also over 4,000 ceramic pieces in this part of the museum, including the De Ciccio majolica collection and examples of the superb porcelain manufactured in Naples at the instigation of Charles III. A fine example of this craftsmanship is Queen Maria Amalia's Porcelain Parlor *(see p99).*

Other decorative arts include ivory, amber, and rock crystal objects as well as medallions, semiprecious stones, and other pieces such as the 17th-century gilded silver table trophy of Diana by Jacob Miller.

***Diana on a Deer* table trophy**

Judith and Holofernes by Artemisia Gentileschi (1597–1651)

THE COLLECTION OF DRAWINGS AND PAINTINGS

AMONG THE MUSEUM'S huge inheritance there are about 2,500 drawings and watercolors and 22,000 prints and engravings. One of the most famous works is a cartoon (a preparatory drawing made with charcoal or chalk) made by Michelangelo around 1546. It was drawn for part of the fresco of *The Crucifixion of St Peter* in the Cappella Paolina in the

THE ROYAL PORCELAIN FACTORY

King Charles III promoted and fostered the manufacturing of decorated porcelain in Naples. The "soft-paste" porcelain, produced with the aid of leading chemists and mineralogists in the Kingdom of Naples, allowed the Real Fabbrica to vie with such top European manufacturers as Meissen. A new pavilion for the Royal Factory was opened in the royal park of Capodimonte in 1743, and

***The Biscuit Vendor* (1750–51)**

the fame of Neapolitan porcelain continued to grow. By 1759, when the king returned to Spain, the factory had become so important to him that he had it dismantled and took it, as well as its staff, with him. The factory was reopened in 1771 by Ferdinand, and production of top-quality pieces began again. Today the Royal Factory is the home of the Institute for the Porcelain and Ceramics industry.

VOMERO

IN 1885 THE Town Council of Naples approved a plan for a new district to be developed "in the rise between Castel Sant'Elmo, the village of Vomero and Antignano," which, once completed, would accommodate 30,000 inhabitants. So began the story of the district of Vomero, which soon became famous for its scenic beauty and healthy climate. These qualities have

Detail of the cloister, Certosa di San Martino

since been partly ruined (especially since World War II) by chaotic, uncontrolled property development with total disregard for the natural surroundings. Yet, some interesting areas are preserved. At the top of the hill is one of the most important monuments in Naples, the Certosa di San Martino, with its splendid Baroque church, fine museum, and its elegant residence called the Quarto del Priore.

SIGHTS AT A GLANCE

Historic Buildings
Castel Sant'Elmo 4
Certosa and Museo Nazionale di San Martino pp108–111 5

Parks and Gardens
Villa La Floridiana 2

Streets and Squares
Pedamentina 6
Via Luigia Sanfelice 7
Via Scarlatti 1

Museums and Galleries
Museo Nazionale della Ceramica Duca di Martina 3

GETTING THERE
The fastest way to reach Vomero is via the funiculars: the Chiaia route from Parco Margherita, the Centrale from Via Toledo, and the Montesanto from the historic center. To get to Castel Sant'Elmo and the Certosa you can also take the circle bus line VI from Piazza Fuga, which connects with the Centrale funicular.

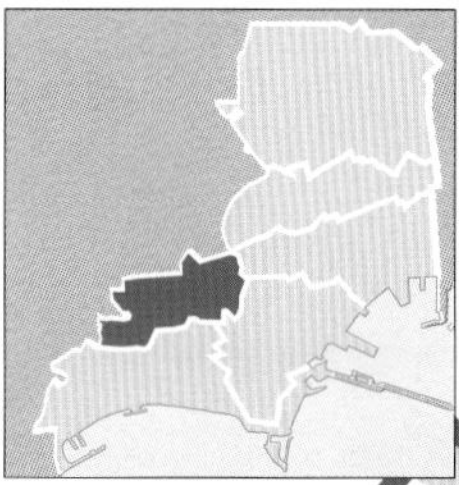

KEY

	Street-by-Street map *See pp104–5*
P	Parking
M	Metro station
🚠	Funicular

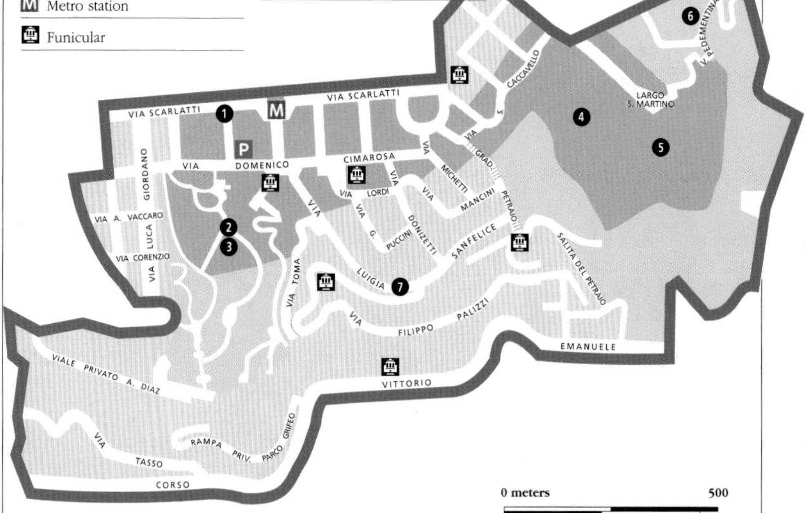

0 meters 500
0 yards 500

Street-by-Street: Vomero

T AKE ONE OF THE funicular lines up the hill to Vomero for some fine views of the city center and the Bay of Naples. Art lovers will find that Neapolitan masters are well represented in the museums of the Certosa di San Martino and Villa La Floridiana (the Duca di Martina). Meanwhile, a walk along the atmospheric streets in the heart of the district reveals an eclectic range of shops and goods, including the Daniele pasticceria in Via Scarlatti, known for its delectable cakes. In Via Luigia Sanfelice is the villa of the Neapolitan comic Eduardo Scarpetta.

Eduardo Scarpetta

Montesanto funicular

Via Scarlatti
This street is the main thoroughfare through Vomero ❶

Vanvitelli

VIA SCARLATTI

PIAZZA VANVITELLI

VIA BERNINI

VIA MORGHEN

VIA CIMAROSA

Centrale funicular

VIA L. SANFELICE

Chiaia funicular

Museo Nazionale della Ceramica Duca di Martina
This is one of Italy's most important collections of decorative arts ❸

★ Villa La Floridiana
The villa, rebuilt by Antonio Niccolini in the early 19th century, now houses the Duca di Martina museum. It stands in a large park filled with pine, holm-oak, plane, and cypress trees ❷

KEY

- - - - - - - Suggested route

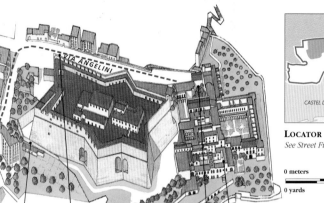

LOCATOR MAP
See Street Finder, maps 1, 2, 5, 6

| 0 meters | 100 |
| 0 yards | 100 |

In Via Tito Angelini are some turn-of-the-century houses, such as Villino Maria (below), which have survived the wave of property development since World War II.

★ **Certosa and Museo Nazionale di San Martino**
After the unification of Italy, this impressive complex – built in the 14th century but drastically restructured later on – became state property and was turned into a museum ⑤

The section of the Museo di San Martino devoted to Neapolitan painting and sculpture of the 19th century includes Vincenzo Gemito's expressive *Head of a Peasant Woman.*

★ **Castel Sant'Elmo**
The patriots of the Parthenopean Republic (see p23) conquered the castle in 1799, but when the revolution was crushed they were imprisoned there ④

STAR SIGHTS

★ **Certosa and Museo Nazionale di San Martino**

★ **Villa La Floridiana**

★ **Castel Sant'Elmo**

Via Scarlatti ❶

Map 2 D5. 🚇 *Centrale: Piazza Fuga; Chiaia: Via Cimarosa.*

THE MOST ELEGANT street in Vomero is lined with tall plane trees and descends from Piazza Vanvitelli toward Via Cilea. Now closed to traffic, Via Scarlatti is the perfect place for a pleasant walk interrupted by an occasional break for shopping. If look beyond the line of stores you will notice the striking contrast between the 19th-century buildings and those constructed in the last 30 years in the wave of property development that has radically altered the face of Vomero.

Villa La Floridiana ❷

Via Domenico Cimarosa 77, Via Aniello Falcone. **Map** 2 C5. 📞 578 55 65. 🚇 *Centrale: Piazza Fuga; Chiaia: Via Cimarosa.* ◯ *9am–1 hr before sunset.*

IN 1817 FERDINAND I acquired an estate on the Vomero hill as a present for his second wife Lucia Migliaccio, the Duchess of Floridia, whom he had married shortly after the death of Maria Carolina of Austria. The estate, which was named La Floridiana in honor of the duchess, included a park with a magnificent view of the

city. There were two buildings on the property. The Villa La Floridiana was rebuilt as a summer residence in the Neo-Classical style by Antonio Niccolini in 1817–19. It now houses the Duca di Martina Ceramics Museum (*see below*). There was also a "Pompeiian" coffee-house, later called Villa Lucia, also designed by Niccolini, which became private property.

The Italian government purchased the Villa La Floridiana in 1919.

Museo Nazionale della Ceramica Duca di Martina ❸

Villa Floridiana, Via Domenico Cimarosa 77, Via Aniello Falcone. **Map** 2 C5. 📞 578 84 18. 🚇 *Centrale: Piazza Fuga; Chiaia: Via Cimarosa.* ◯ *9am–2pm Tue–Sun.* 📷 🚫

PLACIDO DE SANGRO, the Duke of Martina and member of an illustrious noble family, was an avid, passionate collector of decorative art objects, especially porcelain and ceramics. When he died in 1891, his valuable collection of about 6,000 pieces was inherited by his grandson Placido, who donated them to the city of Naples in 1911.

Since the mid-1920s Villa La Floridiana has been the home of the Duca di Martina National Ceramics Museum, where curators aim to reproduce as closely as possible the arrangement and spirit of the collections in the De Sangro residence. The pleasant and unusual atmosphere of a home within a museum has remained unchanged, despite additions and later donations.

The porcelain pieces come from the most important Italian and other

Interior of the Duca di Martina ceramics museum

European factories, while the collection of Oriental art consists mostly of 18th- and 19th-century porcelain and is one of the best in Italy.

The museum also contains 15th-century ivory pieces, majolica, Limoges enamel, leather and tortoiseshell objects, and drawings by 17th- and 18th-century artists, including Solimena, Giordano, and De Matteis.

Castel Sant'Elmo ❹

Via Tito Angelini. **Map** 2 E5. 📞 556 02 03. 🚇 *Montesanto: Via Morghen.* ◯ *9am–2pm Tue–Sun.* 📷 📷

IN THE 1330s the Angevin rulers instigated a flurry of building on the Vomero hill west of Naples : the construction of the Certosa di San Martino and the enlargement and reconstruction of the nearby fortified residence of Belforte, which had been inhabited by Charles I of Anjou's family since 1275.

In the 16th century Pedro Scriba, a leading military architect of the time, completely transformed the 14th-century castle into its present six-pointed star configuration.

Because of its strategic position, Castel Sant'Elmo under viceroy Pedro de Toledo became the focal point of the new defense system for Naples. For centuries it was used as a

Looking across the Floridiana park

prison; among its illustrious "guests" were the great Renaissance philosopher Tommaso Campanella, the 1799 revolutionaries, and patriots involved in the 19th-century Risorgimento.

The entrance bears Charles V's coat of arms and a fine epigraph. The complex, which also contains a large lecture hall, has been the venue for temporary exhibitions and cultural events since 1988. From the castle walls there is a spectacular 360-degree view of Naples and the bay.

Castel Sant'Elmo on the top of Vomero hill

Certosa di San Martino ❺

See pp108–11.

Pedamentina ❻

Map 2 F5. 🚇 *Montesanto: Via Morghen, Corso Vittorio Emanuele.*

THE STEPS CONNECTING Castel Sant'Elmo and the city sprawling below still make for a delightful walk "descending toward the sea amidst the green slopes," as old guidebooks put it, even though the landscape has changed considerably in the meantime. Descent being easier than ascent, you may choose to go down rather than climb the 414 steps from San Martino to Corso Vittorio Emanuele and take in the glimpses of beautiful panoramic views that change at every stage. The walk down passes by dilapidated buildings and slum housing, but the spectacular views of the bay are rewarding.

Via Luigia Sanfelice ❼

Map 2 D5 & 2 E5. 🚇 *Centrale: Piazza Fuga; Chiaia: Via Cimarosa.*

IF YOU ASK for the "Santarella," people will point to Via Luigia Sanfelice. The key to this riddle lies in a curve in the road where there is a villa with a curious nameplate: "Qui rido io" (this is where I laugh). This was the home, built in 1909, of the well-known Neapolitan author and comic actor Eduardo Scarpetta (the father of Eduardo De Filippo), whose best-known work is *Na santarella (see p37)*. In Via Luigia Sanfelice and nearby Via Filippo Palizzi there are a number of elegant houses that are interesting examples of Neo-Renaissance or Art Nouveau styles.

Nameplate at the villa of comic actor and author Eduardo Scarpetta

FROM THE "FERROVIA DI DELIZIA" TO THE FUNICULAR

In 1875 the engineers Bruno and Ferraro designed a rail system to take passengers up the Vomero hill along the Chiaia and Montesanto slopes, using two funiculars, connected so that the ascent of one line caused the descent of the other. The "train of delights,"

The present-day funicular

as it was called, allowed travelers to admire the magnificent views of the bay while crossing the hill, in those days a rural area. The initial plan gradually evolved into two independent funicular lines that ran through a tunnel, providing a rapid and efficient means of transportation between Vomero and the city center. The Chiaia funicular was opened in 1889 and the Montesanto line in 1891. In order to improve connections with what in the meantime had become the most rapidly expanding district in the city, the Centrale funicular was built in 1928. Centrale was the longest of the three; from its starting point in Via Toledo it reaches a point halfway between the other two. There is also a fourth line, the Mergellina funicular, which connects the waterfront with Via Manzoni.

Certosa di San Martino ❺

I N 1325 CHARLES Duke of Calabria began construction of what is one of the richest monuments in Naples. The Carthusian monks were forward looking, and from the 16th to the 18th centuries the greatest artists of the time worked at the

Procession tray

Certosa (charterhouse) of San Martino. The original look of San Martino was gradually altered by Mannerist and Baroque rebuilding. The most radical redecoration and enlargement was carried out by the architects Giovanni Antonio Dosio, at the end of the 16th century, and Cosimo Fanzago, who took over in 1623. The 17th and 18th centuries brought further changes.

The French deconsecrated the monastery in 1806, and since 1866 it has housed the San Martino museum, with displays of Neapolitan art and history.

Chiostro dei Procuratori
This cloister was built in the late 16th–early 17th century by Giovanni Antonio Dosio.

Nativity section

Historical section

The Prior's garden

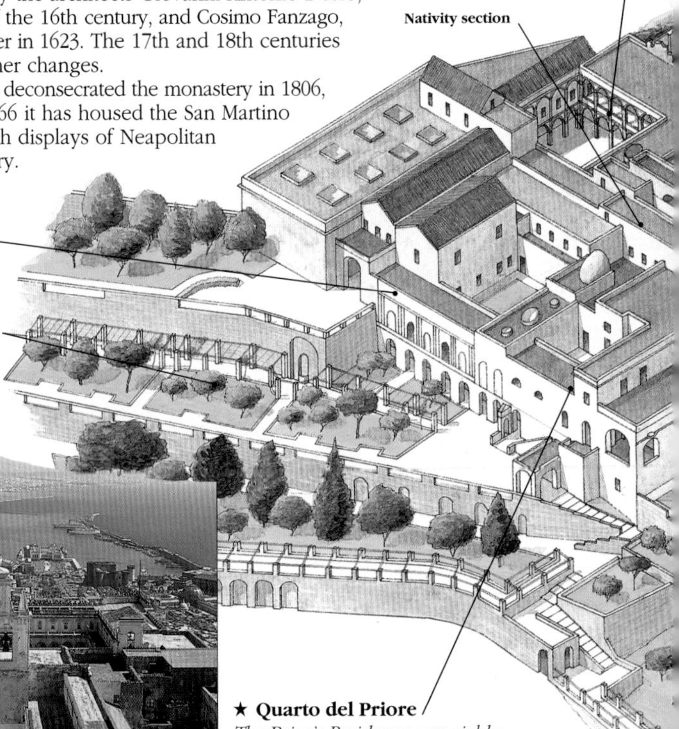

★ Quarto del Priore
The Prior's Residence was richly decorated and had a wide view of the bay of Naples (see p111).

TIMELINE

1325 Construction begun under Charles of Anjou	**1578** Decoration and enlargement by Dosio and Conforto	**1631–56** Complex rebuilt and redecorated by Cosimo Fanzago		**1807** The last monks forced to leave the monastery	*Chain of the Order of the Two Sicilies*
1300		**1600**			**1800**
	1368 Consecration of the church	**1623** Cosimo Fanzago begins work on the Chiostro Grande		**1799** Monastery damaged during Parthenopean revolution	**1866** The Certosa becomes state property and part of it is turned into a museum

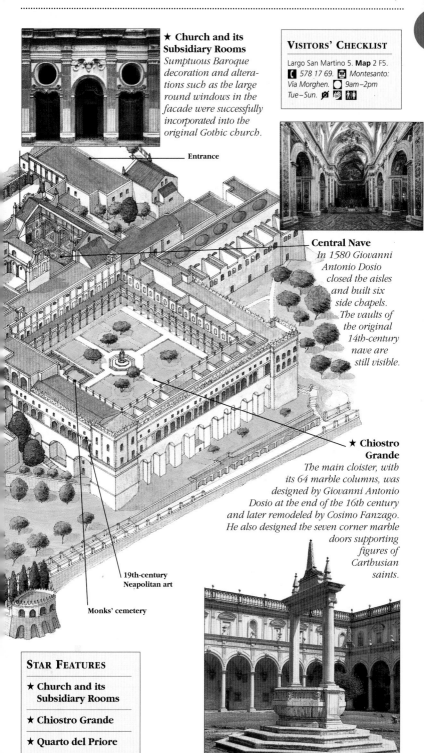

★ **Church and its Subsidiary Rooms**
Sumptuous Baroque decoration and alterations such as the large round windows in the facade were successfully incorporated into the original Gothic church.

VISITORS' CHECKLIST

Largo San Martino 5. **Map** 2 F5.
578 17 69. Montesanto:
Via Morghen. 9am–2pm
Tue–Sun.

Entrance

Central Nave
In 1580 Giovanni Antonio Dosio closed the aisles and built six side chapels. The vaults of the original 14th-century nave are still visible.

★ **Chiostro Grande**
The main cloister, with its 64 marble columns, was designed by Giovanni Antonio Dosio at the end of the 16th century and later remodeled by Cosimo Fanzago. He also designed the seven corner marble doors supporting figures of Carthusian saints.

19th-century Neapolitan art

Monks' cemetery

STAR FEATURES

★ **Church and its Subsidiary Rooms**

★ **Chiostro Grande**

★ **Quarto del Priore**

Exploring the Certosa di San Martino and the Museum

FROM THE OUTSET the Carthusian monks intended San Martino to be a storehouse for Neapolitan history and civilization. The collections document the rich and varied forms of artistic expression found in Naples from the 15th to 19th centuries: from paintings to coral jewelry, traditional creche scenes *(presepi)*, porcelain, prints, and ivory carvings. There is also a fascinating collection of maps. Other parts of the museum are devoted to Neapolitan costumes, festivals, and theater. The minor arts section contains an interesting collection of glass from Venice and other European sources.

Although a large part of the collections in the San Martino Museum is closed to the public as a result of restoration work, the beauty of the church, the Quarto del Priore (Prior's Residence), the cloisters, and the gardens will more than make up for what you miss.

Detail of the inlaid wood paneling in the sacristy (1587–98)

THE CHURCH AND ITS SUBSIDIARY ROOMS

AT THE END OF THE 14th century, the prior Severo Turboli set up an elaborate plan for the complete restructuring of the San Martino charterhouse. The original Angevin church was enlarged and modernized and its Gothic structure almost completely disappeared under the multitude of frescoes, stuccowork, and marbles produced by leading artists of the time.

The most radical changes to the building were carried out in the 17th century by architect and sculptor Cosimo Fanzago, who worked at San Martino from 1623 to 1656. He designed the interior of the church and its lavish decoration. Colored marble adorns the nave and chapels, such as in the Cappella di San Bruno. The rooms adjacent to the church are also richly decorated. In the sacristy the panels of the beautiful inlaid walnut wardrobes contain 56 intarsia scenes with striking perspective effects (16th century). The fresco of *The Triumph of Judith* on the vault of the brightly lit Cappella del Tesoro was painted by Luca Giordano in 1704.

HISTORICAL SECTION

THESE INTERESTING rooms dedicated to the history of the Kingdom of Naples are temporarily closed to the public. Paintings, furnishings, sculptures, medallions, arms, and memorabilia re-create the key moments in the political, social, and cultural history of Naples, from the Aragonese to the Bourbon dynasties. The importance of this valuable collection is exemplified in two famous works that combine historical and artistic

The Cappella di San Bruno, designed by Cosimo Fanzago (1631)

Statue of Charles III of Spain (1754)

documentary significance: *The Revolt of Masaniello (see pp20–21),* painted in 1647, and *Piazza del Mercatello during the 1656 Plague,* both painted by Micco Spadaro. These dramatic compositions tell the story of two important events in the history of 17th-century Naples. They are also an accurate and useful representation of what the city looked like at that time.

Panorama of Naples Viewed from the Conocchia, by Giacinto Gigante

THE NATIVITY SCENES

ONLY TOWARD the end of the 19th century did the *presepe* or nativity scene begin to be considered an artistic genre in its own right, worthy of a museum. This section of the San Martino museum has one of the most important public collections of its kind, with displays of entire nativity scenes as well as individual figures such as Mary and Joseph, the Three Kings, or the shepherds. Many animals and the creche, are also displayed.

Among the most important nativity scenes is one by the Neapolitan playwright, Michele Cucinello. Many of the statuettes were executed by famous Neapolitan artists. *Blind Beggar with Cataracts* (c.1780), in the Perrone Collection *(see p39),* is by the artist Giuseppe Sanmartino, who sculpted the *Veiled Christ* in the Cappella Sansevero *(see p63).*

Blind Beggar with Cataracts by Giuseppe Sanmartino

NINETEENTH-CENTURY NEAPOLITAN ART

THIS COLLECTION of paintings and sculpture also displays pieces that are significant from both an artistic and historical standpoint. The collection consists of purchases made by the Italian government but it owes its strength primarily to donations of important private Neapolitan collections.

All the schools of painting that flourished in this area during the 19th century are represented here. A recurring theme was the Campania landscape, a favorite with local artists. The paintings usually depict a serene and beautiful landscape, such as in Giacinto Gigante's *Panorama of Naples Viewed from the Conocchia.* Among the pieces of sculpture, those by Vincenzo Gemito are not to be missed. *Il Malatiello* (The Sick Child) and *Testa della Popolana* (Head of a Peasant Woman) portray the expressive intensity characteristic of this artist's work.

THE QUARTO DEL PRIORE

The prior, the only person who was allowed contact with the outside world, governed the life of the monastery from his apartments. This was a fabulous residence, filled with artistic treasures and opening onto lush gardens overlooking Naples and the sea.

Built in the 17th century and enlarged the following century, the luxurious quarters have undergone scrupulous restoration. Originally, this part of the complex was used to exhibit the rich art collection of the Carthusian monks. Following the restoration, an attempt

Triptych by Jean Burdichon (c.1414) in the art gallery of the Quarto del Priore

was made to re-create the Quarto del Priore as it was when inhabited by the prior, with paintings, sculpture, fabric, and furniture decorating the rooms.

The art collection and high-quality furnishings reflect the refinement and great artistic sensitivity of the Carthusian monks as well as their ability to keep abreast of the latest artistic and architectural developments. With its stunning decor, works of art and sculpture, and spectacular panoramic views of the city, the Quarto del Priore is one of the highlights of a visit to the Certosa di San Martino.

The Borgo Marinaro and Castel dell'Ovo

SIGHTS AT A GLANCE

Historic Buildings
Castel dell'Ovo ❷

Historic Streets and Sites
Lungomare ❸
Mergellina ⓫
Piazza dei Martiri ❹
Santa Lucia ❶

Museums and Galleries
Museo Diego Aragona Pignatelli
  Cortes and Museo delle
  Carrozze in Villa Pignatelli ❼

Churches
Santa Maria del Parto ⓬
Santa Maria di
  Piedigrotta ❾
Santa Maria in Portico ❽

Parks and Gardens
Parco Virgiliano ❿
Villa Comunale ❺

Aquarium
Stazione Zoologica ❻

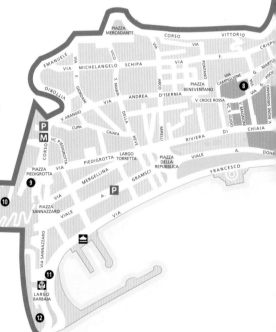

CASTEL DELL'OVO AND CHIAIA

THE CHIAIA AREA grew to its present extent in the 19th century, although there had been buildings along the waterfront outside the city walls since the 16th century. In the late 18th century the construction of the Villa Reale (now called the Villa Comunale) along the Riviera di Chiaia changed the face of this part of Naples.

In the meantime, the city was becoming popular with tourists: 8,000 per year were reported by 1838, which is a significant number of

Decorative detail in the Stazione Zoologica

visitors for that time. In the second half of the 19th century, the development of the Amedeo quarter and the elegant streets that radiate from Piazza Amedeo made this the favorite residential area of the upper middle class. The Chiaia area also bears traces of the distant past: Castel dell'Ovo, the fortress jutting into the water in front of Santa Lucia and the oldest castle in Naples, and the Parco Virgiliano in Mergellina, said to be the place where the Roman poet Virgil was buried.

GETTING THERE

The fastest way to get to this area is by metro (Mergellina station for Mergellina and waterfront area; Piazza Amedeo station for the Chiaia area). The funicular from the Parco Margherita station takes you from Vomero to Chiaia. The R3

bus route, tram 1, and bus 140 run along the Riviera di Chiaia and skirt the Villa Comunale. The C4 bus route and routes 120 and 128 cross Santa Lucia. The Mergellina funicular takes you from Mergellina to Via Manzoni.

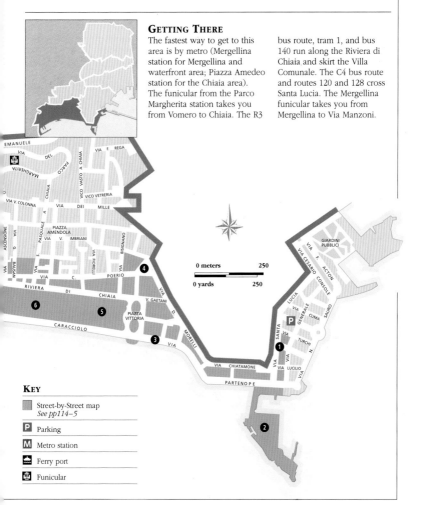

KEY

	Street-by-Street map *See pp114–5*
P	Parking
M	Metro station
	Ferry port
	Funicular

Street-by-Street: Lungomare

B ESIDES BEING a pleasant way of spending the time,
walking along the waterfront is a tradition handed
down over generations of Neapolitans. However, the
sea is not just something to look at here: in the
summer, despite the many "no swimming" signs, it is
filled with swimmers. Every day of the year huge
quantities of fish are sold on the beach and in
Mergellina, and then served in the many neighboring
restaurants. At the Villa Comunale you can combine a
walk in the park with a visit to Europe's oldest
aquarium. Nearby Villa Pignatelli has stupendous
rooms with 19th-century furnishings and decorations.

San Pasquale was built
for Charles III in 1749,
on the occasion of the
birth of his first son.

Villa Comunale
*The kiosk,
known as the
Cassa Armonica
or sound box,
was built in the
gardens during
the 19th-century
restoration of
the villa.* ❺

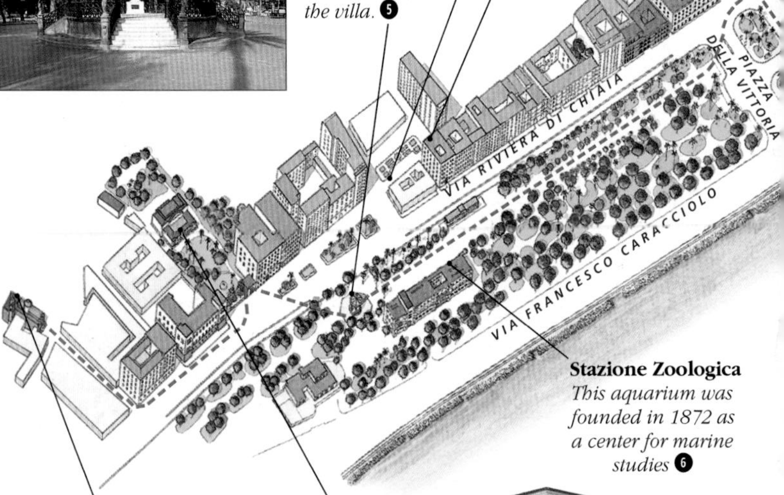

**Palazzo
Pignatelli**

VIA RIVIERA DI CHIAIA

VIA FRANCESCO CARACCIOLO

PIAZZA DELLA VITTORIA

VIA MO

Stazione Zoologica
*This aquarium was
founded in 1872 as
a center for marine
studies* ❻

Santa Maria in Portico
*The church is built on a
Latin cross plan with one
nave, and its dome is
covered with multi-
colored tiles* ❽

KEY

－－－－－   Suggested route

0meters	200
0 yards	200

★ **Villa Pignatelli**
*Originally called Villa Acton, this house was
modeled on an ancient Pompeiian design,
with the side facing the sea consisting of a
loggia supported by Doric columns* ❼

Santa Lucia
There are shrines all over Naples, such as this one in Via Santa Lucia, dedicated to St. Lucy ❶

LOCATOR MAP
See Street Finder, maps 5–7

Borgo Marinaro is a characteristically lively place to wander around, with its small harbor, cafés, and trattorias.

Piazza dei Martiri
The lovely façade of Palazzo Calabritto enlivens this popular square ❹

VIA CHIATAMONE

VIA SANTA LUCIA

VIA PARTENOPE

★ Castel dell'Ovo
The unmistakable bulk of the castle dominates the surrounding area ❷

STAR SIGHTS
★ Castel dell'Ovo
★ Lungomare
★ Villa Pignatelli

★ Lungomare
This column, taken from a building in Via Anticaglia (see p84), is dedicated to those who died at sea ❸

Santa Lucia ❶

Map 7 A4. 🚌 *C4, 120, 128.*

O NE OF the most famous streets in Naples, Santa Lucia exemplifies the city's striking contrasts. Luxury hotels that were built for the elite in the 19th century and imposing buildings for the regional government rub shoulders with the Pallonetto di Santa Lucia slum area where the poor eke out a living. This quarter is named after the church at the beginning of the street, Santa Lucia a Mare, whose history goes back to the 9th century. It has been rebuilt several times. Before you reach the waterfront, on the right you will see the tall rocky face of the hill of Pizzofalcone, the site of the oldest part of Naples *(see p59).*

Castel dell'Ovo with its tall tufa curtain walls

result of the rebuilding carried out after 1503, the year the fortress was almost destroyed during a siege by Ferdinand II of Spain.

Despite the rebuilding, there followed a period of decline that lasted until 1871, at which point the castle was so run-down that one urban renewal plan actually proposed its demolition. Thorough restoration work was begun just over a century later in 1975, and succeeded in bringing the site back to life. It is now used for cultural events. Around the castle is the picturesque Borgo Marinaro quarter, built at the end of the 19th century for the fishermen of Santa Lucia. It is a popular place with visitors because of its restaurants, cafés, and lively atmosphere.

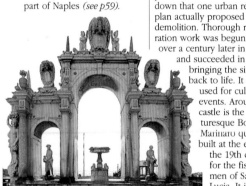

The Immacolatella Fountain

Castel dell'Ovo ❷

Borgo Marinaro. **Map** 7 A5.
☎ 41 50 02. 🚌 *C4, 120, 128, R3.*

T HE OLDEST CASTLE in Naples is built on the islet of Megaris, once the site of a villa belonging to the Roman patrician Lucullus. Later, in the 5th century, a community of monks founded the San Salvatore monastery, the only remaining part of which is the church. The oldest part of the castle dates from the 9th century. Under the Norman, Hohenstaufen, Angevin, and Aragonese rulers, the castle underwent continuous changes, according to the requirements of each dynasty. The present appearance is the

Lungomare ❸

Maps 5 & 6.
🚌 *C4, 120, 128, R3, 140.* 🚋 *1.*

A WALK ALONG the road skirting the coast from Santa Lucia to Mergellina is another experience you must not miss while in Naples. The view of the city and the bay is breathtaking. The first stretch of the waterfront – which corresponds to Via Nazario Sauro and Via Partenope – was built in the 19th century as a result of reclamation along Via Santa Lucia and Via Chiatamone. The two ends of this long and pleasant waterfront promenade are marked by two beautiful 17th-century fountains: the Immacolatella, which was built by Michelangelo Naccherino and Pietro Bernini in 1601, and the Sebeto fountain, which was the work of Cosimo Fanzago (1635–7).

THE LEGEND OF THE EGG

Opinions vary as to the origin of the curious name given to Castel dell'Ovo, or Castle of the Egg, which first appears in 14th-century documents. One possible explanation is the shape of the castle. However, popular tradition has it that the name derived from a magic egg hidden in the castle, which determined the castle's fate and that of the entire city: as long as the egg remained intact, both would be protected from catastrophes. The magic spell was supposed to have been originally cast by the Latin poet Virgil, who, according to medieval legends, possessed supernatural powers and the gift of divination.

The castle in the 1800s

Piazza dei Martiri ❹

Map 6 F2. 🚌 *C4, 120, 128.*

THE SQUARE OF MARTYRS is the heart of the "chic" commercial center of Naples. Its focal point is the Monumento ai Martiri Napoletani designed by Enrico Alvino in 1866–8, with four lions at the base symbolizing the anti-Bourbon uprisings of 1799, 1820, 1848, and 1860. Palazzo Calabritto (No. 30), built by Luigi and Carlo Vanvitelli, dominates the square on the seaward side.

Along the streets that radiate from the square, historic palazzi alternate with elegant shops and cafés. Palazzo Portanna (No. 58), built in the 18th century by Mario Gioffredo, was rebuilt by Antonio Niccolini for Lucia Migliaccio, the morganatic wife of Ferdinand IV. Among the Neo-Renaissance and Liberty style buildings along Via Filangieri and Via dei Mille, Palazzo Mannajuolo (No. 36 Via Filangieri) is worth seeing for its beautiful inner staircase. In nearby Via Poerio and Via San Pasquale are the Lutheran and Anglican churches, founded in 1861–2.

19th-century statue at the Villa entrance

Villa Comunale ❺

Map 6 E2. 🚌 *C4, R3, 140.* 🚋 *1.*

THE FIRST DESIGN for this park area dates from 1697, during the rule of viceroy Luis de la Cerda, but it was Ferdinand IV who, almost a century later, asked architect Carlo Vanvitelli and landscape gardener Felice Abate to lay out the Real Passeggio di Chiaia as a public park.

The Villa Reale, subsequently the Villa Comunale, was completed in 1781 and enlarged in the following century. Among the pine, monkey puzzle, palm, and eucalyptus trees there are 19th- and early 20th-century sculptures and several fountains. These include the so-called *Paparelle*, which in 1825 replaced the famous *Farnese Bull* sculpture group now in the Museo Archeologico *(see p86)*. The park, extends from the Riviera di Chiaia to panoramic Via Caracciolo, where the Neo-Classical buildingoccupies the Stazione Zoologica and the iron and glass kiosk, or the Cassa Armonica, designed in 1877 by Enrico Alvino. Of the many pavilions planned for the park in the 19th-century restoration, this was the only one built.

Facade of the Stazione Zoologica

Stazione Zoologica ❻

Villa Comunale. **Map** 6 E2.
📞 *583 32 63.* 🚌 *C4, R3, 140.*
🚋 *1.* 🕐 *Nov–Feb: 9am–5pm Tue–Sat; 10am–2pm Sun, Mar–Oct: 9am–6pm Tue–Sat; 10am–6pm Sun.* 🎫

THIS INSTITUTE, run by the Consiglio Nazionale delle Ricerche (National Research Council), is one of the oldest and best known of its kind in the world. It was established in 1872–4 by the German scientist Anton Dohrn to study marine environments. The building, designed by Adolf von Hildebrandt, was enlarged and remodeled in 1888, 1904, and again in 1957. It contains research labs, a small exhibition, and the oldest aquarium in Europe, with specimens from the Bay of Naples. The frescoes of marine and rural scenes in the reading room of the library were painted by Hans von Marées in 1873.

The park area of Villa Comunale with the Riviera di Chiaia along the waterfront

Museo Diego Aragona Pignatelli Cortes and Museo delle Carrozze in Villa Pignatelli **❼**

Riviera di Chiaia 200. **Map** 6 D2.
📞 66 96 75. 🚌 C4, R3, 140. 🚋 1.
🕐 9am–1pm Mon–Sat. 🚫 ♿

THE NEO-CLASSICAL villa was built in 1826 by Pietro Valente for the illustrious Acton family. The Rothschilds became the new owners 20 years later and changed the furnishings and internal decoration. Prince Diego Aragona Pignatelli Cortes then purchased the villa, which is named after him. In 1952 his granddaughter donated it to the Italian state. The loveliest rooms are the red hall in Louis XVI style, the smoking room with leather-lined walls, and the ballroom with its large, elegant mirrors and magnificent chandeliers. Villa Pignatelli is often used for temporary exhibitions, concerts, and other cultural events. A small building nearby is occupied by the **Museo delle Carrozze** (Carriage Museum), which has an interesting collection of Italian and French coaches dating from the late 1800s to the early 1900s.

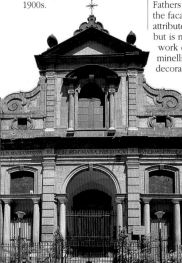
The facade of Santa Maria in Portico

Presbytery and apse of the Chiesa dell'Ascensione a Chiaia

Santa Maria in Portico **❽**

Via Giuseppe Martucci 17. **Map** 6 D2.
📞 66 92 94. 🚌 C4, R3, 140. 🚋 1.
Ⓜ Amedeo. 🚇 Chiaia: Parco Margherita. 🕐 7:30–10:30am, 5:30–7pm Mon–Sat; 7:30am–1pm, 6–8pm Sun. ♿

IN 1632 THE DUCHESS of Gravina Felice Maria Orsini donated some of her property to the Padri Lucchesi della Madre di Dio congregation so they could build a monastery and church. The name "in Portico" refers to the Roman church of Santa Maria in Campitelli al Portico d'Ottavia, where the Lucca Fathers came from. For years the facade in piperno was attributed to Cosimo Fanzago but is now known to be the work of Arcangelo Gugliel-minelli. The interior is decorated with fine 18th-century canvases and stuccoes by Domenico Antonio Vaccaro, who also designed the high altar. A creche with 17th-century figures is in the sacristy. A short walk down nearby Via Piscicelli takes you to the **Chiesa dell'Ascensione a Chiaia**, with fine paintings by Luca Giordano. The 14th-century church was rebuilt in the 1600s by Cosimo Fanzago.

Santa Maria di Piedigrotta **❾**

Piazza Piedigrotta 24. **Map** 5 B3.
📞 66 97 61. 🚌 C4, R3, 140. 🚋 1.
Ⓜ Mergellina. 🕐 7am–noon, 5:30–8pm Mon–Sat; 7am–1:30pm, 5:30–8pm Sun. ♿

THIS CHURCH is mentioned in a letter written by Giovanni Boccaccio in Neapolitan dialect in 1339 in which he mentions the "Madonna de Pederotta." Much altered over the years, Santa Maria di Piedigrotta is commonly believed to have been rebuilt in 1353 to re-place a church founded in 1207. It was again rebuilt in the mid-1400s and in the early 1500s. The orientation of the church, which had faced the "grotta" (cave), was altered the following century.

Fresco by Belisario Corenzio in Santa Maria di Piedigrotta

The present facade is the result of 19th-century resto-ration by Enrico Alvino. Gaetano Gigante decorated the vault. Inside is the 15th-century wooden panel *Descent from the Cross*, by an unknown Neapolitan artist.
The church's great popular-ity is linked to a beautiful 14th-century wooden sculp-ture of the *Madonna and Child*, made by the Siena School, which dominates the church from a high tabernacle. The worship of the Piedigrotta Madonna culminates in the September 7th feast (see p42). In the past, even the royal family took part in the solemn procession. Worshipers did not appreciate the statue's restoration in 1976 to its original state, because the Virgin's large blue mantle and luminous halo were removed.

Parco Virgiliano ⑩

Via Salita Grotta 20. **Map** 5 A2.
【 66 93 90. 🚌 C4, R3, 140. 🚋 1.
Ⓜ Mergellina. ◯ 8am–1:30pm daily.

View of the Parco Virgiliano

MYTH, LEGEND, traces of the past, and natural beauty are what make this park one of Naples's most intriguing sites. It officially became a park after restoration work in 1930. In 1939 a monument to the poet Giacomo Leopardi was erected, and his remains were transferred here from Recanati, his home town.

The park is primarily famous because, according to legend, the poet Virgil is buried here. However, the so-called Tomb of Virgil is in fact an anonymous Roman funerary monument and has nothing at all to do with the great poet.

Another legend involving Virgil is that with a single gesture he created the *Crypta* *Neapolitana*, a tunnel about 700 m (2,300 ft) long. This was, in reality, built by the Roman architect Cocceius in the 1st century BC to connect Neapolis and Puteoli. In the 1920s the tunnel caved in and is now inaccessible. The entrance with its medieval frescoes and epigraphs, can still be seen from the park.

Mergellina ⑪

Map 5 B4. 🚌 C4, R3, 140. 🚋 1.
Ⓜ Mergellina.

THE FISHERMEN'S quarter that developed over the inlet at the foot of Posillipo hill, and was hailed by poets and writers for its beauty, was a popular place for pleasure trips from the Angevin age on. The harmony of the landscape was broken by 19th-century land reclamation that extended the coastline farther into the sea. However, Mergellina is still enjoyable to walk around. The numerous cafés, called *chalet* by the locals, offer excellent ice cream and fresh fruit.

Hydrofoil boats for the islands and other destinations in the bay depart from the docks in the harbor.

St Michael and the
"Mergellina devil"

Santa Maria del Parto ⑫

Via Mergellina 21. **Map** 6 B4.
【 66 46 27. 🚌 C4, R3, 140.
🚋 1. Ⓜ Mergellina. ◯ 7:30–11am, 5:30–7:30pm Mon–Sat; 8am–12:30pm, 6–7:30pm Sun. 🚻

THE HISTORY of the church of Santa Maria del Parto is closely linked with the figure and works of Jacopo Sannazaro (1458–1530), the famous Neapolitan humanist and poet in the service of the Angevin court. The church was built in the 1520s, upon the initiative of Sannazaro, on a plot of land donated by Frederick of Aragon and was named after one of the poet's works, *De Partu Virginis*. Behind the high altar is the tomb of the poet himself, a fine marble group sculpted by Giovan Angelo Montorsoli and Francesco del Tadda in 1537, and probably designed by Sannazaro himself. Before leaving, don't forget to look at the "Mergellina devil" depicted in a wooden panel by Leonardo da Pistoia on the right-hand altar. The panel shows St. Michael, who has just vanquished the devil – the devil has assumed the guise of a beautiful woman.

The small harbor of Mergellina, filled with fishing boats and pleasure craft

Two Trips Around Posillipo

THE PENINSULA that juts into the sea, separating the Bay of Naples from Pozzuoli, was called *Pausilypon* ("respite from pain") by the ancient Greeks because of the great beauty of the site. As can be seen by the many ruins along the coast, in Roman times a huge settlement grew up along the westernmost edge of what is now called Posillipo and was connected to the neighboring Phlegraean Fields (*see pp132–5*). Posillipo was occupied by religious communities and suburban villages during the Middle Ages, and became the favorite vacation resort of the Spanish aristocracy in the 17th century, when luxurious seaside villas and aristocratic palaces were built here. In the following century, the area began to decline, and it was only in the early 19th century that it regained its former popularity. This was partly the result of improved access, thanks to the new coastal road opened in 1812 by Joachim Murat, ruler of Naples from 1806. However, from the 1950s on (during the era when Achille Lauro, *see pp26–7*, was mayor of Naples), the upper part of the hill between Via Orazio, Via Petrarca and Via Manzoni was overtaken by unregulated, unscrupulous property development that has sadly ruined an area of unsurpassed scenic and historic beauty.

Sant'Antonio campanile

Getting Around
The best way to take in the fascination and beauty of the Posillipo coast is by boat; however, excursions can be made only in the summer (for information: **Ascultur Campania**, Via F Galiani 20, **☎** 66 55 32). Otherwise, take bus 140 down Via Posillipo and Via Santo Strato and then walk toward the sea along Via Ferdinando Russo and Via Marechiaro.

Sights at a Glance
Capo Posillipo ③
Marechiaro ④
Palazzo Donn'Anna ①
Posillipo Park ⑥
Santa Maria del Faro ⑤
World War I Memorial ②

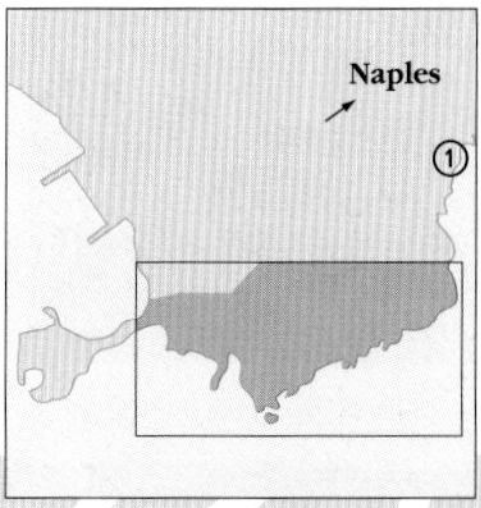

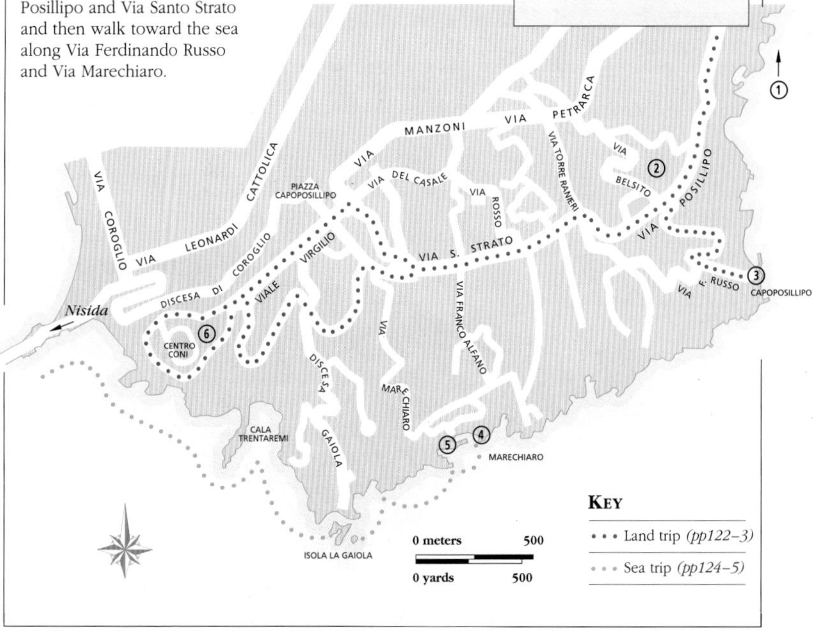

Key
• • • Land trip (*pp122–3*)
• • • Sea trip (*pp124–5*)

◁ The small island of Gaiola and the rocky Posillipo coastline

Posillipo by Land

IF YOU DECIDE to explore Posillipo by land, bear in mind that the complete itinerary shown here would make a very long walk. The best way to get around, in the following order, is by scooter, taxi (agree on the fare beforehand), bus route 140, or a rented car. This is the least popular option because traffic can be heavy and parking difficult. Many of the old villas, now privately owned, are hidden from view and only a few can be seen from the road. However, the views are stupendous and the routes down to Capo Posillipo and Marechiaro, though demanding, very rewarding.

Palazzo Donn'Anna ①

Palazzo Donn'Anna on the water

In 1637 the Spanish viceroy Ramiro Guzman, Duke of Medina, married the Neapolitan princess Anna Carafa. To celebrate, Don Ramiro asked the architect Cosimo Fanzago to build the large Palazzo Donn'Anna at the water's edge. Construction began in 1642, but the building was never completed and never used by the couple. The viceroy returned to Spain in 1644, and Donn'Anna died soon after.

The palazzo was damaged during the 1647 uprising and again as a result of the 1688 earthquake. It was partly restored in the early 1700s, but decades later it was still being described in tourist guides as a building in a state of total neglect.

Its air of mystery gave rise to the rumor that in its past the palace had been used by Queen Joan II for secret assignations with her lovers. Popular belief has it that after these men had served their purpose, they were thrown into the sea below the palace. Palazzo Donn'Anna suffered further damage in the early 19th century when part of the facade was demolished to build the Via Posillipo. In 1870 attempts were made to turn it into a hotel, but the idea was abandoned.

Despite its tormented history and the damage wrought by time and neglect, the massive tufa palace with its cavernous vaults is still majestic and one of the city's celebrated sights.

World War I Memorial ②

From Piazza San Luigi you can see how property development has spoiled the view of the hill. Past the piazza is the Ara Votiva, or War Memorial, set in a small park. The middle of the park is dominated by the large Egyptian-style mausoleum that Matteo Schilizzi began building in 1883 as a tomb for his brother Marco. This impressive monument was purchased and finished in 1923 by the Naples city council in order to house the remains of soldiers who had died in World War I.

Capo Posillipo ③

After Piazza Salvatore di Giacomo, a square with a small garden in the middle, go down Via Ferdinando Russo toward the bay of Capo Posillipo and Villa Volpicelli. The villa, first built in the 17th century, was rebuilt in the 19th century by Raffaele Volpicelli and gives the impression of a castle floating on the water.

The Neapolitans call the area around the Villa Volpicelli the Riva Fiorita, or flowered shore. In summer the little harbor, the beach, and the cliff area opposite hum with life. Cafés and the famous restaurant Giuseppone a Mare (see p184) lend atmosphere to this area at all times of the year. To reach the fishing village of Mare-chiaro, take the road that curves down to the left.

The 17th-century Villa Volpicelli, built on the water's edge

The Bay of Naples viewed from Posillipo in a 1920s photograph

Marechiaro ④

A famous Neapolitan song says this coastline is so romantic, even the fish make love in the moonlight. Going down Via Marechiaro by day, you will see elegant villas surrounded by greenery and beautiful panoramic views.

Toward the sea is a small square with the remains of a Roman column from the so-called Temple of Fortune. Farther down, in the fishing village of Marechiaro, there are cafés, restaurants, and swimming facilities. The village has been made famous by a song of the same name by Salvatore di Giacomo.

Santa Maria del Faro ⑤

This church, recorded in documents as far back as the 1300s, was probably built over the remains of an ancient Roman lighthouse (*faro* in Italian). It was restored by Sanfelice in the 18th century but the facade dates from the

Santa Maria del Faro

19th century. From here you can go down the Calata del Ponticello, which brings you close to the water's edge.

Parco di Posillipo ⑥

After going back up Via Marechiaro along Via Boccaccio, you will arrive at the park of Posillipo, also known as Parco Virgiliano or Parco della Rimembranza. It sits on the top of the hill overlooking the water and offers a spectacular view from the Bay of Naples to Vesuvius and the Sorrento peninsula on one side, and the Bay of Pozzuoli and the Phlegraean Fields on the other. Below are the island of Nisida, formed from an ancient volcanic crater, and the remains of the now-abandoned ILVA steelworks. At sunset, the views toward Ischia are stunning.

THE VILLAS OF POSILLIPO

The northern stretch of Via Posillipo is dominated by **Villa Doria D'Angri**, built in 1833 by Bartolomeo Grasso for Prince D'Angri and now the Istituto Santa Dorotea. Farther down, on the seaward side, is 17th-century **Villa Quercia**, painted a Pompeiian red. A hunting lodge built by the Duke of Frisio in the 1700s was bought at the end of the 19th century by Count **Pavoncelli**, who gave the villa at No. 43 his name. **Villa Grottamarina** (No. 33) was the home of Maria Anna, sister of King Philip IV of Spain, in the 1630s. The French engineer Alfredo Cottreau built the **Villa Cottreau** (No. 35) in the late 1800s; several wings on different levels descend toward the sea. Pompeiian red is again the color of the **Villa Bracale** (No. 37), whose original 17th-century structure is almost unrecognizable today. The pagoda-shaped **Villa Rocca-romana** (No. 38a) was built in 1814 for Prince Caracciolo. **Villa d'Abro** (No. 46) was named after the nobleman Aslan

Villa Rosebery, now state property

d'Abro, who bought it in 1870 and had it restored in Neo-Romantic style. Beyond Capo Posillipo is **Villa Rosebery** (No. 26 Via Russo), the Neapolitan residence of the President of the Italian Republic. It was here, on May 9, 1946, that King Vittorio Emanuele II abdicated in favor of his son Umberto. At No. 27 Via Russo is the 17th-century **Villa Emma**, the summer residence of the painter Jakob Philipp Hackert. Fringed palms give a tropical feel to the **Villa Gallotta**, built close to the water's edge.

Villa Gallotta

Viewing Posillipo from the Sea

Neapolitan gozzo boat

F ROM THE SEA, Naples and the bay can be viewed in all their splendor. To the west of the city, from Castel dell'Ovo north to Nisida and beyond, as far as the Phlegraean Fields, the coast is dotted with grottoes and inlets. Beyond Capo Posillipo you can see the fishing village of Marechiaro, Roman ruins, and the small islands of Gaiola and Nisida. Bars and beaches lure visitors here in summer. In winter the dramatic coastline can still be admired from a hydrofoil or ferry on an excursion to Procida and Ischia *(see pp164–7)*.

Cala di Trentaremi
The tufa cliffs of Cala di Trentaremi are reflected in the sea, which gleams blue and green. This cove is particularly sheltered and is a favorite with swimmers.

Nisida
The ancients called this place Nesis, or little island. It was here that Brutus and Cassius, in the Brutus's villa, plotted to kill Caesar in 44 BC. The Angevin building that dominates the island became a prison under the Bourbons.

← Nisida

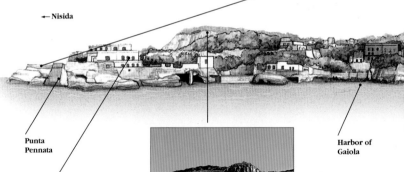

Punta Pennata

Harbor of Gaiola

Gaiola
The presence of ruined ancient buildings between the tufa island of Gaiola and the village of Marechiaro has led scholars to suggest that a complete Roman city once existed here.

Posillipo Park
A well-equipped sports center is one of the attractions in the park at Posillipo on the Coroglio summit.

Marechiaro

The original name for the water by this fishing village was
Mare planum *(calm sea), which was translated literally in*
Italian as "Marepiano." With usage it became "Marechiaro,"
the name now used for the area as a whole. On weekends
Neapolitans love to come and dine out here (see p184).

DIRECTORY

Bagno Elena
Via Posillipo 14.
575 35 20.

Bagno Ideal
Via Posillipo 18.
575 36 17.

Bagno Sirena
Via Posillipo 357.
575 12 55.

Bagno Rocce Verdi
Via Posillipo 68.
575 67 16.

Bagno Marechiaro
Discesa Marechiaro.
769 12 15.

**Church of Santa
Maria del Faro**

Beach at Marinella

Palazzo degli Spiriti

*The remains of the "palace
of the spirits" are visible only
from the sea. This name was
given to the three-story
Roman ruins because of
their mysterious appearance.*

SWIMMING AND RELAXING

If sightseeing in Naples in midsummer becomes too much,
take a break at one of the *stabilimenti balneari* (swimming
spots) along the Posillipo coast. Rent a deckchair and an
umbrella and swim in the sea or in the pool. Neapolitans
started this habit in the 19th century at the **Bagno Elena**,
which first opened 150 years ago. A short distance away
are the **Bagno Ideal** and the **Bagno Sirena**. For those who
prefer cliffs to sand, there are the **Bagno Rocce Verdi**, with
two saltwater pools, and **Bagno Marechiaro** *(see p178)*, with
its restaurant overlooking the bay.

The rocks at Posillipo

POMPEII & THE AMALFI COAST

POMPEII & THE AMALFI COAST

T O THE NORTH OF NAPLES *fertile plains sweep down to the town of Santa Maria Capua Vetere, home to one of the largest remaining Roman amphitheaters in Italy. The remote hinterland to the east is wild, mountainous, and lonely country. To the south is the breathtaking Amalfi coast and the dramatic seaboard of the Cilento. Buried Roman towns and Greek ruins reveal the region's ancient history.*

From the 17th century on Naples was an increasingly crowded and often tormented metropolis. By contrast, the countryside around the city managed to retain its charm and attracted visitors, especially foreigners, many of whom made Campania their home. "A brief sojourn in Naples," the German historian Gregorovius wrote in the mid-1800s, "is enough to demonstrate that not all life is concentrated in the city but flows mightily into the surroundings."

Today, a visit to Pompeii, buried by an erupting Vesuvius in AD 79, is a high priority for tourists, but this was not always so. Travelers on the Grand Tour in the 1600s and early 1700s preferred the volcanic phenomena of the Solfatara crater and the Phlegraean Fields to the west of Naples. Even in the late 18th century Goethe described the area around Paestum, southeast of Naples, as "anything but picturesque," populated by "buffaloes that look like hippopotami, with wild, bloodshot eyes." Only when the first archaeological digs unearthed the remains of Paestum and the buried cities around Mount Vesuvius, did a tour of the ancient ruins become popular.

The beautiful color, light, and atmosphere found on the islands of Capri and Ischia, and the Sorrento peninsula began to interest landscape painters in the 19th century. The southern flank of the peninsula – the Amalfi coast – remained isolated, regarded by many as barren, until the mid-1960s when it attracted visitors in search of an alternative, remote lifestyle. Ironically, the Amalfi coast has since become a very popular vacation spot.

Paestum, south of Naples; in the background are the temples of Neptune and Hera

◁ The fishing harbor of Corricella on the island of Procida

Exploring the Coast

THE MAIN CENTER from which to explore
Campania is Naples itself, well situated in
the middle of the bay. Road and rail links are
generally good in the region, with both
state railroads (FS) and privately run lines
serving a variety of destinations. The
Circumvesuviana railroad connects all
the sights in the area of Vesuvius,
including Pompeii. The three islands
in the bay are accessible by
hydrofoil (half an hour's trip) and
by ferry (one hour) from
Mergellina. Connections are also
possible from Sorrento, Positano,
Amalfi, and Salerno.

Castello Aragonese in Ischia

SIGHTS AT A GLANCE

The Amalfi Coast ⑫
Bagnoli ❶
Baia and Bacoli ❸
Capri ⑯
Caserta ⑮
Cumae ❹
Herculaneum ❾
Ischia ⑰
Paestum ⑭
Pompeii ❿
Portici and the
  Vesuvian Villas ❺
Pozzuoli ❷
Procida ⑱
The Sorrento Peninsula ⑪
Torre Annunziata ❻
Torre del Greco ❼
Vesuvius ❽

Tours
Along the Sorrento Coast ⑬

The Solfatara at Pozzuoli

SEE ALSO

- **Where to Stay** pp170–71

- **Where to Eat** pp178–89

- **Shopping in Campania**
  pp194–5

0 kilometers   20

0 miles   20

View of the Phlegraean Fields at Cumae

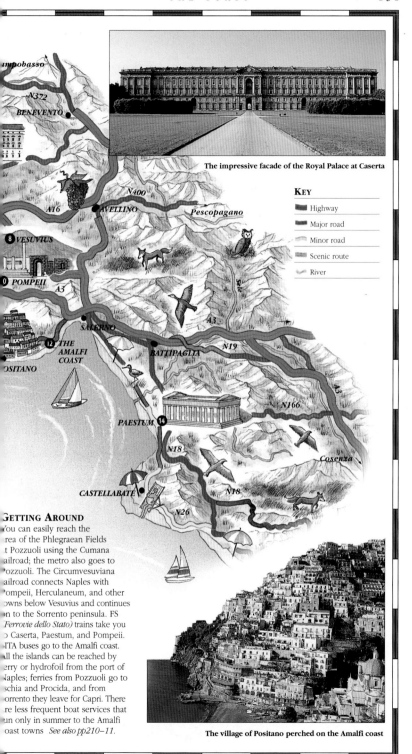

impobasso

N372

BENEVENTO

A16

N400

AVELLINO

Pescopagano

8 VESUVIUS

0 **POMPEII**

A3

SALERNO

12 THE AMALFI COAST

OSITANO

BATTIPAGLIA

N19

A3

N166

PAESTUM 14

N18

Cosenza

N18

CASTELLABATE

N26

The impressive facade of the Royal Palace at Caserta

KEY

	Highway
	Major road
	Minor road
	Scenic route
	River

GETTING AROUND

You can easily reach the area of the Phlegraean Fields at Pozzuoli using the Cumana railroad; the metro also goes to Pozzuoli. The Circumvesuviana railroad connects Naples with Pompeii, Herculaneum, and other towns below Vesuvius and continues on to the Sorrento peninsula. FS (*Ferrovie dello Stato*) trains take you to Caserta, Paestum, and Pompeii. SITA buses go to the Amalfi coast. All the islands can be reached by ferry or hydrofoil from the port of Naples; ferries from Pozzuoli go to Ischia and Procida, and from Sorrento they leave for Capri. There are less frequent boat services that run only in summer to the Amalfi coast towns *See also pp210–11*.

The village of Positano perched on the Amalfi coast

Bagnoli ❶

Road map C3. 🚌 *C1, F9.* 🚊
Cavalleggeri Aosta. 🚃 *Cumana:*
Bagnoli.

THE AREA WEST of Naples,
beyond Posillipo, is called
"de' Bagnoli" because of the
fumaroles and hot springs
there. In 1907 the ILVA
steelworks was built here *(see
pp24–5)*, blighting a beautiful
natural setting. Eventually, the
factory was closed down.
Today part of the site is taken
up with the **Città della
Scienza** (Science City), first
opened in 1996. A series of
tours feature education
through games involving
science, aimed at both
children and adults.

🏛 Città della Scienza
Via Coroglio 104. 📞 *081-230 10
19.* 🕐 *9am–7pm Tue–Sun
(Oct–Mar: until 5pm).*
🖼 📷 🎫 ♿

Pozzuoli ❷

Road Map C3. 🏠
76,045. 🚉 *Azienda
Autonoma di Soggiorno e
Turismo, Via Campi Flegrei 3.*
📞 *081-526 14 81/24 19,
Via Matteotti 1.* 📞 *081-526 66 39/
50 68.* Ⓜ 🚃 *Cumana: Pozzuoli.* ⛴
to Ischia & Procida.

The amphitheater
stage entrance

The *macellum* at Pozzuoli, commonly known as the Temple of Serapis

AROUND THE 7th century BC,
the Greek colony of
Dicearchia was founded on
this site overlooking the port.
By 194 BC Roman Puteoli
was a flourishing trade center
with luxurious villas.
The town later
became the Rione
Terra quarter.
Abandoned in
1971 because of
the underground
volcanic activity
that has always
affected Pozzuoli,
the place is now
under restoration.
A Roman temple can still be
seen under the San Procolo
cathedral. The amphitheater,

one of the oldest in Italy,
shows how important the city
once was.

🏛 Anfiteatro Grande
Via Terracciano 75. 📞 *081-526 23
41.* 🕐 *9am–4pm daily.* 🖼
The amphitheater had a
seating capacity of 40,000.
The underground area was
used for the caged animals
and the equipment to lift
them up to the arena, as well
as a sophisticated drainage
system to collect rainwater.

🏛 Temple of Serapis
Piazza Serapide. 📞 *081-44 01 66.*
🕐 *daily.* 🎫
The Temple of Serapis (2nd
century AD), actually the

The Anfiteatro Grande at Pozzuoli, with three tiers of seats

The Solfatara in Pozzuoli, known as *Forum Vulcani* in ancient times

macellum, or food market, is all that remains of the ancient port district.

🏛 Solfatara
Via Solfatara 161. 📞 *081-526 23 41.*
⭕ *8:30am–1 hr before sunset daily.* 📷
This volcanic crater was an obligatory stop for those making the Grand Tour. It is now dormant, but you can see phenomena created by the still-molten underground magma and water seepage: fumaroles and sulfur fumes.

🦌 Riserva degli Astroni Oasi WWF
Bypass (tangenziale; 1 km from Agnano exit). 📞 *081-588 37 20.*
⭕ *10am–2pm.* 🎫 *holidays & holiday eves; groups by appt.*
This wildlife preserve lies in an extinct crater covered with trees. It was once an Aragonese hunting ground.

Baia and Bacoli ❸

Road Map B3. 🗺 *26,699.*
🚉 *Cumana: Baia, Bacoli.*

ALONG THE COAST between Pozzuoli and Capo Miseno there are many places that were well known in antiquity. Baia boasted sumptuous Roman villas with terraces overlooking the water, famous therapeutic springs (still in use in the Middle Ages), and an Aragonese castle, now an archaeological museum.

Bacoli lies along the coast and runs into the modern town of Miseno, which developed over the site of the Roman town of Bauli. At the time of the Emperor Augustus, the port of Miseno was connected to Lake Miseno in the interior. The

The Bath of Mercury at Baia

port was planned so to avoid silting from volcanic movement; it replaced Porto Giulio (*see p135*), the headquarters of the Roman navy. The Arco Felice, which was the gateway to Cumae (*see pp134–5*), is on the peninsula protecting the Bay of Pozzuoli.

Beaches and clubs make this area a summer favorite.

⛲ Casino Vanvitelliano del Fusaro
Via Fusaro 162, Baia. 📞 *081-868 70 80.* 🚉 *Cumana: Baia.*
⭕ *8am–8pm.*

In 1794 Vanvitelli built a casino, or hunting lodge, on an island in Lake Fusaro for Ferdinand IV. This is the only nonvolcanic lake in the area.

🏛 Parco Archeologico di Baia
Via Fusaro 35, Baia. 📞 *081-868 75 92.* 🚉 *Cumana: Baia.* ⭕ *9am–1 hr before sunset.* 📷
The large domes at this archaeological site were once thought to be temples but are now known to be the remains of a spa that included baths named after Venus and Mercury and the so-called Temple of Diana.

This monumental complex was built, from the late 2nd century–early 1st century BC, on two levels, with terraced land descending to the water.

The site is now used to exhibit excavation finds from the Phlegraean Fields area.

🏛 Museo Archeologico dei Campi Flegrei
Via Castello, Baia. 📞 *081-523 37 97.* 🚉 *Cumana: Baia.* ⭕ *9am–1 hr before sunset.* ⭕ *Mon.* 📷
The Castello di Baia was once an Aragonese fortress.

View of the city of Baia; in the foreground, the Roman ruins

Hall in the Museo Archeologico

It was totally rebuilt in the 1600s and then used as an orphanage from 1927 to 1975. It is now an Archaeological Museum, with finds from the Phlegraean Fields *(Campi Flegrei)*. Also on display are the Roman plaster casts of Greek statues found in Baia. From the northwest tower you can see the reconstructed Sacello degli Augustali, used for worship of the emperor, found near the Forum at Miseno. The zone is now partly under water.

Piscina Mirabilis
Via A Greco, Bacoli. ◯ 9am–1 hr before sunset. ☐ for inquiries: custodian Ida Basile.
This enormous reservoir, divided into five longitudinal sections supported by pillars, collected water brought by Roman aqueduct from the Serino River, then supplied it to the fleet at Miseno.

Cento Camerelle
Via Cento Camerelle 165, Bacoli. ☐ for inquiries: custodian Scotto di Vetta. ☎ 081-523 36 90.
The tunnels dug out of the tufa contained a series of cisterns placed at different levels. They originally supplied a villa dating back to the Republican era.

The *Piscina Mirabilis* at Bacoli

Cumae ❹

Road map B3. 🚌 Cumana: Baia. 🚌

FOUNDED IN the 8th century BC, probably by Greeks stationed on Ischia, Cumae is one of the oldest known colonies of Magna Graecia. An important port for centuries, Cumae resisted the Etruscans but succumbed to the Romans in the 3rd century BC and became a Roman colony. A village grew up over the ruins of the upper city in the 5th–6th centuries, but it was totally destroyed by the Saracens in 915. The ancient settlement has not yet been completely excavated.

The tufa corridor in the Sibyl's Grotto

The best-known areas are the acropolis on the rise to the northwest and the necropolis in the plain. The acropolis walls, partly rebuilt, and two huge temples are well preserved. The Temple of Apollo lies on the lower terrace, the Temple of Jupiter on the upper one; both were rebuilt in the age of Augustus and the pre-Christian era. At the foot of the acropolis is the entrance to the so-called Sibyl's Grotto.

The lower city, inhabited at a later period, is still being excavated and studied. There is a forum, various baths, and an amphitheater. There are also remains of different epochs: the Samnite-age forum conceals the more ancient *agora*, or Greek city center. In recent years a sanctuary dedicated to Isis,

destroyed with the rise of Christianity, was discovered in the port area.

Archaeological Park
Via Acropoli. ☎ 081-854 30 60. ◯ 9am–1 hr before sunset.

Temple of Apollo
Most of the finds from the Temple of Apollo date from the Roman era, when a terrace overlooking the city was added. In the early Christian period the temple was turned into a basilica, and burial pits were hewn out of the ancient foundations.

The Sibyl's Grotto
According to myth this was where to find the Cumaean Sibyl, the oracle consulted by Aeneas. The tufa passageway, trapezoid in section, is illuminated by narrow

ARCHAEOLOGICAL PARK

Acropolis

Temple of Jupiter

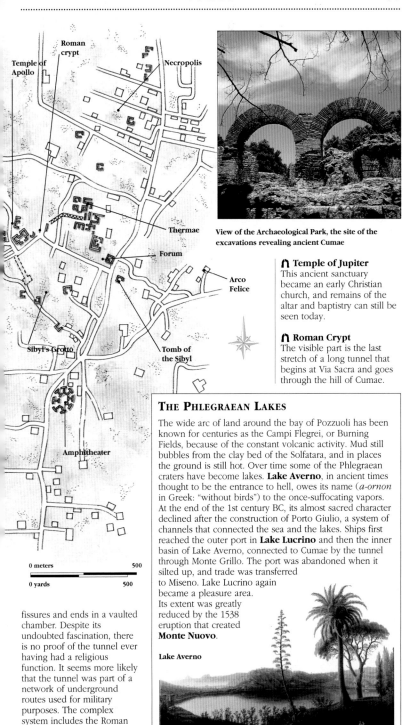

View of the Archaeological Park, the site of the excavations revealing ancient Cumae

⋔ Temple of Jupiter
This ancient sanctuary became an early Christian church, and remains of the altar and baptistry can still be seen today.

⋔ Roman Crypt
The visible part is the last stretch of a long tunnel that begins at Via Sacra and goes through the hill of Cumae.

THE PHLEGRAEAN LAKES

The wide arc of land around the bay of Pozzuoli has been known for centuries as the Campi Flegrei, or Burning Fields, because of the constant volcanic activity. Mud still bubbles from the clay bed of the Solfatara, and in places the ground is still hot. Over time some of the Phlegraean craters have become lakes. **Lake Averno**, in ancient times thought to be the entrance to hell, owes its name (*a-ornon* in Greek: "without birds") to the once-suffocating vapors. At the end of the 1st century BC, its almost sacred character declined after the construction of Porto Giulio, a system of channels that connected the sea and the lakes. Ships first reached the outer port in **Lake Lucrino** and then the inner basin of Lake Averno, connected to Cumae by the tunnel through Monte Grillo. The port was abandoned when it silted up, and trade was transferred to Miseno. Lake Lucrino again became a pleasure area. Its extent was greatly reduced by the 1538 eruption that created **Monte Nuovo**.

Lake Averno

fissures and ends in a vaulted chamber. Despite its undoubted fascination, there is no proof of the tunnel ever having had a religious function. It seems more likely that the tunnel was part of a network of underground routes used for military purposes. The complex system includes the Roman crypt and the Grotto of Cocceius that connected Cumae to Lake Averno.

Portici and the Vesuvian Villas ❺

Road Map C3. 🚟 *67,934.* 🛈 *Ente Ville Vesuviane Napoli, Piazza del Plebiscito.* 📞 *081-40 53 93.* 🚆 🚉 *Circumvesuviana: Portici.* 🚌 *city buses.*

THE COAST east of the city, up to the foot of Mount Vesuvius, has always been dotted with rural estates, owned by the nobility but used for agriculture as much as rural retreats. The luxurious villas, now known as the Ville Vesuviane, were built in the early 1700s, when the value of land in the area rose because of the interest in the archaeological excavations around the volcano. Prince d'Elboeuf, who discovered Herculaneum in 1709, built a villa here. A few decades later, after the building of the Royal Palace at Portici, these aristocratic villas grew in number, transforming the road between Resina and Torre del Greco into what became known as the **Miglio d'Oro**, or Golden Mile. The presence of the Bourbon palace and the location of these villas, with fine views of, and often access to, the countryside and sea, made this area a favorite resort of the aristocracy. A port was built here in 1773.

Over 100 of the villas are of considerable architectural interest; unfortunately, only a few can be visited. Many are either inhabited or in a state of decay. Some are well worth a visit, if only to see the decorations on the facade or the magnificent gardens that have survived massive urbanization.

🏛 Reggia di Portici

Via Università 100, Portici. 📞 *081-775 12 51.* ⏰ *by appt.*

The Royal Palace *(reggia)* was built between 1738 and 1742 in the center of a splendid park at the foothills of Vesuvius and overlooking the water.

The Royal Palace in Portici

Two villas had occupied the site, and a road still crosses the large inner courtyard and continues toward Herculaneum. Originally, finds from the site at Herculaneum and the other archaeological sites in the area

were kept in Maria Amalia's Porcelain Parlor in the palace, but these have since been transferred to the museum at Capodimonte *(see p99).*

The palace did not have a mooring, so the sovereigns bought the Villa d'Elboeuf for this purpose. Designed by Ferdinando Sanfelice, the villa incorporates some splendid stuccowork and a magnificent circular staircase. In 1839 the Naples-Portici *(see p23)* railroad was built, separating the villa from the waterfront.

In 1873, the Royal Palace and its park became the home of the Faculty of Agriculture of the University of Naples.

🏛 Villa Campolieto

Corso Resina 283, Ercolano. 📞 *081-732 21 34.* ⏰ *10am–1pm Tue–Sun.*

Begun in 1755 by Gioffredo and completed by Vanvitelli in 1775, the Villa Campolieto has since been completely restored. A monumental staircase links the ground floor and upper floor. Vanvitelli's elegant portico hosts the Festival delle Ville Vesuviane *(see p41)* each summer, and the villa sometimes hosts other events such as the *Terraemotus* modern art exhibition.

🏛 Villa Favorita

Corso Resina 291, Ercolano. 🚫 *to the public.*

This villa, set in an extensive park, was designed by Ferdinando Fuga in 1768 as a royal residence. Ferdinand IV decorated it with paintings, silk from San Leucio (*see p159*), and a mosaic removed from the Villa Jovis in Capri (*see p163*). His son Leopold supervised the layout of the park and stables. The villa was restored in 1854.

🏛 Villa Prota

Via Nazionale 1009, Torre del Greco. 🚫 *to the public.*

This is one of the most spectacular of the Vesuvian villas. Through the large portal, built with balconies and a gateway, you can see the driveway and park. The main wing was built to one side so not to obstruct the views from the villa.

Vanvitelli's curved portico in Villa Campolieto

Torre Annunziata ❻

Road map D3. 🚂 50,607. ℹ️ Pro Loco Ufficio Informazioni Turistiche: Via Sepolcri 16. 📞 081-862 31 63. 🚆 Ⓜ️ Circumvesuviana: Portici.

THE TOWN WAS built over the ruins of ancient Oplontis, which was destroyed in the eruption of Vesuvius in AD 79. Its name derives from a watch-tower *(torre)*, built to warn the populace of any imminent Saracen raids, and a chapel consecrated to the Annunziata (the Virgin Mary), around which the town grew up.

In the 18th century Charles III founded an arms factory here, designed by a pupil of Vanvitelli and finished by Ferdinando Fuga. In the late 1700s and early 1800s Torre Annunziata became a center for pasta production. Toward the waterfront are the spas, Terme Vesuviane Nunziante, named after the general who discovered the ruins of a Roman baths complex here in 1831. He was responsible for the present-day structure, which is still in operation.

∩ Oplontis Excavations

Via Sepolcri 1. 📞 081-862 17 55. 🕐 9am–1 hr before sunset daily. Ⓜ️

The excavation area includes the villas of Poppaea , who was Nero's second wife, and Craxus. Brought to light in 1964, the Oplontis complex reflects the elegant taste of its owners. As well as large gardens and por-ticoes, the private baths of the house can also be seen, complete with *calidarium* (the hot room) and *tepidarium* (the warm room). Also interesting are the 1st century BC–1st century AD wall paintings. These frescoes depict still lifes and scenes combining architecture and figures, in some cases with illusionistic effects around the doorways or windows. The rooms in the Villa of Craxus were once used as storerooms or shops, and many amphoras were found there.

The harbor at Torre Annunziata

Torre del Greco ❼

Road map C3. 🚂 103,605. ℹ️ Via G Marconi 14. 📞 081-881 46 76. 🚆 Ⓜ️ Circumvesuviana: Portici.

THE NAME DERIVES from a watchtower built by Frederick II and from the vineyards that produce wine from a grape variety called Greco. Torre del Greco is mainly known for its fine coral manufacturing. The old town, rebuilt several times after the various eruptions of Vesuvius, lines the coast, while the newer districts, with villas surrounded by gardens, lie on the slopes of the volcano itself. Don't miss Palazzo Vallelonga in Via Vittorio Emanuele and the Camaldoli alla Torre monastery, both 18th-century buildings. The poet Giacomo Leopardi lived in the Villa delle Ginestre (on a road crossing Via Nazionale) and wrote his last poems there, including *La Ginestra* (The Broom).

The imperial villa of Poppaea Sabina at Torre Annunziata

THE RED GOLD AT TORRE DEL GRECO

By the 15th century the main trade in Torre del Greco was coral fishing. Over the centuries the town became a collection point for coral, and other coastal towns followed suit. The first factories were established by foreigners during the 1800s, and later, the Bourbon rulers set up their own factories. Local designs were at first inspired by classical models, and subsequently influenced by the Art Nouveau style. As well as coral work, there were designs in mother-of-pearl, turtle shell, and ivory The *coralline* boats that used to collect the coral have been modernized and reequipped, but today most of the raw material comes from Japan. Admirers of red gold can visit the numerous workshops *(see pp194–5)* in town or the museum at No. 6 Piazza Palomba.

Carved piece of coral

Mount Vesuvius 8

IN ANCIENT TIMES Vesuvius was simply "the mountain," covered with vegetation and vines. The first person to understand its volcanic nature was the Greek geographer Strabo (AD 19), who suggested that its rocks had been burned by fire. In AD 79 an enormous eruption smothered the cities on its foothills and greatly altered the surrounding landscape. Ash and debris showered Pompeii, and Herculaneum was

Carbonized eggs from Pompeii

buried by a landslide of thick mud. Pliny the Younger recorded the cloud of black smoke that rose "like an umbrella pine" from the mountain. His uncle, Pliny the Elder, was suffocated by the gaseous vapors that engulfed the area. Today, the volcano is constantly monitored, bit it still inspires both fear and fascination.

Layers of ash alternate with lava flow, settle on the sides of the volcano and gradually build up the cone.

Vineyards
The land around volcanoes, rich in alkali and phosphorus, is extremely fertile. On the slopes of Vesuvius, the grapes produce the Lacrima Christi, *once considered one of Italy's best wines.*

Layers of lava

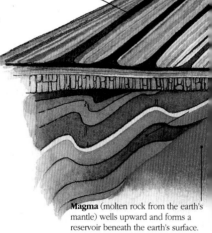

Magma (molten rock from the earth's mantle) wells upward and forms a reservoir beneath the earth's surface.

HISTORY OF THE VOLCANO

These sections show the changes in the structure of Vesuvius following the most significant eruptions, from prehistoric times to the formation of the present-day cone.

First eruptions began 35,000 years ago

Further ash and lava flows built up a second cone

8th century BC: Monte Somma is a single cone

After AD 79: Monte Somma is an open caldera

Today's cone, Vesuvius, formed in the old caldera

Vesuvius Observatory
The observatory on the slopes of Vesuvius was built by Ferdinand II between 1841 and 5. The Neo-Classical building has a well-stocked library, an interesting collection of minerals., and splendid views from the square. Today it is used only as a base for recording data; the research section has been transferred to Naples.

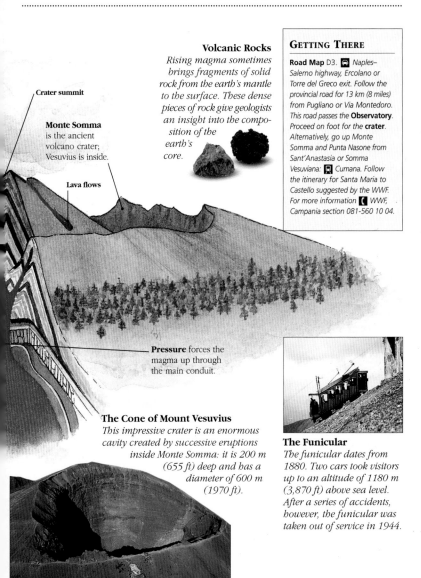

Volcanic Rocks

Rising magma sometimes brings fragments of solid rock from the earth's mantle to the surface. These dense pieces of rock give geologists an insight into the composition of the earth's core.

Crater summit

Monte Somma is the ancient volcano crater; Vesuvius is inside.

Lava flows

Pressure forces the magma up through the main conduit.

The Cone of Mount Vesuvius
This impressive crater is an enormous cavity created by successive eruptions inside Monte Somma: it is 200 m (655 ft) deep and has a diameter of 600 m (1970 ft).

GETTING THERE

Road Map D3. 🚆 Naples–Salerno highway, Ercolano or Torre del Greco exit. Follow the provincial road for 13 km (8 miles) from Pugliano or Via Montedoro. This road passes the **Observatory**. Proceed on foot for the **crater**. Alternatively, go up Monte Somma and Punta Nasone from Sant'Anastasia or Somma Vesuviana: 🚆 Cumana. Follow the itinerary for Santa Maria to Castello suggested by the WWF. For more information 📞 WWF, Campania section 081-560 10 04.

The Funicular
The funicular dates from 1880. Two cars took visitors up to an altitude of 1180 m (3,870 ft) above sea level. After a series of accidents, however, the funicular was taken out of service in 1944.

TIMELINE (1600–Present day)

1694 Another eruption, with lava flow from the crater

1794 Torre del Greco destroyed

1906 Another eruption: the crater widens by 300 m (985 ft)

1933 A series of shocks shows the volcano is active once again. Lava appears on June 3

1600 1700 1800 1900

1631 On December 16 the lava claims 600 victims. Naples is saved, and the Guglia in Piazza Sforza is built in thanks to San Gennaro (see p62)

1767 The lava reaches San Giorgio a Cremano and approaches Naples

1880 The funicular opens to public

1944 After a final violent explosion, the trail of smoke disappears

Herculaneum ➒

Silver disk of Apollo

Ancient Herakleion fell under Greek influence around the 5th century BC and then under Samnite rule. In 89 BC the town became part of the Roman Empire: a residential *municipium* and resort. The town's quiet existence was brought to an abrupt halt in AD 79, when the eruption of Vesuvius that buried Pompeii covered Herculaneum with a deep layer of lava and mud.

Excavations began in the 18th century and uncovered Roman houses built around a rectangular plan. Perhaps the best known is the Villa dei Papiri, the inspiration for the J. Paul Getty museum in Malibu. Sculptures found in the villa are now in the Museo Archeologico Nazionale *(see pp86–9).*

The city baths, built in 10 BC, are divided into two sections. The one for men is larger and decorated and includes a gymnasium; the women's section is smaller and better preserved.

Decumanus Maximus

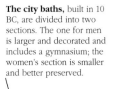

★ **Trellis House**
A typical example of an inexpensive Roman multiamily dwelling, the Trellis House has wood and reed laths in the crude tufa and lime masonry.

House with the Mosaic Atrium
This house has a famous mosaic floor with geometric patterns. There are also living rooms with a portico and terrace facing the water.

0 meters 50
0 yards 50

★ **House of the Stags**
The name derives from the beautiful sculpture groups of stags found here. The house is one of the more elaborate: the inner porticoed garden connects the north section (entrance, indoor triclinium, and smaller rooms) to the south side, which has bedrooms and an arbor with a view of the water.

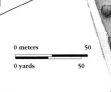

★ House of the Neptune and Amphitrite Mosaic

This mosaic is in the summer dining room. The building and a shop, with wooden shelves for amphoras, are among the best preserved.

VISITORS' CHECKLIST

Road Map C3. **FS** *Portici-Ercolano.* 🚉 *Circumvesuviana: Ercolano-Scavi.* **Digs**: Piazza Museo. **📞** 081-739 09 63. 🕐 9am–1 hr before sunset. 📷

House of the Bicentenary
This patrician residence, excavated 200 years after digging began, had mosaic floors and wall paintings.

Decumanus Inferiore

The Gymnasium area is dominated by the hall, used as the refectory, and the large central pool for the athletes, fed by a bronze fountain.

STAR SIGHTS

- ★ House of the Neptune and Amphitrite Mosaic
- ★ House of the Stags
- ★ Trellis House

The Excavation Area
The site of ancient Herculaneum is well below the level of the modern town. The area is still being excavated, and some buildings, like the Villa dei Papiri, northwest of the site, remain underground.

The House of Telephus contains a 1st-century BC relief narrating the myth of Achilles and Telephus.

The House of the Gem is named after a cameo portrait from the era of Claudius that was found here.

Pompeii ⑩

"Samovar" from Pompeii

A N EARTHQUAKE in AD 62, which shook Pompeii and damaged some of its buildings, was merely a prelude to the tragic day in AD 79, when Vesuvius erupted, engulfing the city and its inhabitants in a terrible storm of cinders and ash. When the remains of Pompeii were discovered around 1750, it looked as though a spell had been cast to freeze all life. The bodies of people and animals were unearthed along with their houses, temples, works of art, and everyday objects. The first archaeologists removed the most important finds. These artifacts became part of the royal collection and were transferred to the Museo Archeologico Nazionale *(see pp86–9)*. This illustration shows the western end of the archaeological site.

The House of the Golden Cupids *(see pp146–7)* is named after the delightful images in the bedroom.

House of the Faun *(see p146)*

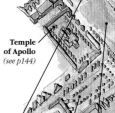

Plaster Casts
Since 1863, plaster cast techniques have enabled researchers to re-create body shapes. Many were killed by the toxic fumes while engaged in everyday tasks.

★ **House of the Vettii**
This is one of the most famous places in Pompeii (see p146). *It has rich wall decorations dating from the last Pompeiian period after AD 62. The array of themes includes Daedalus and Pasiphaë, shown here.*

Temple of Apollo *(see p144)*

Macellum
The macellum was the covered meat and fish market. Fronted by a portico with two moneychangers' kiosks, it opened onto the Forum near the weights and measures office and the Forum Holitorium vegetable market.

Forum *(see p144)*

Basilica *(see p144)*

Temple of Venus *(see p144)*

STAR SIGHTS

★ **House of the Vettii**

★ **Via dei Sepolcri**

Fresco from a Lupanare
Most of the guests at the inn – called hospititium *or* caupona *– were gladiators, since more important visitors were put up in private homes. Here and in the* lupanares, *or brothels, paintings and graffiti depict this world and the services offered by waitresses and prostitutes, as well as boys, to satisfy their clients and lovers.*

VISITORS' CHECKLIST

Road Map C3. **FS** *Pompei-Scavi.* **圓** *Circumvesuviana: Pompei-Villa dei Misteri.* **Digs:** *Porta Marina, Piazza Esedra, Porta Anfiteatro, Piazza Immacolata.* **☎** *081-861 07 44.* **◷** *9am–1 hr before sunset.* **✍ ℹ** *Azienda Autonoma di Soggiorno e Turismo, Via Sacra 1.* **☎** *081-850 72 55; Via Porta Marina Inferiore 1.* **☎** *081-861 09 16.*

Modesto's Bakery, where carbonized bread was found, is one of several bakeries in Pompeii with wood-fired ovens and millstones.

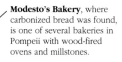

The Stabian Baths *(see p145)*, the oldest in the city, had separate sections for men and women.

Small Theater *(see p145)*

The Forum
Originally the market place, the Forum (see p144) became the focus for the most important civic functions, both political and religious.

0 meters 50
0 yards 50

The Large Theater *(see p144)* was built in the hollow of a hill for good acoustics.

Triangular Forum *(see p145)*

Gladiators' courtyard and barracks *(see p145)*

★ Via dei Sepolcri
"Twenty steps wide, 500 long, the entire length still furrowed by the ancient carriage wheels, completely furnished with pavements like ours, and lined throughout, at left and right, with funerary monuments." This is how an awestruck Alexandre Dumas described Via dei Sepolcri, outside the northwest city wall, which was discovered in the first digs.

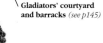

Exploring Pompeii

THANKS TO ITS STRATEGIC position near the Sarno River, Pompeii was a center of commerce for inland areas. The first town plan (6th century BC) was irregular, but, from the 4th century BC on, building developed on a Greek-inspired grid plan. Slabs of old lava from Vesuvius were used to pave the roads. Large villas and houses of different periods and styles, made of brick, stone, and cement, and often richly decorated, offer an unparalleled view of ancient domestic architecture *(see pp146–7)*. Furthermore, the streets, workshops, and public areas are in an excellent state of preservation. Finds such as furnishings, tools, jewelry, and even food and drink reveal how the people of Pompeii lived, from the ruling class down to the slaves.

The Forum viewed from the Temple of Apollo

The Basilica, Pompeii's ancient judicial seat opening onto the Forum

THE FORUM

THE FORUM, a rectangular paved area, was the center of public life and the oldest part of Pompeii, built on the highest spot. Arranged around it are a number of important administrative and religious institutions. To the south is the Basilica, or law court, and opposite are the temples of Apollo, Jupiter, and Vespasian, and the Sanctuary of the Lari. The Eumachia building was perhaps used by the wool merchants' guild or, more likely, for commercial transactions. On the other side of the Basilica is the site of the Temple of Venus. The goddess was the protectress of the city, but in tandem with the fate of Pompeii, her temple was badly damaged in the earthquake of AD 62, then totally devastated by Vesuvius.

TRIANGULAR FORUM

SURROUNDED BY columns and built on a steep-sided lava mass, the Triangular Forum was the focal point for leisure activities. In front of the Doric temple is a well and also a curious building that scholars think was revered by Pompeiians as the sanctuary of the mythical founder of the city. The sacred area might have been dedicated to the gods Hercules and Athena.

THEATERS

THE LARGE THEATER (2nd century BC) was rebuilt several times in its history and in modern times has once again been put to use for summer cultural events. It was built to seat about 5,000 people. The quadrangular portico behind the stage, originally designed as a space

The Forum, with Vesuvius in the background

The gladiators' barracks, part of the Large Theater complex

swimming pool in the middle, are in an outlying area between the Nocera and Sarno gateways. The amphitheater was used for gladiatorial combat and is the oldest one of its kind in existence. The stone tiers were separated into different sections for the various social classes. A large cloth canopy (*velarium*) shaded spectators from the sun.

VIA DELL'ABBONDANZA

A public fountain in Via dell'Abbondanza

for the audience to stroll in during intermissions, was turned into a barracks for the gladiators after AD 62. Skeletons, including one of a baby, have been excavated here.

Next door is the indoor theater, or Small Theater, used for music concerts. Behind this is the Temple of Isis, the locally worshiped goddess.

VIA STABIANA

THIS AVENUE, passing through the Porta di Stabia, to the south, was a major thoroughfare used by carriages traveling between Pompeii and the port and coastal districts.

On the west side of the avenue are the Stabian Baths, the most ancient in Pompeii; the original structure dates from the 4th century BC. Behind the baths, in the alley, is the best preserved of the city's many brothels. It is the only one with two levels, two entrances, and an independent stairway – all designed to provide greater privacy for clients. Erotic wall paintings and a dish of pasta were found in this building. At the junction with Via di Nola are the central baths, which were

under construction at the time of Vesuvius' devastating eruption.

Near Porta Vesuvio you can see the remains of an aqueduct. This channeled water from the Serino River aqueduct, built in the era of Augustus, into three conduits that served both private homes and public fountains. The aqueduct fell into disuse after being damaged by the earthquake of AD 62.

An inn in Via dell'Abbondanza

AMPHITHEATER AND GREAT GYMNASIUM

THE AMPHITHEATER (80 BC) and the Augustan era Great Gymnasium, with a

THE LIVELIEST street in Pompeii was lined with private homes (see pp146–7) and stores selling a wide range of goods. The buildings and contents present a vivid picture of everyday life, down to the cart tracks in the street.

You can visit the shop of Verecundus, who made felt and tanned hides; Stefano's well-preserved laundry, where urine was used as a cleaning agent; or the bakery run by Sotericus, where bread was baked but not sold retail. Among the inns, the most famous belonged to Asellina, whose obliging foreign waitresses are depicted in graffiti on the wall. The inn (*thermopolium*) still has the record of the proceeds of that fateful day in AD 79: "683 sesterces."

The Houses in Pompeii

M ANY LARGE HOUSES of great historical value and
architectural interest are concentrated in the area
between Via di Mercurio (the most elegant *cardo*,
reserved for pedestrians, in the northwest of Pompeii)
and Via Stabiana, and along Via dell'Abbondanza.
Wealthy residents had houses with courtyards, living
rooms, and gardens *(see pp16–17)*, often with
decorated walls. A typical Pompeian house was constructed around two open courts: the atrium, an Italic
feature, and the colonnaded garden, a feature of Greek
origin. The suburban farmstead layouts were different;
the Villa of the Mysteries is one of the most famous.

Bronze statue, House of the Faun

HOUSE OF THE VETTII

The lari shrine, House of the Vettii

T HE OWNERS of the House of
the Vettii were freedmen
who had become rich mer
chants. The house has been
carefully restored, and its
interior walls are adorned
with splendid paintings
and friezes featuring
mythological themes.

In the atrium of the more
rustic part of the house is
the altar of the lari – the
deities who protected the
place. This depicts the
ancestral spirit of the
pater familias with two
lari and, below, a serpent.

HOUSE OF THE FAUN

T HE NAME comes from a
bronze statue in the
middle of the impluvium
(pond) in one of the atria.
The original is in the
Museo Archeologico
Nazionale, as are many of the
mosaics, including the famous
*Battle of Alexander (see
pp86–9)*. Built in the 2nd
century BC, this is one of the
largest private dwellings here.

HOUSE OF THE TRAGIC POET

T HE ENTRANCE has a mosaic
of a dog with a "beware
of the dog" inscription, but its
many frescoes are in the
Museo Archeologico. The
name derives from a mosaic
showing a drama rehearsal.

HOUSE OF THE GOLDEN CUPIDS

T HIS HOUSE, owned by the
Poppaea family, was
decorated with the elegant
taste characteristic of Nero's
era. It is not large and is built
on an irregular plan because
of the limited space. The
name derives from the cupids
(amorini) in gold
leaf that decorate
the bedroom.

The peristyle in the House of the Golden Cupids

Gardens were an important feature at that time, and this garden was well tended and adorned with sculptures, marble tables, and a pool.

HOUSE OF THE CITARISTA

NAMED AFTER the bronze statue of *Apollo the Lyre Player* found in the central peristyle and now in the Museo Archeologico *(see pp86–9)*, this was in fact two houses. It is distinguished by the number of open courts: two atria and three peristyles.

HOUSE OF MENANDER

Silver goblet found in the house

THE WEALTH of decoration and the grandeur of its atrium, peristyle, and the rooms facing east make this one of Pompeii's most interesting houses. The walls of this home were decorated with lovely paintings, including a portrait of the Greek playwright after whom it has been named and images of Ulysses in the Trojan War. A treasure trove of 115 silver objects was also found here in 1930. The bath is quite unusual; it lies on the western side of the peristyle, around a porticoed atrium that still has traces of a fresco portraying divine and mythological figures. The dressing room affords access to the frescoed *calidarium* (warm room).

On the same street is the Samnite period **House of the Labyrinth**. This has two atria and a spacious peristyle with a mosaic on the floor representing *Theseus and the Minotaur in the Labyrinth*.

HOUSE OF THE CRYPTOPORTICUS

THE "hidden portico" that characterizes this house lies under the garden. In AD 79 the owner was probably converting it into a wine cellar, as can be seen by the supply of amphoras. The showcases in the corridor contain plaster casts *(see p142)* of the inhabitants who took shelter in the *cryptoporticus* during the eruption, but who suffocated from the ashes that made their way in through an air vent.

In the *triclinium* (dining room) you can still see frescoes and traces of the rich stuccowork on the vault.

HOUSE OF JULIA FELIX

THE PATRICIAN villas such as this one in Pompeii were usually built outside the town center. The House of Julia Felix, a wealthy resident of Pompeii, occupies an entire block, divided into the owner's quarters and rented dwellings and shops. An inscription with the rental regulations was found here. The house also had baths that were rented and open to the public, who probably flocked here after the Forum Thermae had been damaged by the AD 62 earthquake. The clients waited for their turn in the vast porticoed courtyard, where you can still

Mosaic of Theseus, House of the Labyrinth

see the seats. From here they went to the outdoor pool and then to the baths proper, with a *frigidarium* (cold pool) and *tepidarium* (warm pool).

VILLA OF THE MYSTERIES

THIS LARGE VILLA outside the city walls on Via dei Sepolcri was built in the early 2nd century BC. It was converted from an urban dwelling into an elegant country house. The interesting architecture and beautiful paintings make it one of the most famous houses in Pompeii. It contains a well-known cycle of frescoes with 29 brightly colored life-size figures against a red background, who represent a bride's initiation to the Dionysian mysteries or a postulant's initiation to the Orphic mysteries. Some scholars say this subject was depicted because the owner was a priestess of the Dionysian cult, which was widespread in Southern Italy.

Scene from the famous fresco cycle in the Villa of the Mysteries

The Sorrento Peninsula ⓫

Lemons at Sorrento

THE PENINSULA created by the Lattari hills forms a boundary between the bays of Naples and Salerno. The soft tufaceous northern side has been inhabited for centuries and is dotted with ancient villas dedicated to leisure and culture. The coast becomes rugged and precipitous on the southern side *(see pp150–3)* after Punta della Campanella *(see pp154–5)*, which was fairly isolated until the 19th century. The old Bourbon road passed through Castellammare di Stabia (Roman Stabiae) and served Vico Equense and Sorrento, while the more recent road is higher up and continues to the Amalfi coast via Sant'Agata sui due Golfi.

Vico Equense

CASTELLAMMARE DI STABIA
Road map D4.

🏛 *68,887.* 🚆 *Circumvesuviana: Castellammare.* ℹ️ *Azienda Autonoma di Soggiorno e Turismo, Piazza Matteotti.* 📞 *081-871 13 34.*
Castellammare was completely rebuilt in the 9th century as was its castle that defended the most important of its many sources of therapeutic waters. The old **thermal baths** are still in use today. The Bourbon rulers built major shipyards here that were later abandoned. Ancient Stabiae, an agglomeration of villas and farmsteads, lies outside the modern town on the Varano plain. Stabiae was destroyed by the Vesuvius eruption of AD 79 and was only partly excavated in the 18th century. After World War II more ancient houses were found along the coast and in the interior. The oldest is the **Villa di Arianna** on the Varano hill, with a 1st-century BC nucleus and 13 rooms overlooking the bay. Many of these villas were richly decorated and placed in splendid scenic positions.

♨ Thermal Baths
Piazza Amendola. 📞 *081-871 44 22.* 🕐 *Jun–Oct 7am–1pm.*
⛪ Villa di Arianna
Via Passeggiata Archeologica. 📞 *081-871 45 41.* 🕐 *9am–1 hr before sunset.*

VICO EQUENSE
Road map D4. 🏛 *19,120.* 🚆 *Circumvesuviana: Scraio, Vico Equense.* ℹ️ *Via San Ciro 16.* 📞 *081-879 93 51, 879 88 26, 801 57 52.*
On a rocky spur with sheer cliffs, this town of Etruscan origin, famous in antiquity for its wine, is now a tourist resort with popular bars and restaurants. At nearby Scraio freezing sulfurous water continues to flow into the sea.

🗻 Monte Faito
The best hiking trail to the chestnut and beech woods begins near the Angevin Villa Quisisana. The cable car, which operates from April to

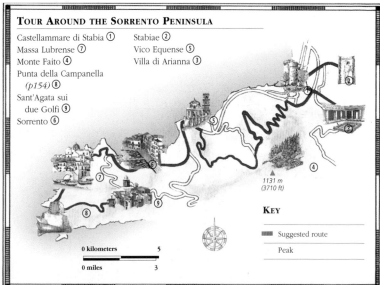

TOUR AROUND THE SORRENTO PENINSULA

Castellammare di Stabia ①
Massa Lubrense ⑦
Monte Faito ④
Punta della Campanella (p154) ⑧
Sant'Agata sui due Golfi ⑨
Sorrento ⑥

Stabiae ②
Vico Equense ⑤
Villa di Arianna ③

1131 m (3710 ft)

KEY

▬▬ Suggested route

▲ Peak

0 kilometers   5
0 miles   3

View of the Sorrento coast

October, departs from the Circumvesuviana train station.

SORRENTO

Road map C4. 🚶 *17,101.*
🚉 *Circumvesuviana: Sorrento.*
🚢 *from & to Naples.*
ℹ️ *Azienda Autonoma di Soggiorno Sorrento e Sant'Agnello, Via De Maio 21.* 📞 *081-807 40 33;*
Azienda Autonoma di Soggiorno e Turismo, Via de Maio 35.
📞 *081-877 33 97.*

You can still distinguish the original Greek town plan in the old center of Sorrento.

Advertisement for a Sorrento hotel

In the summer months the town is filled with tourists strolling along Corso Italia or seated at the cafés in Piazza Tasso. The **Sedile Dominova**, in the square of the same name, is a 15th-century building once used as an assembly hall for the nobility. The **duomo** is of ancient origin and was rebuilt in the 1400s and then remodeled several times. Inside the cathedral is the archbishop's marble throne, sculpted in 1537, and fine marquetry-decorated choir stalls.

The cloister in the church of San Francesco is a mixture of styles and periods: rounded arches on two sides and interlaced Arabic ones on the other two. The **Museo Correale di Terranova** contains 17th–19th-century objets d'art. Outside the town, toward Capo di Sorrento, you can visit the **Bagno della Regina Giovanna**, with the ruins of Pollius Felix's residence.

Many other ancient villas along the coast were absorbed into more recent ones and were sometimes converted into hotels. Sorrento has been a popular resort town since the 1700s: Casanova and Goethe were guests of Sir William and Lady Hamilton, and the French generals lodged at the Cocumella, the town's oldest hotel, opened in 1798. Other historic hotels are the Imperial Tramontano *(see p174)* and the Excelsior Vittoria.

🏛 Duomo
Via Santa Maria della Pietà 44.
📞 *081-878 22 48.*
🕐 *8am–noon, 3–10pm.*

🏛 Museo Correale di Terranova
Via Correale 50.
📞 *081-878 18 46.*
🕐 *9am–12:30pm, 5–7pm Apr–Sep; 3–7pm Oct–Mar.* 📷

🏛 Bagno della Regina Giovanna
Punta del Capo descent (Calata).

MASSA LUBRENSE
Road map C4. 🚶 *11,869.* ℹ️ *Viale Filangieri 11.* 📞 *081-878 91 23.*
Massa is a market town and beach resort at the western end of the peninsula.

SANT'AGATA SUI DUE GOLFI
Road map C4.
Perched on a hill with views north and south, Sant'Agata is a favorite with Neapolitans. It is also famous for the Don Alfonso restaurant *(see p184).*

The harbor at Sorrento

The Amalfi Coast ⑫

Portal of Amalfi Duomo

Suspended between sea, sky, and earth, state road 163 twists and turns along the full length of the Amalfi coast, offering stunning views at every corner. Until the 19th century, this stretch of the "divine coast" was isolated and could be reached only by going up difficult mountain paths on mules. By the early 1900s, this very isolation had become the main appeal and the coast began to attract travelers, artists, and writers. Visitors of all kinds were drawn to steep-stepped Positano; to Amalfi with its glorious past as a marine republic; and to Ravello, which Wagner chose as "the magic garden of Klingsor," the setting for *Parsifal*. The limestone islands called Li Galli, southwest of Positano, are traditionally the home of the Sirens made famous by Homer in his accounts of the trials of Odysseus. Exploring by boat *(see pp154–5)* enables you to appreciate this astonishing coast at closer quarters.

A stretch of state road 163

NERANO

Road map D4. 🚌 *Sita.*

The first stop on the Amalfi coast road is the quiet village of Nerano, administratively part of Massa Lubrense. The road to Nerano goes upward from Sorrento and cuts across the end of the peninsula near the small village of **Termini**. The sea sparkles in the distance, and the panoramic views are stunning. You can even see Capri and the rocky islands of Li Galli *(see p155)*.

Nerano is perched on a ridge; below is the beach and the town of **Marina del Cantone**, popular because of its small water-front restaurants, some supported by stilts. Hikers can descend on paths among the olive trees to the bay of **Ieranto**.

POSITANO

Road map D4.
👥 3,621. 🚌 *Sita.* ⛴ *from Capri & Naples.* 🛈 *Azienda Autonoma di Soggiorno e Turismo, Via Saraceno 1.*
📞 089-87 50 67 or 87 57 60.

In 1953 John Steinbeck wrote that Positano "bites deep. It is a dream place that isn't quite real when you are there and becomes beckoningly real after you have gone." The town climbs the hill in steps, with the oldest houses in the upper part of Positano, either faded red or pink, decorated with Baroque stuccoes. The traffic-free street going down to the sea, Via Pasitea, penetrates the atmospheric heart of town with its narrow stepped alleys, houses with vaulted roofs, terraces, and tiny gardens that defy the

rock. The brightly colored articles Positano is famous for (such as cloth bags and beachwear) on display inside and outside the many shops blend well with the pastel-colored houses, and the local craftsmen are only too happy to make sandals for you while you wait.

Near the beach is the small church of Santa Maria dell'Assunta, whose cupola is covered with yellow, blue, and green majolica tiles. The descent ends at Marina Grande, a pebble beach used by fishing boats, lined with bars and restaurants.

If you want to go to inlets inaccessible by land, or to the little islands of **Li Galli**, or take a trip along the coast, boats are always available. If you prefer to walk, take the easy path to Fornillo beach with its two watch-towers, and swim at Ciumicello or Arienzo. There are also craggy grottoes in the inlets, including La Porta,

Typical Amalfi scenery, with sheer cliffs overlooking the water

where there are Paleolithic and Mesolithic ruins. From Montepertuso, a village above Positano, you can walk along a spectacular scenic path to **Nocelle**. For those who love good food, there are plenty of bars and restaurants, including Buca di Bacco *(see p185)*, famous for its *arancini* rice croquettes.

The beach at Marina di Praia

PRAIANO
Road map D4.
🏠 *1,899.* 🚌 *Sita.*

This fishing village is perched on the ridge of Monte Sant'Angelo and stretches toward Capo Sottile. The church of San Luca, with 16th-century paintings by Giovan Bernardo Lama, lies in the upper part. In an inlet just outside Praiano is **Marina di Praia**, a small beach surrounded by fishermen's houses. On the road from Positano there are more delightful beaches; just before Praiano is **Vettica Maggiore** and farther on, Conca dei Marini. The views are splendid from the terraced square of Vettica Maggiore, by the church of San Gennaro. Before you reach Amalfi, the road widens into an open space. Here you can take the elevator down to the **Grotta dello Smeraldo**, where stalagmites and stalactites merge to form great columns in the emerald-green water.

🏊 **Grotta dello Smeraldo**
⬆️ **State road** 163,
4 km (2 miles) from Amalfi. 🖋

AMALFI
Road map D4.
🏠 *5,615.* 🚌 *Sita.*
ℹ️ *Azienda Autonoma di Soggiorno e Turismo, Corso Roma 19/21.* ☎ *089-87 11 07 or 87 26 19.*

Tucked in between mountains and sea, Amalfi is a perennial favorite with visitors for its scenic beauty

The rocky Amalfi coastline

and original architecture. It also has a glorious history as a powerful maritime republic; in the 11th century Amalfi was a rival to the ports of Venice and Genoa.

Little remains to show for the colorful trading history of this small town, whose inhabitants once numbered 60,000. Amalfi's cathedral, the **Duomo di Sant'Andrea**, founded in the 9th century, was rebuilt in Romanesque style in the 11th century and then altered several times. The facade and atrium date from the late 1800s, but the carved bronze doors were cast in Constantinople around the year 1000. The campanile (1276) is decorated with Arabic-like interlaced arches, typical of southern Italian Romanesque. To the left of the porch, the Chiostro del Paradiso (Paradise cloister)

was built around 1266 for Bishop Augustariccio as a cemetery for prominent citizens. The garden is surrounded by an ornate colonnade with interlaced arches supported by paired columns and with fragments of sculpture from different periods. Near Piazza Duomo is the Arsenal; here you can see the ruins of two naves and the vault. Heading inland from Amalfi, you can visit the Valle dei Mulini (Valley of the Mills), famous for its traditional paper production and the **Museo della Carta**, or Paper Museum.

🔔 **Duomo di Sant'Andrea**
Piazza Duomo.
🕘 *9am–1pm, 3–8pm daily.*
🏛 **Museo della Carta**
Valle dei Mulini.
☎ *089-87 26 15.* 🕘 *9am–1pm Mon, Fri.* ⚫ *Tue–Thu, Sat & Sun.*

Piazza Duomo in Amalfi and the wide steps leading to the cathedral

RAVELLO

Road map D4. 🏘 *2,430.* 🚌 *Sita.*
ℹ️ *Azienda Autonoma di Soggiorno
e Turismo, Piazza Duomo 10.*
📞 *089-85 70 96 or 85 79 77;
Ente Provinciale di Turismo, Piazza
Vescovado 1.* 📞 *089-85 76 57.*

Ravello's history is entwined
with that of Amalfi: Ravello
became part of the Duchy of
Amalfi in the 9th century. The
period of greatest splendor
was the 13th century, when
trade with Sicily and the
Orient was at its height.
Somewhat off the beaten
track, Ravello is for those
who love peace and quiet
and stupendous views.

The **Duomo** is dedicated to
San Pantaleone, the town's
patron saint, and the blood of
the saint is kept here. The
church dates from 1086 and
its bronze doors from 1179.
Inside is a splendid raised
pulpit, the work of Niccolò di
Bartolomeo da Foggia from
1272. The twisted columns,
patterned with mosaics, rest
on sculpted lions.

Walking around the town,
Moorish details are evident in
the buildings, in the inner
courtyards and gardens, and
in the many churches. The
narrow streets and pathways
offer occasional, often
unexpected, glimpses of
marvelous coastal views. Two
highlights are Villa Rufolo
and Villa Cimbrone. **Villa**

The view from the terrace at Villa Rufolo

Rufolo, originally built for
the Rufolo family, is a mixture
of 13th- and 14th-century
constructions. It was
remodeled in the 19th century
by a Scottish enthusiast, who
preserved the Arabic
elements. It is famed not only
for the courtyard with its
double arches but also for the
tropical gardens, which
inspired Wagner's *Parsifal*
(see p35). The Wagner festival
is now an annual event.

On Via San Francesco,
which takes you to Villa
Cimbrone, are the churches
of San Francesco, of Gothic
origin but rebuilt in the 18th
century, and Santa Chiara, the
only one on the coast that has
retained its *gynaeceum*
(women's gallery).

Villa Cimbrone was built
in the late 1800s by the
Englishman Lord Grimthorpe.
An assortment of ancient
architectural elements were
incorporated in the house.
From the villa's clifftop
terrace there is a spellbinding
view of the coast to Punta
Licosa and the Paestum plain.
Villa Cimbrone is now a small
hotel *(see p175).*

Another place well worth
visiting is the church of San
Giovanni del Toro, in the
square of the same name,
with its three tall semicircular
apses and decorated domes.

🔒 **Duomo**
Piazza Duomo. 📞 *089-85 83 11.*
⏰ *8:30am–1pm, 3–8pm Dec–Feb;
3–6:30pm Mar–Nov.*

🏛 **Villa Rufolo**
Piazza Duomo. 📞 *089-85 78 66.*
⏰ *9am–8pm May–Feb; 9am–5pm
Mar–Apr.* 🔖

🏛 **Villa Cimbrone**
Via Santa Chiara 26.
📞 *089-85 71 38.* ⏰ *9am–1 hr
before sunset.* 🔖

The picturesque village of Cetara; standing out among rooftops is the dome of San Pietro

MAIORI, MINORI, AND CETARA

Road map D4 & E4.
Maiori: 5,757; Minori: 3,106; Cetara: 2,520. Sita. **Maiori:** *Azienda Autonoma di Soggiorno e Turismo, Viale Capone (Palazzo Zitara).* 089-87 74 52; **Cetara:** *Pro Loco, Via San Francesco 15.* 089-26 14 74.

Ancient *Reginna Minor* and *Maior* are now two popular seaside resorts with a long and noble history. **Minori**, where the Amalfi Maritime Republic arsenals were located, dates back to Roman times. Near the waterfront is the basilica of Santa Trofimena, built in the 12th–13th centuries and then rebuilt in the 1800s. The relics of the ancient patron saint of Amalfi are here.

Maiori is like an amphitheater at the end of the Tramonti valley. It was founded in the 9th century but is now a modern town, rebuilt after a flood in 1954. The fine beaches and swimming facilities have made it one of the most visited towns on the coast. The 18th-century campanile on 12th-century Santa Maria a Mare towers over the Maior stream.

After the lovely beach of Erchie, **Cetara** was the easternmost possession of Amalfi. At the end of the 9th century it was also a stronghold for the Saracens, who anchored their ships at Cala di Fuenti cove. The name may derive from the Latin *cetaria*, or tuna-fishing net; the fish, salted and sold in ceramic pots, is a typical local product.

A typical ceramics shop in Vietri

VIETRI

Road map E4. *9,421.* Sita.
The majolica-decorated dome and bell tower of San Giovanni Battista (1732) have come to symbolize this town overlooking the Bay of Salerno. Vietri is famous as a seaside resort and especially for its ceramics. Cooking utensils, plates, vases, and tiles have been manufactured here since the 1400s. In the mid-18th century, Vietri became known as the majolica-makers' district, a suburb of the Cava de' Tirreni (see below). The most original items made were the extremely popular tiles painted with religious subjects. You can still see these tiles in streets, private homes, and churches.

Porcelain plate made in Vietri

Today you can find ceramics of all kinds, either traditional or experimental in color and shape, catering to all tastes. The green donkey used as the logo of local production is a relatively recent invention, inspired by the 1930s creations of Dutch and German ceramicists. The Villa Guarigli park is home to the **Museo della Ceramica** (Ceramics Museum) featuring local products from the 1600s to the present day.

Museo della Ceramica
Torretta di Villa Guariglia.
089-21 18 35.
9am–1pm, 3–7pm daily.

CAVA DE' TIRRENI

Road map E4.
52,502. Sita.
Lying in a valley in the interior, Cava de' Tirreni is the only town in Southern Italy to have streets lined with porticoes. Go and see the 11th-century abbey of Santissima Trinità and the old Scacciaventi quarter, whose winding streets block the wind (*scacciaventi* means "wind-chaser").

View of Vietri, with the dome and campanile of San Giovanni

Along the Sorrento Coast ⓭

A boat trip

THE BEST WAY to take in all the beauty of the bay is by sea – to discover the isolated beaches, villages perched on the hillsides, and ancient watchtowers. From Amalfi, Sorrento, and Capri you can rent a launch or a slow *gozzo* boat. In the summer the major centers offer organized excursions on larger boats with a guide, but you cannot stop where you like. A favorite excursion is from the Amalfi coast to Capri (or vice versa), an all-day trip with evening meal at one of the coastal restaurants; the return in the moonlight is an unforgettable experience.

Sorrento Peninsula
An excellent way of seeing the coast from the sea is to take a fast motorboat and travel the full length of the Sorrento coastline, rounding Campanella point.

Marina di Massa Lubrense, a picturesque fishing harbor, is now a popular resort.

Sorrento

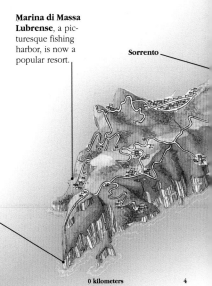

Punta della Campanella
An ancient temple of Minerva stood on this rocky cliff; before that time the site may have been dedicated to the indigenous cult of the Sirens. Some scholars think the Latin name for Sorrento, Surrentum (see p149), is derived from the association with Sirens.

0 kilometers   4

0 miles   2

Capri
The island of Capri (see pp162–3) is also associated with the Sirens: the promontory of Marina Piccola is called Scoglio delle Sirene. Those who want to stroll on the "blue island" can get off here, otherwise take a boat trip around the island, or simply stop for lunch at one of the many restaurants along the coast (see pp186–7).

Marina del Cantone is an
excellent place to stop for
lunch: the local specialty is
pasta with zucchini. The small
Recommone restaurant in the
nearby cove is also good.

VISITORS' CHECKLIST

At **Positano** you can rent a boat
from **Lucibello** on the large beach
☎ 089-87 50 32; or **Grassi**, on
Fornillo beach. ☎ 089-81 16 20.
At **Capri**, from **Sercomar**, Piazza
Fontana 64. ☎ 081-837 87 81;
from **Banana Sport**, Via Marina
Grande 12. ☎ 081-837 51 88;
and from **Whaels**, Via Colombo
17. ☎ 081-837 88 94.

Positano
*The square, pastel-colored
houses of Positano (see
pp150–51) cling to the steep
slopes of Monte Sant'Angelo a
tre Pizzi and Monte Comune
overlooking the sea. Lush
gardens and bougainvillea
fill the terraces of these
charming houses. This is one
of the most popular resorts on
the Amalfi coast, famous for
its bright, patterned textiles.*

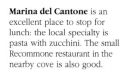

Isca
*Just offshore is the small island of
Isca, where the Neapolitan actor
and playwright Eduardo De Filippo
(see p37) lived. The house now
belongs to his son Luca.*

The Li Galli Archipelago
*These islands, known as the Sirenuse until the 19th century, were once considered to be
the home of the mythical Sirens who lured sailors onto the rocks. The clear water between
the three crags, Gallo Lungo, La Rotonda, and Castelluccia, makes swimming irresistible.*

Paestum ⑭

ANCIENT POSEIDONIA, founded along the Sele River by Greek colonists from Sybaris around 600 BC, became the Roman colony of Paestum in 273 BC. The town began to decline in the 1st century BC after a malaria outbreak. Earthquakes and deforestation (the local pines made excellent raw material for building ships) had gradually turned the area into marshland. The inhabitants tried to combat the rising water level; they raised their streets and homes, or went to live on higher ground. It was at this time that the Temple of Hera was made into a church by the converted population. Eventually, however, Paestum was abandoned for the nearby town of Capaccio.

Red-figure lekythos

This ancient site was first unearthed in the 18th century during the building of a road, but most of it remained undiscovered until the 1950s.

★ **Temple of Ceres**
This temple was built around 500 BC and dedicated to Athena. For centuries, until a votive offering was found nearby, it had been attributed to Ceres.

Temple of Neptune
The name of this temple has been a subject of debate. It was probably dedicated to Apollo or Zeus, but it is commonly known as the Temple of Neptune. Built in 450 BC, it is one of the most complete Greek temples in Europe.

THE THREE TEMPLES AT PAESTUM

These plans compare the structure of the 3 main temples at Paestum. The Temple of Hera (6th century BC) has 9 front columns, 18 side columns, and 2 aisles divided by a row of columns. The Temple of Ceres (6th century BC) has 6 fluted columns at the front, 13 lateral ones, and an undivided *cella.* The largest, Temple of Neptune (5th century BC), has 6 front columns, 14 side ones, and its *cella* is divided into 3 aisles by 2 rows of 2-tier columns.

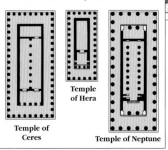

Temple of Ceres

Temple of Hera

Temple of Neptune

STAR SIGHTS

★ **Temple of Ceres**

★ **Temple of Hera, the "Basilica"**

★ **Tomb of the Diver**
(funerary fresco in Paestum Museum)

Museum

VISITORS' CHECKLIST

Road map F5. Via Magna Grecia.
🚆 *Napoli–Salerno: Capaccio.*
Site ⊙ *9am–1 hr before sunset.*
📞 *0828-81 10 23.* **Museum**
⊙ *9am–6:30pm daily.* ● *1st &*
3rd Mon of month. 🎫
ℹ️ *Azienda Autonoma di*
Soggiorno e Turismo, Via Magna
Grecia 152. 📞 *0828-72 23 22.*

Metope with Dancing Girls
This metope, on display in the Paestum Museum, comes
from one of the two temples in the sanctuary of Hera
Argiva at the mouth of the Sele River. Founded by the
first colonists, the complex was discovered in 1934–40
after almost two centuries of searching.

The amphitheater
(1st century BC–1st
century AD) has been
only partly excavated.

Forum

Baths

★ **Tomb of the Diver**
The frescoed slabs of the
Tomb of the Diver, which
date from about 480 BC,
were discovered in 1968
about 1 km (half a mile)
from Paestum. The image
of the diver on the lid
symbolizes the passage to
the afterlife. These unique
examples of Greek
funerary painting can be
seen in the site's museum.

★ **Temple of Hera, the "Basilica"**
The absence of religious features
led the first archaeologists to believe
this was a civic building, when in
fact it is the oldest temple in
Paestum, built around 530 BC.

Antonio Joli, The Temples of Paestum (1758)
Temple ruins had a profound effect on local landscape painters,
who often used them in their art. Antonio Joli's painting shows the
Basilica, the Temple of Neptune, and the
Temple of Ceres.

0 meters   100

0 yards   100

Billboards and shop signs in present-day Caserta

Caserta ⓯

Road map C2. 🏛 69,181.
🚉 *Caserta.* ℹ *Ente Provinciale per il Turismo, Palazzo Reale.* 📞 *0823-32 22 33.*

Caserta was once known as the village of La Torre, named after a medieval tower of the Acquaviva family. In the middle of the 18th century, Charles III, Bourbon king of Naples, chose the plain at the foot of the Tifatini mountains as the

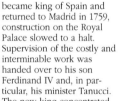

Facade of the cathedral of San Michele, Caserta Vecchia

site for his new center of administration. The town began to flourish and expand; not long afterward it took the name of the nearby medieval village of Caserta Vecchia.

Present-day Caserta is a modern agricultural town that reflects the major rebuilding carried out in the 1950s. A few older buildings remain, such as the church and monastery of Sant'Agostino in Via Mazzini and the former residence of the Acquaviva family in Piazza Vanvitelli. However, the main reason to visit Caserta is the Royal Palace (*see pp160–61*). Conceived by Charles III as the heart of his new administrative center, the palace was to be a leading European court, modeled on Versailles and linked to the capital and other cities by radial roads and protected by the fortress at Capua. This plan to move power away

from the capital city was influenced by the apparent vulnerability of the Palazzo Reale on the Naples waterfront (*see pp50–51*), a fact that came to light in 1742 when the English fleet threatened to attack. Once this danger had passed, however, attention was turned to the style of the palace. The king summoned Luigi Vanvitelli, technical adviser at the Vatican, to draw up designs. The palace and the new city were begun in 1752.

When Charles III became king of Spain and returned to Madrid in 1759, construction on the Royal Palace slowed to a halt. Supervision of the costly and interminable work was handed over to his son Ferdinand IV and, in particular, his minister Tanucci. The new king concentrated on the magnificent park and bothered little about the unfinished palace.

Some additional work was carried out, but as the two semicircular buildings at the entrance to the grounds illustrate, these were poor substitutes for the splendid buildings proposed in Vanvitelli's original designs.

ENVIRONS
🏛 Caserta Vecchia
Road map C2.
The fascination of Caserta Vecchia, 10 km (6 miles) along a winding road northeast of Caserta, does not lie in the individual monuments but the town itself, which has a remarkably well-preserved medieval character. This small hilltop town was probably founded by the Lombards in the 8th century and then came under Norman rule. When Charles III designed his new palace, activity in this lively community moved into the new town in the plains.

Caserta Vecchia revolves around the main square where the cathedral of San Michele stands. Nearby is the Gothic church of Annunziata with a marble portal opening onto a 17th-century portico. On the eastern side of the village are the ruins of a 13th-century castle, dominated by a 30-meter (98-ft) turret.

🏛 Cathedral of San Michele
🕐 *9am–1pm, 3–7:30pm daily.*
The cathedral in Caserta Vecchia was completed in 1153. The faded yellow and gray tufa façade is simple, with three marble portals. Columns on the triangular tympanum above the middle portal are supported by lions.

Caserta Vecchia, dominated by the cathedral of San Michele

The 14th-century dome has the interlaced Arabic arches often seen on Romanesque buildings in Southern Italy.

The interior of the church is lined with irregular columns and stunning majolica tiles. A starlit sky is represented in the dome, with gray stone for the night and white marble stars.

To the right of the cathedral stands the dark stone bell tower, added a century later, with an archway over the road.

Village of San Leucio
Road map C2.
This area, 3 km (2 miles) north-west of Caserta was purchased by Charles III in 1750. Five years later Ferdinand IV built a royal lodge here, Casino di Belvedere. In 1789, he founded a progressive community with enlightened laws and based on the production of silk. An existing building was re-designed as a silk factory to be used by the local artisans. Today, all that is left of this ambitious project are the workmen's dwellings and the Belvedere lodge on the slopes of the hill. The royal lodge was also the residence of the silk factory management.

The Belvedere lodge, San Leucio

Sant'Angelo in Formis
Road map C2. ☐ *daily (ask the caretaker in house opposite).*
The small, Romanesque church of Sant'Angelo in Formis lies 10 km (6 miles) northwest of Caserta. Built on the ruins of an ancient temple to Diana, Roman goddess of the forest, it was reconstructed in 1073. Many beautiful features of the temple were incorporated into the church, such as the mosaic floor and the Corinthian columns on the portico.

Inside, a cycle of 11th-century frescoes, painted in Byzantine style by artists from the School of Montecassino, depict stories from the Bible.

THE IDEAL VILLAGE OF SAN LEUCIO

Attractive street in the village of San Leucio

San Leucio was founded in 1789 by Ferdinand IV as a village for workers in the local silk factory. The aim of this social experiment was to create a community dedicated to the pursuit of happiness instead of personal profit. The community had its own laws, attributed to the king but in fact written by Antonio Planelli. These were based on reason and morality, included compulsory education, equal inheritance rights for men and women (who, however, had to marry within the community), the abolition of the dowry, and medical assistance for the aged and disabled. The 1799 revolution brought about the end of the most ambitious project of the founders, the creation of an entire model city, Ferdinandopoli, although the designs survive. San Leucio is famous for its silk manufacturing, and the articles produced here are still very much in demand.

Roman Amphitheater
Piazza Adriano, Santa Maria Capua Vetere. 📞 0823-79 88 64. ☐ 9am–1 hr before sunset.
The amphitheater at Santa Maria Capua Vetere, 6 km (4 miles) west of Caserta, dates from the 1st century BC. Restored by Hadrian and Antonius Pius, it is still well preserved today, especially its underground structure. Second in size only to the Colosseum in Rome, it had four levels: the first three were travertine arches with busts and statues of the gods, while the last was solid but decorated with pilasters. Statues of Eros, Venus, and Psyche found here are on display in the Museo Archeologico Nazionale (*see pp86–9*).

Ponti della Valle
This viaduct, 2 km (1 mile) from Maddaloni, is over 500 m (1640 ft) long and is supported by three arches. It was built in 1753–8 by Vanvitelli to bring water to the Royal Palace at Caserta.

Ruins of the amphitheater at Santa Maria Capua Vetere

Royal Palace of Caserta

Statue on a fountain

IN HIS MEMOIRS, the architect Vanvitelli says it was the king who designed the Royal Palace. This may have been adulation, or perhaps Charles III knew what he wanted – to emulate his favorite models, the Buen Retiro in Madrid and Versailles in France. Vanvitelli drew inspiration from Buen Retiro for this quadrangular, 1,200-room structure, which was finally completed in 1852. The lower ground floor now houses a museum, with photos and exhibits relating to the palace and Caserta culture.

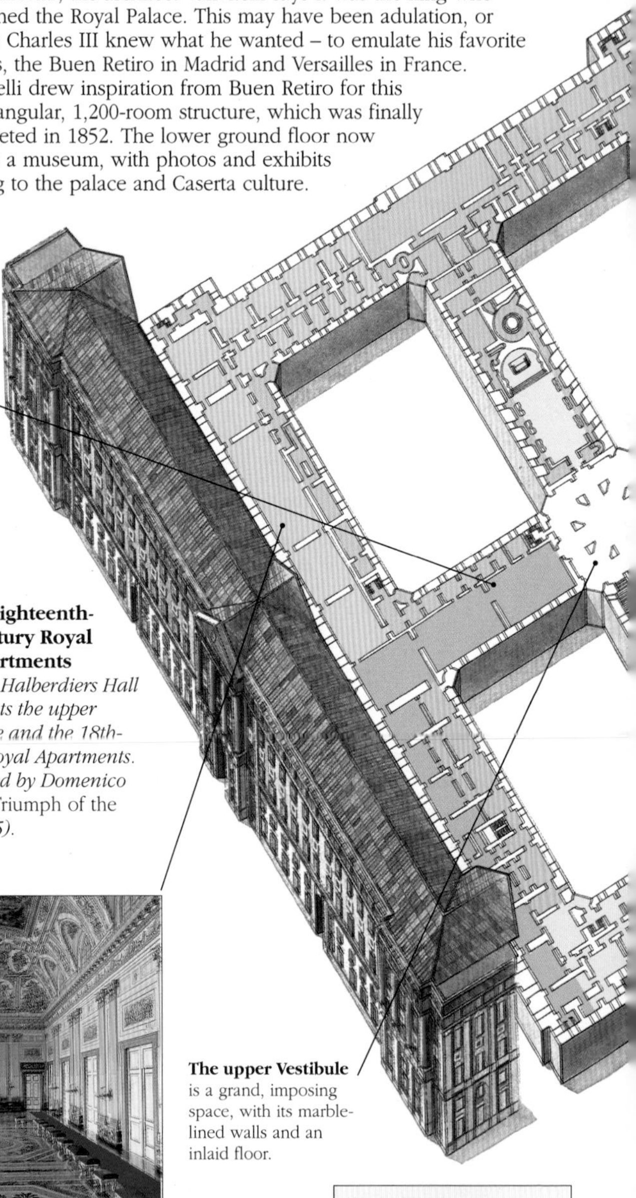

★ Eighteenth-century Royal Apartments
The Halberdiers Hall connects the upper vestibule and the 18th-century Royal Apartments. The ceiling is adorned by Domenico Mondo's fresco The Triumph of the Bourbon Arms *(1785).*

★ Throne Room
This is one of the large 19th-century salons – in contrast with the smaller 18th-century rooms – in the palace. It was decorated by Gaetano Genovese in 1844–45 and was once filled with elegant French furniture.

The upper Vestibule
is a grand, imposing space, with its marble-lined walls and an inlaid floor.

STAR FEATURES

★ Eighteenth-century Royal Apartments

★ Throne Room

★ Court Theater

Great Staircase
The staircase is positioned to one side so it does not interrupt the splendid view of the park from the main doorway.

Art Gallery
Among the portraits in the Art Gallery is that of Maria Carolina, Ferdinand IV's wife, who occupied four elaborate rooms in the 18th-century apartments.

KEY (UPPER FLOOR)

▢ 18th-century Royal Apartments
▢ 19th-century Royal Apartments
▢ *Terraemotus* exhibition
▢ Cappella Palatina
▢ Biblioteca Palatina
▢ Art Gallery
▢ Non-exhibition space

★ Court Theater
The theater is on the ground floor. The rear of the stage could be opened to the air, creating a natural backdrop.

THE PARK

Luigi Vanvitelli designed this famous park, one of the last examples of the fashion for a regimented garden in the Italian or French style. The long central axis is designed on descending levels, creating a remarkable effect with pools and fountains ornamented with splendid sculptures. The play of flowing water culminates in the **Grande Cascata** waterfall, almost 80 m (260 ft) high, also known as the Fountain of Diana. Next to this is the English Garden, perhaps the first of its kind in Italy. The idea was suggested to Queen Maria Carolina by her friend Lord Hamilton; the landscaping work began in 1768.

Flowing water with fountains and waterfalls, the park's central feature

Capri

Excursion taxi

THE FIRST illustrious residents in Capri were the Roman emperors Augustus and Tiberius. For the last decade of his life, Tiberius ruled Rome from Capri, and the ruins of his luxurious villa can still be seen today. Despite this noble history, the island saw few visitors until the 19th century, when a poet named August Köpisch found the Grotta Azzurra, which was known to locals but not to travelers on the Grand Tour. Tourism began to flourish, and Capri became the haunt of foreign politicians, artists, and intellectuals, Alexandre Dumas and Oscar Wilde among them. The singer Gracie Fields and the writer Norman Douglas, author of *Siren Land*, made the island their home.

Marina Grande
Capri's main harbor is a colorful village with seafood restaurants and some Roman and Byzantine remains. A funicular takes you to central Capri in a few minutes.

Rocky Beaches
Sunbathers lounge among the rocks on this island with few sandy beaches.

The Grotta Azzurra,
or Blue Grotto, owes its name to the blue color of the water, the result of light refraction.

0 meters   1000

0 yards   1000

Anacapri
On the slopes of Monte Solaro (see p167) is the second largest town on the island, Anacapri. Here you can visit the church of San Michele, the Villa San Michele (home of the Swedish physician Axel Munthe), the excavations at the imperial villa of Damecuta, and appreciate the magnificent view from the top of the hill.

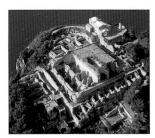

Villa Jovis
The retreat built by Emperor Tiberius stands on the mountain named after him. Excavations have unearthed baths, apartments, and "Tiberius's drop," from which his victims were supposedly thrown into the sea.

Writer Curzio Malaparte gave this villa, shaped like a hammer with a sickle on the roof, to the Chinese government in 1957.

I Faraglioni, Capri's most striking offshore rocks, soar up to 109 m (360 ft) out of the sea.

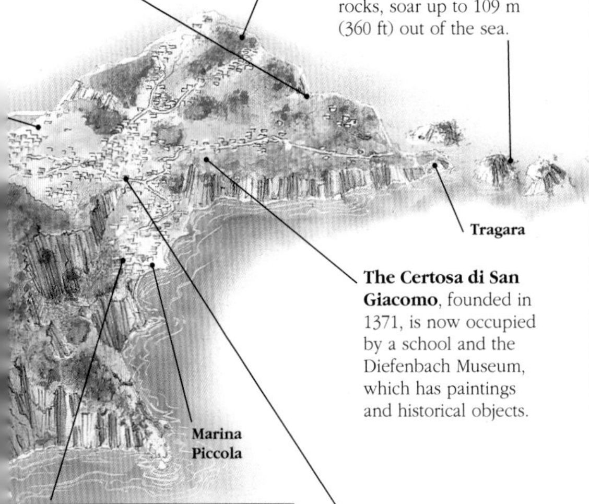

Tragara
Marina Piccola

The Certosa di San Giacomo, founded in 1371, is now occupied by a school and the Diefenbach Museum, which has paintings and historical objects.

Visitors' Checklist

Road map C4.
Capri 7,063; Anacapri 5,351.
from Naples & Sorrento.
Azienda Autonoma di Soggiorno e Turismo: **Capri**, *Via Marina Grande/Piazza Umberto I.*
081-837 06 34 or 837 06 86;
Anacapri, *Via Orlandi 19a.*
081-837 15 24.
Grotta Azzurra: *from Marina Grande.* *from Anacapri, 9am–1 hr before sunset.* *if the sea is particularly rough.*
Certosa di San Giacomo: Viale della Certosa, Capri. *081-837 62 18.* *9am–1pm Tue–Fri, 9am–2pm Sat & Sun.*
Villa Jovis: Via A Maiuri, Capri. *9am–1 hr before sunset daily.*
Villa San Michele: Via Capodimonte 34, Anacapri. *081-837 14 01.* *Nov–Feb: 10:30am–3:30pm daily; Mar: 9:30am–4:30pm daily; Apr, Oct: 9:30am–5pm daily; May–Sep: 9am–6pm daily.*
Monte Solaro: Anacapri. *Chair lift from Via Caposcuro.* *081-837 14 28.* *Jun–Oct: 9:30am–5:30pm daily; Oct–Jun: 11:30am–3pm daily.* *in bad weather conditions.*

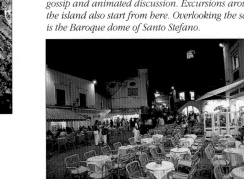

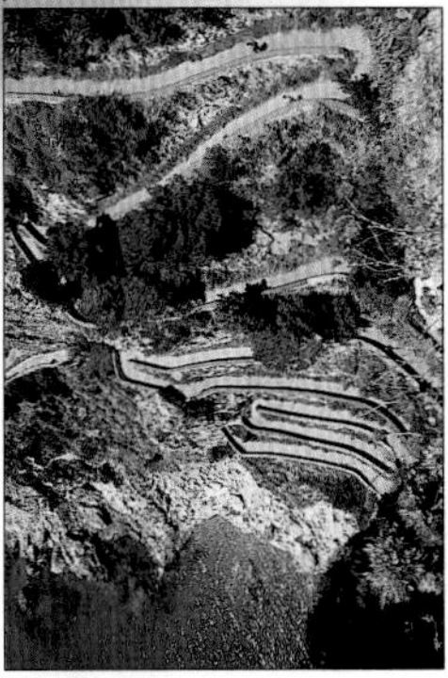

Via Krupp
Commissioned by the German industrialist Krupp, this famous road makes its vertiginous descent toward the sea in a series of hairpin bends.

The "Piazzetta" in Capri
In the heart of town the famous "Piazzetta," officially Piazza Umberto I, is an outdoor living room, crowded day and night, packed with café tables buzzing with gossip and animated discussion. Excursions around the island also start from here. Overlooking the scene is the Baroque dome of Santo Stefano.

Ischia ⑰

Bougainvillea

THE HOT SPRINGS on the volcanic island of Ischia were famous in antiquity and still draw visitors today. Ancient Pithecusa was founded here in the 8th century BC by the same Greek traders who later founded Cumae on the mainland *(see pp134–5)*. Repeated attacks in the early 1300s forced people to take refuge on the small offshore island that the Aragonese later turned into a castle. A favorite with Bourbon royalty, Ischia also enchanted landscape painters and visitors such as the Irish philosopher Berkeley and the French poet Lamartine. The island is green and rugged, and each coast has a different character, offering beaches or steep hills, busy nightlife, or quiet seclusion.

Fungo di Lacco Ameno
This "mushroom" rock is a prominent landmark outside Lacco Ameno, where the Greek colonists first landed.

Lacco Ameno is home to the Museo Archeologico di Villa Arbusto where items from the Greek settlement are held.

Forio

The beach at Citara is generally considered the most beautiful in Ischia.

Santa Maria del Soccorso
This small sanctuary in the town of Forio combines elements of Gothic, Renaissance, and Baroque and is known for its collection of votive offerings from sailors. The English composer Sir William Walton lived just north of here, at La Mortella.

0 kilometers   2

0 mile   1

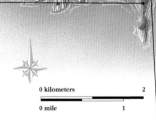

Sant'Angelo
Originally a fishing village and now a thermal spa resort, Sant'Angelo lies west of the long Maronti beach. Here "taxi boats" can be rented to take you to coves otherwise inaccessible by land. Nearby are the Nitrodi hot springs.

Monte Epomeo
(see p167) is an extinct volcano. According to mythology, the eruptions and quakes were caused by the wails and sighs of the giant Typhoeus, imprisoned under the island.

Casamicciola Terme
*Despite the damage caused by the 1883 earthquake,
the spa town of Casamicciola has retained its
atmosphere and some Art Nouveau architecture.
The Norwegian writer Ibsen wrote* Peer Gynt *here.*

Ischia Porto is the
island's main town
where ferries dock.

Ischia Ponte
*This village is connected to
the small offshore island of
Castello Aragonese by a
causeway built in 1438.*

Castello Aragonese
*Different architectural styles can be
seen inside the fortified walls of the
island: the Angevin cathedral of the
Assunta, a monastery, and the church
of San Pietro a Pantaniello. There is a
lovely view from the Carta-
romana belvedere.*

Maronti beach

Procida ⑱

Road map B3. 🏘 *10,459.* ⛴ ⛴
from Naples & from Pozzuoli.
ℹ *Azienda Autonoma di Soggiorno
e Turismo, Via Roma, Stazione
Marittima 1.* ☎ *081-810 19 68.*

M UCH SMALLER than Capri
and Ischia and also
much less affected by
tourism, the third island in
the Bay of Naples is a favorite
with those who love the
simplicity and traditions of
the local culture. This is the
enchanting world that author
Elsa Morante, recollecting her
many visits here, evoked in
Isola di Arturo (Arthur's
Island). Procida's economy is
sustained not only by tourism
but, to a large extent, by the
money its emigrants send
back home to the family.

Deeply rooted local
traditions are evident in
the various festivals: for
example, the Good
Friday procession *(see
p40)* that descends to the
modern port from so-called
Terra Murata – the rise
dominated by the Abbey of
San Michele – or the Graziella
celebration that takes place
in the port in mid-August.

The multicolored houses
resting against the tufa rock
make the island architecture
one of the most distinctive
in the region. Unique to the
island are the vaulted

**The fortified rise of Terra Murata
with the Abbey of San Michele**

Capo Bove

Marina di
Sancio Cattolico

Punta di Mezzogiorno

Vivara Nature
Reserve

Chiaiolella

Centane

Punta
Solchiaro

| 0 meters | 1000 |
| 0 yards | 1000 |

buildings. Originally built as
winter boat shelters and later
enlarged, they acquired
among other things facades
with arches and half-arches
that frame the doors and
windows, terraces, loggias,

and long external staircases.
On your arrival in Procida
you can see this type of
architecture, albeit in a
partially modernized version,
in Marina di Sancio Cattolico,
the area built up in the 17th
and 18th centuries, and at the

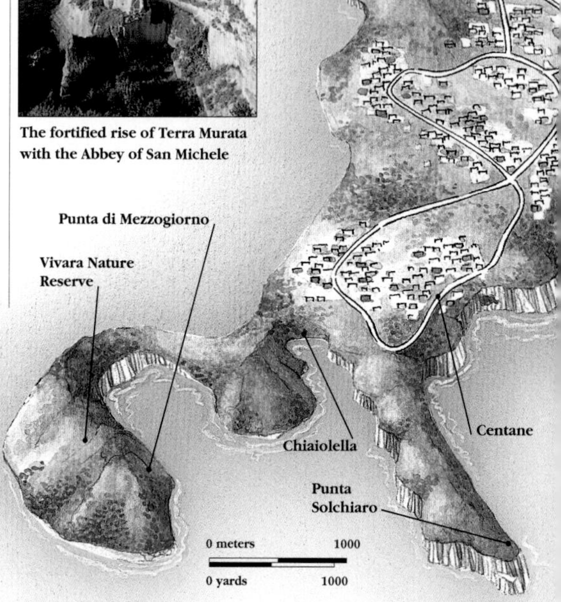

View of Marina di Sancio Cattolico

Procida

Punta della
Lingua

Punta di
Pizzaco

Marina
Corricella

Terra
Murata

Typical Procida architecture

small, popular Chiaiolella port
on the other side of the
island. The Abbey of San
Michele, dominating Terra
Murata, dates back to 1026,
though it has since been
rebuilt. Marina Corricella,
at the foot of Terra Murata,
has been virtually untouched
by modern times. The soil is
very fertile, and the gardens
here are filled with lemon
trees. You can also visit the
luxuriant **Vivara Nature
Reserve**, a small island
connected to Chiaiolella by
a bridge, with its specimens
of Mediterranean flora and an
ornithological center. It was
here that intriguing remains
of a late Bronze Age
Mycenean settlement were
found a few years ago.

🏛 **Abbey of San Michele**
Via Terra Murata. 📞 *081-896 76 12.*
🕐 *9am–12:30pm, 3:30–7pm daily.*
🦋 **Vivara Nature Reserve**
🕐 *ask the Protezione Civile (which
manages the park) for permission.*
📞 *081-896 74 00.*

WALKING ON THE ISLANDS

While Procida is almost flat – the highest point, Terra
Murata, is 91 m (300 ft) above sea level – Capri and Ischia
are steep-sided. On Capri *(see pp162–3)*, the path
connecting Monte Solaro (589 m/1930 ft)) to Anacapri is
delightful and easy even for lazy visitors, although there is
always the option of the chairlift. Hikers will be well
rewarded by the striking view and the 14th-century Santa
Maria di Cetrella monastery on Marina Piccola (a detour
halfway up). Experienced hikers come back down by the
"Passetiello" path that includes a stretch directly above the
sea and leads to Capri.

The highest mountain in the bay is the extinct Epomeo
volcano (788 m,/2580 ft) on Ischia *(see pp164–5)*. A climb
up the cone starts off at night from Fontana in order to
admire the view at dawn. The view takes in the island
itself, the Bay of Naples, and the Tyrrhenian coast up to
Roccamonfina and the Pontine Islands. A rough dirt track
leads to the church of San Nicola (1459) and the adjoining
monastery, both hewn out of tufa rock. On your way
down you can choose the road to Forio or Casamicciola.

Looking out over Capri from the Monte Solaro chairlift

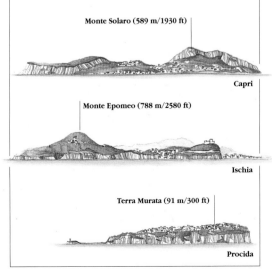

Monte Solaro (589 m/1930 ft)

Capri

Monte Epomeo (788 m/2580 ft)

Ischia

Terra Murata (91 m/300 ft)

Procida

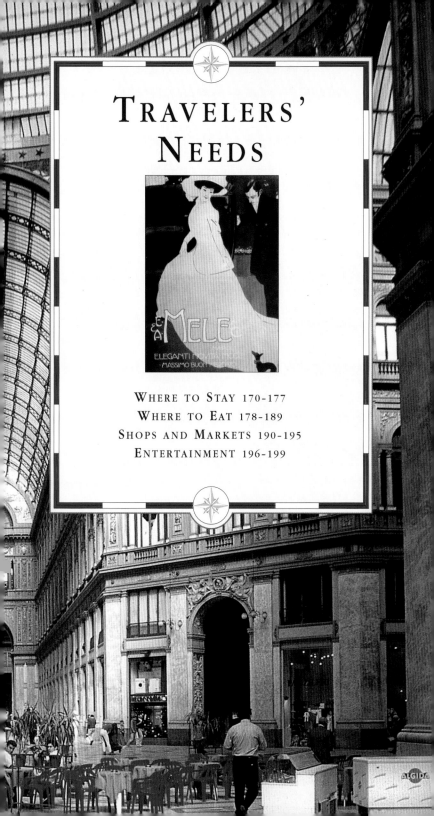

TRAVELERS' NEEDS

WHERE TO STAY

THE FASCINATION and enchantment of Naples and the surrounding countryside have drawn visitors here for many centuries. Kings and queens, revolutionaries in exile, poets, writers, and composers are among the host of celebrities who have wintered at the foot of Mount Vesuvius since the 18th century. Hotels and pensioni in the center of Naples tend to be fairly expensive, but efforts are being

PRESTIGE
hotels

**Logo of the
Prestige hotels**

made to widen the range of available facilities . Along the Amalfi coastline, around Sorrento, and on the islands, traditional vacation areas, the range of accommodations is much wider. Choices offered cover all price categories, from simple pensioni to a grand luxury hotel with pools and magnificent views along the coast. This section and the list of hotels on pages 172 - 177 will help you make your choice.

The 5-star Hotel Excelsior *(see p173)*
overlooking the waterfront

WHERE TO LOOK

OUTSIDE NAPLES there is no lack of choice of hotels, from luxury chains to less expensive, family-run pensions. These are clean and comfortable and often have fine panoramic views. In Naples itself, however, the range is limited. Hotels can often be expensive and sometimes are short on good service. The most exclusive hotels are usually located on hills or on the waterfront with spectacular views.

If you plan to spend a lot of time visiting museums, churches, and galleries, it is best to stay in the center of Naples. You will be within easy reach of the most important sights, and you can go back to your hotel to relax between bouts of sightseeing. For those who don't mind the walk, a hotel in the commer-

cial district is ideal; it may not have the characteristic charm of an older establishment but will be modern and comfortable. The Prestige hotel chain, such as the Grand Hotel Vesuvio, the Excelsior, and the Majestic, offer excellent service to an international clientele, and include 42 suites and 22 conference halls. The information offices of the Ente Provinciale per il Turismo (**EPT**, the Italian Tourist Board – *see p203)* prints lists of hotels, pensioni, and campsites. For more information you can also make inquiries at the **Associazione Albergatori Napoletani** (Neapolitan Hotel Owners' Association).

PRICES AND GRADING

ITALIAN HOTELS are classified by a star-rating system with one to five stars, one being the lowest. Prices including taxes are displayed inside each room. Breakfast is often

**The Hotel Pension Pinto Storey
(see p172), opened in 1878**

not included and may be an expensive item compared to a coffee and croissant in the nearest local bar. In Naples there is no difference between tourist and off season, but it is always worth asking about discounts. It is often possible to negotiate special rates for groups or for longer stays. On the average, single rooms cost two-thirds of the double room rate; rooms without a bathroom may cost up to 30 percent less. In resorts prices differ in tourist season; during the peak summer months you may be expected to take some meals at the resort restaurant.

HOTEL FACILITIES

THANKS TO THE World Cup and then the G7 summit, almost all the middle-range and luxury hotels in Naples underwent renovation and now provide a high level of comfort, including sound-proofing. The less expensive hotels (one or two stars) have clean but simple rooms, often with shared bathroom. Hotels outside Naples usually offer better facilities for less money.

*Breakfast on the terrace of the
Hotel Executive (see p172)*

The elegant foyer in Parker's Hotel *(see p173)*

RESERVING AND PAYING

Y OU SHOULD RESERVE well in advance if you have special requests such as a room with a good view. During July and August, the peak vacation season, hotels along the coast and on the islands get very full, so you must reserve your room well ahead of time. If there are no special events scheduled in Naples, advance booking won't be necessary, and you can choose your hotel when you arrive. The local tourist offices will advise you.

If you do reserve in advance, you will probably be asked to pay a deposit, which can be done by credit card or international money order. When you arrive at your hotel, the reception will ask for your passport; this is to register travelers with the police, a legal formality. By law, the hotel must give you a receipt when you check

out. Telephone calls from the room and drinks from the minibar can be very expensive, so it is advisable to check beforehand.

BUDGET ACCOMMODATIONS

I F YOU ARE on a tight budget you can stay in a hostel. The **Associazione Italiana Alberghi per la Gioventù** (Youth Hostel Association) has lists of hostels. In Naples, the Ostello Mergellina, near the Mergellina train station and close to the Parco Virgiliano *(see p119)*, is highly recommended. Rooms have washing-up facilities and breakfast is included. There are also inexpensive family-run pensions with clean, basic rooms, but in general bathrooms are communal.

Interior of the Cappuccini Convento in Amalfi *(see p174)*

View from the terrace of the Hotel Poseidon in Positano *(see p175)*

Choosing a Hotel

T HE HOTELS in this guide have been carefully selected across a wide price range for the quality of service and location. They are listed by area. For more detailed information on exact locations in Naples, see the Street Finder on pages 212–27; for towns and islands in the rest of the region, see the Road Map on the inside back cover.

	CREDIT CARDS	GARDEN OR TERRACE	PRIVATE PARKING	RESTAURANT	BAR

NAPLES					
TOLEDO AND CASTEL NUOVO: *Jolly* ⓁⓁⓁ Via Medina 70. **Map** 7 B2. 【 *081-41 60 00.* **FAX** *081-551 80 10.* Situated in the heart of the city, in a skyscraper built in the 1950s, this hotel is popular with business people. Well-equipped, modern rooms with views. 🔛 TV 🗐 **Rooms:** *252*	V AE DC			●	▦
TOLEDO AND CASTEL NUOVO: *Mercure Angioino* ⓁⓁⓁ Via A Depretis 123. **Map** 7 B2. 【 *081-552 95 00.* **FAX** *081-552 95 09.* Located between the university area and the port, offering good lodgings. Pleasant, light-filled public rooms; the bedrooms are tastefully furnished and soundproofed. 🔛 TV 🗐 **Rooms:** *85*	V AE DC		▦		▦
SPACCANAPOLI: *Soggiorno Sansevero* Ⓛ Via San Domenico Maggiore 9. **Map** 3 B5 (9 C3). 【 *081-551 59 49.* This pension is in an 18th-century building overlooking elegant Piazza San Domenico. Simple, unpretentious rooms for those who want to stay in the historic center. Family atmosphere. 🔛 **Rooms:** *6*					
SPACCANAPOLI: *Executive* ⓁⓁⓁ Via del Cerriglio 10. **Map** 7 B1 (9 C5). 【 *081-552 06 11.* **FAX** *081-552 06 11.* Next to Santa Maria la Nova monastery (and occupying part of it), the Executive makes for a comfortable stay with its well-kept rooms, gym with sauna, and terrace overflowing with flowers. 🔛 TV 🗐 **Rooms:** *19*	V AE DC	●	▦		▦
SPACCANAPOLI: *Terminus* ⓁⓁⓁ Piazza Garibaldi 91. **Map** 4 E4. 【 *081-28 60 11.* **FAX** *081-20 66 89.* This hotel facing the train station is used mostly by businessmen. Well-furnished rooms, each with its own balcony. 🔛 TV 🗐 **Rooms:** *170*	V AE DC	●	▦	●	▦
DECUMANO MAGGIORE: *Hotel Duomo* Ⓛ Via Duomo 228. **Map** 3 C4. 【 *081-26 59 88.* On the first floor of a 19th-century building, this small family-run hotel has pleasantly spacious and quiet rooms. 🔛 TV **Rooms:** *10*			▦		
CAPODIMONTE AND I VERGINI: *Villa Capodimonte* ⓁⓁⓁ Via Moiariello 66. **Map** 3 C1. 【 *081-45 90 00.* **FAX** *081-29 93 44.* Close to the Palace of Capodimonte, dominating the Sanità district. Its unusual location is ideal for those seeking good hospitality, quiet surroundings, and something more unusual. 🔛 TV 🗐 **Rooms:** *58*	V AE DC	●	▦	●	▦
CASTEL DELL'OVO AND CHIAIA: *Canada* ⓁⓁ Via Mergellina 43. **Map** 5 B3. 【 *081-68 20 18.* **FAX** *081-68 09 52.* Opposite the small Mergellina port and the hydrofoil embarkation point. Rooms with good views but rather small public areas. 🔛 TV **Rooms:** *12*	V AE DC		▦		▦
CASTEL DELL'OVO AND CHIAIA: *Pinto Storey* ⓁⓁ Via G Martucci 72. **Map** 6 D2. 【 *081-68 12 60.* **FAX** *081-66 75 36.* A pension with a homely atmosphere in the elegant part of town. Opened in 1878, Pinto Storey is on the third floor and has a small lobby with plants and antique furniture. The rooms are simple, brightly lit, and spacious. 🔛 TV **Rooms:** *25*	V AE DC		▦		▦

Price categories for a standard double room per night, with tax, breakfast, and service included: Ⓛ under L100,000 ⓁⓁ L100,000 – 199,000 ⓁⓁⓁ L200,000 – 299,000 ⓁⓁⓁⓁ L300,000 – 399,000 ⓁⓁⓁⓁⓁ over L400,000.	**PARKING** Private parking on premises or in nearby garage. Hotels usually charge for parking facilities. **GARDEN OR TERRACE** Public area outdoors reserved for guests. **RESTAURANTS** The hotel has a restaurant that is also open to nonresidents. **BAR** The hotel has a bar also open to nonresidents.	CREDIT CARDS	GARDEN OR TERRACE	PRIVATE PARKING	RESTAURANT	BAR

CASTEL DELL'OVO AND CHIAIA: *Britannique*   ⓁⓁⓁ
Corso Vittorio Emanuele 133. **Map** 6 D1. 📞 *081-761 41 45.* 🆀 *081-66 04 57.*
A hotel with an old tradition. Comfortable, light rooms with a view of the bay. The small, private garden with exotic plants is reserved for residents. 🖥 📺 🈁
Rooms: 90

		V AE DC	●	■	●	■

CASTEL DELL'OVO AND CHIAIA: *Miramare*   ⓁⓁⓁ
Via Nazario Sauro 24. **Map** 7 A4. 📞 *081-764 75 89.* 🆀 *081-764 07 75.*
Located in a pastel-colored Art Nouveau villa on the waterfront. Rooms with every comfort and a view; a terrace for sunbathing in the summer. 🖥 📺 🈁
Rooms: 30

		V AE DC	●	■		■

CASTEL DELL'OVO AND CHIAIA: *Parker's*   ⓁⓁⓁⓁ
Corso Vittorio Emanuele 135. **Map** 6 D1. 📞 *081-761 24 74.* 🆀 *081-66 35 27.*
Traces of its history (the hotel dates from the 1870s) can be seen everywhere, starting in the reception rooms with period furniture and fine paintings. Views of the bay and Capri. 🖥 📺 🈁
Rooms: 80

		V AE DC	●	■	●	■

CASTEL DELL'OVO AND CHIAIA: *Santa Lucia*   ⓁⓁⓁⓁ
Via Partenope 46. **Map** 7 A4. 📞 *081-764 06 66.* 🆀 *081-764 85 80.*
The delicately colored interior with Neo-Classical furnishings creates a romantic atmosphere. One of the historic hotels on the waterfront with elegant, light rooms overlooking Castel dell'Ovo and Borgo Marinaro. 🖥 📺 🈁
Rooms: 100

		V AE DC		■	●	■

CASTEL DELL'OVO AND CHIAIA: *Excelsior*   ⓁⓁⓁⓁⓁ
Via Partenope 48. **Map** 7 A4. 📞 *081-764 01 11.* 🆀 *081-764 97 43.*
A historic hotel with a view of Castel dell'Ovo and Capri, the Excelsior has accommodated many famous guests. The rooms with Belle Epoque marble, mirrors, and curtains are very atmospheric. 🖥 📺 🈁
Rooms: 135

		V AE DC	●	■	●	■

CASTEL DELL'OVO AND CHIAIA: *Vesuvio*   ⓁⓁⓁⓁⓁ
Via Partenope 45. **Map** 7 A4. 📞 *081-764 00 44.* 🆀 *081-764 00 44.*
The great tenor Enrico Caruso spent his last night in the suite named after him. This historic hotel, with fine views over the bay, has been popular with celebrities since it opened in the 19th century. 🖥 📺 🈁
Rooms: 167

		V AE DC	●	■	●	■

POSILLIPO: *Paradiso*   ⓁⓁⓁ
Via Catullo 11. **Map** 5 A4. 📞 *081-761 41 61.* 🆀 *081-761 34 49.*
Near the funicular that takes you to Mergellina in a few minutes, this hotel is in an extraordinary position dominating the entire bay. In the summer, romantic breakfasts are served on the terrace, which has a view of Vesuvius. 🖥 📺 🈁
Rooms: 75

		V AE DC	●	■	●	■

SORRENTO PENINSULA

SANT'AGNELLO (SORRENTO): *Cocumella*   ⓁⓁⓁⓁ
Via Cocumella 7. **Road map** C4. 📞 *081-878 29 33.* 🆀 *081-878 37 12.*
Situated in a former 17th-century monastery surrounded by greenery, this hotel has a private beach. The rooms have terraces overlooking the sea, and the old cloister is now used for functions. ● *Nov–Mar.* 🖥 📺 🈁 🏊
Rooms: 60

		V AE DC	●	■	●	■

SORRENTO: *Hotel del Corso*   Ⓛ
Corso Italia 134. **Road map** C4. 📞 *081-87 07 31 57.* 🆀 *081-807 10 16.*
A family-run hotel conveniently located in the center of town, it has a particularly lovely terrace overlooking the old center. ● *Nov–Jan.* 🖥
Rooms: 20

		V AE DC	●			■

For key to symbols see back flap

Price categories for a standard double room per night, with tax, breakfast, and service included:
Ⓛ under L100,000
ⓁⓁ L100,000 – 199,000
ⓁⓁⓁ L200,000 – 299,000
ⓁⓁⓁⓁ L300,000 – 399,000
ⓁⓁⓁⓁⓁ over L400,000.

PARKING
Private parking on premis
Hotels usually charge for
GARDEN OR TERRACE
Public area outdoors rese
RESTAURANTS
The hotel has a restaurar
nonresidents.
BAR
The hotel has a bar alsc
nonresidents.

SORRENTO: *Loreley et Londres*
Via Califano 2. **Road map** C4. **(** *081-807 31 87.* **FAX** *081-8*
Hotel with panoramic view and elevator that takes
The retreat of writer Sibilla Aleramo in the early 19
Rooms: 23

SORRENTO: *Bellevue Syrene*   ⓁⓁⓁⓁ   V AE DC
Piazza della Vittoria 5. **Road map** C4. **(** *081-878 10 24.* **FAX** *081-878 39 63.*
Surrounded by a garden with elevator access to a private beach, this
19th-century villa has Neo-Classical furnishings and frescoed rooms
(see p149). Each room has a balcony and view of the park or sea. 🛏 📺 ♿
Rooms: 73

SORRENTO: *Excelsior Vittoria*   ⓁⓁⓁⓁ   V AE DC
Piazza Tasso 34. **Road map** C4. **(** *081-807 10 44.* **FAX** *081-877 12 06.*
This old hotel consists of four buildings in different styles and visitors have
included Byron and Goethe, among others. Tastefully furnished rooms,
frescoed salons, and a large terrace jutting out over the sea. 🛏 📺 🗐 ≋
Rooms: 105

SORRENTO: *Imperial Tramontano*   ⓁⓁⓁⓁ   V AE DC
Via Veneto 1. **Road map** C4. **(** *081-878 19 40.* **FAX** *081-807 23 44.*
This historic hotel was the birthplace of poet Torquato Tasso *(see p149).*
Surrounded by an ancient park and full of atmosphere, the Tramontano
offers comfort and elegance and an easy descent to the water. 🛏 📺 ≋
Rooms: 116

AMALFI COAST

AMALFI: *La Bussola*   ⓁⓁ   V AE DC
Lungomare dei Cavalieri 1. **Road map** D4. **(** *089-87 15 33.* **FAX** *089-87 13 69.*
This family-run hotel is located inside a converted mill. The rooms
are clean and simple, and the public areas have a view of the sea.
Guests can take advantage of the sun terrace on the cliff. 🛏
Rooms: 62

AMALFI: *Luna Convento*   ⓁⓁ   V AE DC
Via Comite 33. **Road map** D4. **(** *089-87 10 02.* **FAX** *089-87 13 33.*
Ibsen wrote his play *A Doll's House* in one of the cells in this
former monastery, which many still find inspirational. Breakfast
is served in the impressive Byzantine cloister. 🛏 📺 ≋
Rooms: 54

AMALFI: *Cappuccini Convento*   ⓁⓁⓁ   V AE DC
Via Annunziatella 46. **Road map** D4. **(** *089-87 18 77.* **FAX** *089-87 18 86.*
This old monastery, now a hotel, is surrounded by a garden. There
is a chapel, an Arabesque-Norman cloister, and a spectacular view
of the sea. 🛏 📺 🗐
Rooms: 54

AMALFI: *Santa Caterina*   ⓁⓁⓁⓁⓁ   V AE DC
Strada Statale Amalfitana 9. **Road map** D4. **(** *089-87 10 12.* **FAX** *089-87 13 51.*
About half a mile from Amalfi, this exclusive hotel offers
excellent service: graceful salons, an elegant restaurant, rooms with fine
views, a garden descending to the sea, and a private beach. 🛏 📺 🗐 ≋
Rooms: 70

POSITANO: *Casa Soriano*   Ⓛ
Via Pasitea 212. **Road map** D4. **(** *089-87 54 94.*
This 18th-century villa is a real hideaway. It is in an extraordinary
location, with spectacular balconies overlooking the sea, and its
rooms have vaulted ceilings. ● *Oct–Mar.* 🛏
Rooms: 8

POSITANO: *Casa Albertina* Ⓛ Ⓛ
Via della Tavolozza 3. **Road map** D4. 📞 *089-87 51 43.* **FAX** *089-81 15 40.*
Perched on a ridge 300 steps above the sea, this delightful
family-run hotel is simple and peaceful. 🍽 🛏
Rooms: *19*

V
AE
DC

POSITANO: *Palazzo Murat* Ⓛ Ⓛ Ⓛ
Via dei Mulini 23. **Road map** D4. 📞 *089-87 51 77.* **FAX** *089-81 14 19.*
This 18th-century residence with a courtyard lobby was the home
of Joachim Murat, once ruler of Naples. The rooms in the old wing
are furnished with antiques. ● *Jan–Mar.* 🛏 📺 🍽
Rooms: *30*

V
AE
DC

POSITANO: *Poseidon* Ⓛ Ⓛ Ⓛ
Via Pasitea 148. **Road map** D4. 📞 *089-81 11 11.* **FAX** *089-87 58 33.*
A romantic, cozy Mediterranean hotel a few minutes from the beach,
with a swimming pool, a health spa, and a beauty shop. It is co-managed
by the Tuscan spa baths Terme di Saturnia. ● *Nov–Easter.* 🛏 📺 🍽 🏊
Rooms: *50*

V
AE
DC

POSITANO: *San Pietro* Ⓛ Ⓛ Ⓛ Ⓛ
Via Laurito 2. **Road map** D4. 📞 *089-87 54 55.* **FAX** *089-81 14 49.*
Perched over the water, 1.5 miles from Positano, this luxury hotel offers
every comfort. International stars such as Sting, Mick Jagger, and Tina Turner
have stayed here. ● *Nov–the week before Easter.* 🛏 📺 🍽 🏊
Rooms: *59*

V
AE
DC

POSITANO: *Le Sirenuse* Ⓛ Ⓛ Ⓛ Ⓛ
Via C Colombo 30. **Road map** D4. 📞 *089-87 50 01.* **FAX** *089-81 17 98.*
A noble mansion transformed into an elegant hotel with
precious objects and antique furniture. The rooms all have stunning
views that have enchanted famous guests from John Steinbeck to
Ronald Reagan. 🛏 📺 🍽 🏊
Rooms: *62*

V
AE
DC

RAVELLO: *Graal* Ⓛ Ⓛ
Via della Repubblica 4. **Road map** D4. 📞 *089-85 72 22.* **FAX** *089-85 75 51.*
A pleasant family-run hotel in a peaceful location and with a good
swimming pool. All the rooms have balconies and the restaurant
offers excellent home-cooked food. 🛏 📺 🍽 🏊
Rooms: *35*

V
AE
DC

RAVELLO: *Caruso Belvedere* Ⓛ Ⓛ Ⓛ
Piazza San Giovanni del Toro 2. **Road map** D4.
📞 *089-85 71 11.* **FAX** *089-85 73 72.*
In business for over a century, the Caruso Belvedere has frescoed halls, period
furniture, and a terraced garden. Greta Garbo fell in love with this place. 🛏
Rooms: *24*

V
AE
DC

RAVELLO: *Villa Cimbrone* Ⓛ Ⓛ Ⓛ
Via Santa Chiara 26. **Road map** D4. 📞 *089-85 74 59.* **FAX** *089-85 77 77.*
Once the home of an English lord who wanted to reconstruct the original
building in Neo-Gothic style, this hotel, in the middle of the famous Villa
Cimbrone park, is only a ten-minute walk from town. 🛏
Rooms: *19*

V
AE
DC

RAVELLO: *Palumbo* Ⓛ Ⓛ Ⓛ Ⓛ
Via San Giovanni del Toro 28. **Road map** D4.
📞 *089-85 72 44.* **FAX** *089-85 81 33.*
The 12th-century Palazzo Confalone is now a charming hotel. In
the lobby, traces of Moorish architecture frame a panoramic view
of the coast. The rooms, furnished with antiques, look out onto a
citrus grove that descends to the waterfront. 🛏 📺 🍽
Rooms: *20*

V
AE
DC

CAPRI

ANACAPRI: *San Michele* Ⓛ Ⓛ Ⓛ
Via G Orlandi. **Road map** C4. 📞 *081-837 14 42.* **FAX** *081-837 14 20.*
A late 19th-century hotel with an appealing, old-fashioned atmosphere.
Quiet and simple, the rooms have a view of the sea or of Monte Solaro.
● *Nov–Mar.* 🛏 📺 🏊
Rooms: *60*

V
AE
DC

Price categories for a standard double room per night, with tax, breakfast, and service included:
- Ⓛ under L100,000
- ⓁⓁ L100,000 – 199,000
- ⓁⓁⓁ L200,000 – 299,000
- ⓁⓁⓁⓁ L300,000 – 399,000
- ⓁⓁⓁⓁⓁ over L400,000.

PARKING
Private parking on premises or in nearby garage. Hotels usually charge for parking facilities.

GARDEN OR TERRACE
Public area outdoors reserved for guests.

RESTAURANTS
The hotel has a restaurant that is also open to nonresidents.

BAR
The hotel has a bar also open to nonresidents.

Hotel	Price	Credit Cards	Garden or Terrace	Private Parking	Restaurant	Bar
CAPRI: *Belvedere e Tre Re* Via Marina Grande 138. **Road map** C5. **FAX** 081-837 03 45. Opened in the mid-1800s. Its name *(tre re)* derives from a visit paid by three Scandinavian kings. Rooms with a view, dining room with large windows overlooking the sea, veranda, and piano. 🛏 **Rooms:** 15	Ⓛ		●		●	▪
CAPRI: *La Tosca* Via Birago 5. **Road map** C5. ☎ 081-837 09 89. A secluded place for those who prefer the appealing silence and simplicity of the "other" Capri. Book well in advance for rooms with a view. **Rooms:** 12	Ⓛ		●			
CAPRI: *Villa Krupp* Via G Matteotti 12. **Road map** C5. ☎ 081-837 03 62. **FAX** 081-837 64 89. Once the home of Russian author Maxim Gorky, who entertained Lenin here, the Villa Krupp is quite close to the Piazzetta. Family-run, rooms without frills, and with a view of the sea and the Faraglioni rocks. ● *Nov–Feb.* 🛏 **Rooms:** 12	ⓁⓁ	V	●			
CAPRI: *Gatto Bianco* Via Vittorio Emanuele 32. **Road map** C5. ☎ 081-837 02 03. **FAX** 081-837 80 60. A classic example of Capri hospitality: in the center of town but quiet, with inviting rooms and quaint furniture, wide sofas, and colored ceramics. Almost all the rooms have a terrace. ● *Nov–Easter.* 🛏 📺 **Rooms:** 36	ⓁⓁⓁ	V AE DC	●		●	▪
CAPRI: *La Palma* Via Vittorio Emanuele 39. **Road map** C5. ☎ 081-837 01 33. **FAX** 081-837 69 66. The oldest hotel in Capri, with tastefully furnished rooms. The bar is a fashionable haunt for islanders. 🛏 📺 ▤ **Rooms:** 74	ⓁⓁⓁⓁ	V AE DC	●		●	▪
CAPRI: *Villa Brunella* Via Tregara 24a. **Road map** C5. ☎ 081-837 01 22. **FAX** 081-837 04 30. From the terrace-restaurant a steep stairway leads to the hotel rooms, which are quiet and comfortable. The hotel overlooks a lemon grove and has a large swimming pool. ● *Nov–one week before Easter.* 🛏 📺 ▤ 🏊 **Rooms:** 20	ⓁⓁⓁⓁ	V AE DC	●		●	▪
CAPRI: *Quisisana* Via Camerelle 2. **Road map** C5. ☎ 081-837 07 88. **FAX** 081-837 60 80. In the mid-19th century this was a sanatorium founded by an English physician. Now it is one of the top ten hotels in the world, with large, elegant rooms, a gym, two swimming pools, two restaurants, and an ultrafashionable bar. ● *Nov–one week before Easter.* 🛏 📺 ▤ 🏊 **Rooms:** 150	ⓁⓁⓁⓁⓁ	V AE DC	●		●	▪

ISCHIA

Hotel	Price	Credit Cards	Garden or Terrace	Private Parking	Restaurant	Bar
FORIO D'ISCHIA: *Hotel della Baia* Via San Montano 18/22. **Road map** A4. ☎ 081-98 63 98. **FAX** 081-98 63 42. A Mediterranean style, pastel-colored, pleasant hotel a few steps from the San Montano beach and the Negombo thermal park. ● *Oct–Apr.* 🛏 📺 ▤ **Rooms:** 20	ⓁⓁ	V AE DC	●	▪	●	▪
FORIO D'ISCHIA: *Il Vitigno* Via Bocca 31. **Road map** A4. ☎ 081-99 83 07. **FAX** 081-99 83 07. This is an ancient farmstead surrounded by vineyards. *(vitigno).* The rooms are plain and rustic. The excellent food comes from local produce, and the wine is from vineyards on the property. 🛏 **Rooms:** 6	ⓁⓁ		●	▪	●	▪

FORIO D'ISCHIA: *Mezzatorre*   ⓁⓁⓁⓁ V AE DC
Località San Montano. **Road map** A4. 081-98 61 11. **FAX** 081-98 60 15.
This magnificent hotel lies at the end of San Montano bay, built around
a Saracen tower, between the sea and a thick grove of pine and
holm-oak trees. ● *Nov–Apr.* 🛏 📺 🍴 ♨
Rooms: *50*

ISCHIA PONTE: *Il Monastero*   ⓁⓁ
Castello Aragonese. **Road map** B4. 081-99 24 35.
The plain rooms are offset by the unique position: from the Castello
rock there is a magnificent view of ancient Ponte and the water..
Ideal for those who love secluded spots. ● *mid-Oct–Mar.* 🛏
Rooms: *22*

ISCHIA PONTE: *Miramare e Castello*   ⓁⓁⓁⓁ V AE DC
Via Pontano 9. **Road map** B4. 081-99 13 33. **FAX** 081-98 29 38.
Situated opposite Castello Aragonese, this hotel offers elegant public areas
and rooms as well as perfect service. There is no lack of facilities:
three swimming pools (one with thermal water), a beauty shop, and
a private beach. ● *Nov–Apr.* 🛏 📺 🍴 ♨
Rooms: *40*

ISCHIA PORTO: *La Villarosa*   ⓁⓁⓁ V AE
Via G Gigante 5. **Road map** B4. 081-99 13 16. **FAX** 081-99 24 25.
The original nucleus was a farmhouse. The hotel stands in a shady garden
where there are independent chalets with two-room suites. The rooms,
chalets, and public areas are tastefully furnished. Swimming pool and
water cures are available. ● *Nov–Mar.* 🛏 📺 ♨
Rooms: *37*

ISCHIA PORTO: *Il Moresco Grand Hotel e Terme*   ⓁⓁⓁⓁ V AE DC
Via E Gianturco 16. **Road map** B4. 081-98 13 55. **FAX** 081-99 23 38.
The Moresco, in a pine grove next to the beach, is typical of the high-quality
hotels in Ischia: elegant Moorish-style halls, rooms with terraces, thermal
pools, a beauty shop, and tennis courts. ● *Oct–Mar.* 🛏 📺 🍴 ♨
Rooms: *76*

LACCO AMENO: *Hotel Regina Isabella*   ⓁⓁⓁⓁ V AE DC
Piazza Santa Restituta. **Road map** A4. 081-99 43 22. **FAX** 081-90 01 90.
Directly overlooking the sea, this luxury hotel was a favorite with
film directors and stars in the 1950s. Sophisticated and elegant,
with good facilities: tennis, thermal pools, sauna, and private beach.
● *mid-Jan–Mar.* 🛏 📺 🍴 ♨
Rooms: *134*

SANT'ANGELO: *Casa Conchiglia*   ⓁⓁ V AE DC
Via Chiaia delle Rose 3. **Road map** A4. 081-99 92 70. **FAX** 081-99 92 70.
Overlooking the sea, this small pension has simple, clean rooms,
all with a balcony and view. ● *Dec–Easter.* 🛏
Rooms: *10*

SANT'ANGELO: *Park Hotel Miramare*   ⓁⓁⓁ V
Via Comandante Maddalena 29. **Road map** A4. 081-99 92 19.
Close to the village of Sant'Angelo and one of the loveliest spots on
the island, this hotel overlooks the sea and is a short distance from
the famous spa of Aphrodite-Apollon. ● *Nov–Mar.* 🛏 📺
Rooms: *55*

PROCIDA

MARINA DELLA CHIAIOLELLA: *Crescenzo*   ⓁⓁ V AE DC
Road map B3. 081-896 72 55. **FAX** 081-810 12 60.
In the atmospheric fishermen's quarter opposite the island of Vivara,
this small hotel has only a few charming, light rooms and is well known
because it has one of the best fish restaurants in Procida. 🛏 📺 🍴
Rooms: *10*

MARINA CORRICELLA: *Pensione Gentile*   ⓁⓁ
Road map B3. 081-896 77 99. **FAX** 081-896 90 11.
In the old fishermen's quarter where the steps wind down to the
sea among multicolored houses, this small, secluded pension
offers rooms with a terrace and panoramic views. 🛏 📺
Rooms: *6*

For key to symbols see back flap

RESTAURANTS, CAFÉS, AND BARS

THE REGION KNOWN to the Romans as *Campania felix* (happy country) revels in food, especially the fruit, vegetables, and grapes that grow in abundance on every available slope. Neapolitan cuisine is well known throughout the world, thanks to the emigrants who took pizza and pasta with them wherever they went. Neapolitans have never given up their passion for good food;

Neapolitan pizzeria sign

eating is a social occasion here – all important events are celebrated with huge meals that may last half a day. Key elements in Neapolitan cuisine are pasta, olive oil, and tomatoes, but all along the coast and on the islands you'll find the freshest seafood and fish dishes, from simple pasta sauces to generous fish stews. This is also the home of ice cream and delectable cakes and pastries.

TYPES OF RESTAURANTS AND BARS

NAPLES AND the outlying area offer a wide choice of restaurants, trattorias, and bars to suit all budgets. A *ristorante* may be fancier and more expensive than a *trattoria*, and a trattoria may be more informal. Every part of Campania has its own specialties, and similar recipes may be interpreted in quite different ways in different locations. Family-run trattorias usually offer excellent home-style cooking. Many of the most exclusive restaurants in Naples are located in the waterfront area. In Posillipo the famous restaurants are expensive, but you will be seated in front of breathtaking views. The mild climate means you can eat outdoors practically all year.

The city center is the place to go for less pretentious and cheaper trattorias and pizzerias with typical Neapolitan food. A pizzeria

The Lido Marechiaro *(see p125)* looking out on to the Bay of Naples

will offer pasta, meat, and fish dishes as well as pizza. In the Spaccanapoli and Decumano Maggiore districts there are trattorias known as *vini e cucina* where you can eat quite cheaply. Besides good wine served by the bottle or from the barrel, these are good places for trying genuine Neapolitan home cooking. They are usually family-run and small, located in the popular areas; the interiors may be quite plain, with plastic tablecloths and paper napkins; and the menu will either be written on a blackboard or recited at your table by the waiter. *Vini e cucina* are popular with locals and students, so you can also experience authentic Neapolitan life. At *tavole calde* (snack bars) first and second courses are

economically priced. The food for sale at the stands and *friggitorie* (for fried food) is often very good: potato croquettes, fried pizzas *(pizzelle)*, and *panzerotti* (ravioli). Bars may offer filled rolls *(panini)* and sandwiches *(tramezzini)* as well as cakes and pastries and assorted drinks. Many bars also operate as *gelaterie*, with a tempting range of ice creams.

HOW MUCH TO PAY

THE AVERAGE PRICE for a full meal at a trattoria is about L25,000, and it can be as little as L15,000 in pizzerias and *vini e cucina*. Restaurants cost from L35–40,000 on up. *Vino sfuso*, or house wine, is often served in jugs and is quite inexpensive. Fresh fish is usually sold by weight, which can make calculating the cost of your meal difficult. You may find fish can be somewhat expensive.

The Da Carmine trattoria *(see p182)*

Eating outdoors, one of the many pleasures of Naples

OPENING HOURS

RESTAURANTS ARE generally open from 12:30 to 3:30pm and from 8pm to midnight, but this may vary somewhat, especially on weekends and in summer when you can dine until fairly late. Family-run trattorias have more limited business hours and are usually closed on Sundays and in August, especially around Ferragosto (Aug 15), when many shops in the city are closed for vacations. The restaurants in tourist centers on the islands and along the coast usually close in the winter and open around Easter.

A wood-fired pizza oven

MAKING RESERVATIONS AND PAYING

RESTAURANTS AND pizzerias tend to be very crowded on Saturday evening, so it's best to book in advance or arrive early. It is also a good idea to book during the tourist season or on local feast days. Service charges are included in the prices on the menu, but it is customary to leave a tip of around ten percent. The larger restaurants accept major credit cards.

READING THE MENU

A TYPICAL NEAPOLITAN menu begins with antipasti, which are so varied and interesting they make a meal in themselves: seafood salad, sautéed clams and mussels, or tomatoes, peppers, and eggplant cooked in various different ways. The first course *(primo)* will depend on the season: spaghetti with seafood, *parmigiana di melanzane (see p180)* or a simple tomato, mozzarella, and basil salad *(insalata caprese)* for lunch at the seaside; pasta and meat sauce or *sartù di riso (see p181)* for a heartier winter lunch. Among the main courses *(secondi)*, you can choose calamari or squid in tomato sauce, assorted fried fish *(fritto misto)* or grilled fish *(grigliata mista)*, or fried

> QUI 100 ANNI FA
> NACQUE LA PIZZA MARGHERITA
> 1889   1989
> BRANDI

Centenary of the Margherita pizza

baby mozzarella, artichokes, and potato or rice croquettes. You must try the vegetable pies; the most famous is made with endive and, in the winter, *friarelli*, a type of broccoli found only in Naples. They are sauteed in a pan with *peperoncino* (hot chili pepper) and are usually served with sausages.

PIZZERIAS

NAPLES IS THE ORIGINAL home of authentic pizza, freshly made and baked in wood-fired ovens. Pizza was originally a peasant dish, made very simply from dough spread with olive oil and tomatoes, and dating from the 18th century. Eaten at any hour of the day in the poorer neighborhoods of Naples, it was ignored by everyone else until Queen Margherita, the wife of Umberto I, decided to taste this dish. The famous pizza Margherita, with mozzarella and basil added to create the colors of the Italian flag – red, white, and green – was invented in her honor. It is now found in every pizzeria, not only in Italy but wherever pizza is sold. Neapolitan pizza chefs are famous for their creative flair, and as well as making classic toppings like the Margherita and the Marinara (tomato and anchovies), you may find they offer to create their own chef's specialty.

Inside La Bersagliera restaurant *(see p183)*

What to Eat and Drink in Naples

Colander and oil pourer

NEAPOLITAN CUISINE is based on "the three Ps": pizza, pasta, and *pomodoro* (tomato). Pizza, perhaps the most ingenious gastronomic invention of all time, was first created here and is now known all over the world. Although pasta is not of Neapolitan origin, Naples is its adoptive home. The tomato is a symbol of Southern Italian cooking and is used in an infinite number of ways: fresh with salad, dried, peeled, pulped, or concentrated. But there's much more to Neapolitan cuisine: from very simple dishes that require fresh, top-quality ingredients to the rich, elaborate dishes inherited from the aristocratic cuisine of the past, such as timbales, elaborate stuffings, and deliciously soft pastries.

Frutti di Mare *(Seafood)*
Served with spaghetti or risotto, fried or grilled as a main course, fresh seafood is found all along the coast.

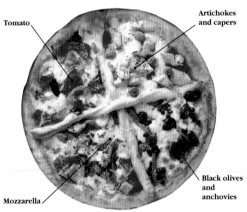

Tomato

Artichokes and capers

Black olives and anchovies

Mozzarella

Quattro Stagioni (four seasons) pizza

Pasta e Fagioli
This is a simple dish of pasta and beans; one of many ideas combining vegetables or beans with pasta.

Pizza
Pizza is eaten everywhere and served with a great variety of typical Mediterranean toppings, such as olives, capers, anchovies, and herbs. Pizza may even be sold by the yard, as at Vico Equense, near Sorrento.

Spaghetti con le Vongole
This is a typical first course: spaghetti and fresh clams, served plain or with tomato sauce, sprinkled with parsley.

Parmigiana di Melanzane
Layers of eggplant, tomato sauce, mozzarella, grated Parmesan, and basil are combined for this dish. Zucchini may be used.

CHEESE AND DAIRY PRODUCE
Mozzarella, made with buffalo milk, is the best of the local cheeses. Fiordilatte and treccia di mozzarella (made from cow's milk) are excellent with tomatoes and basil. There are many types of provolone and scamorza (stuffed, smoked), depending on their origin. Fresh ricotta is used both for savories and sweet pastries. Grated Parmesan is often added to pasta.

Ricotta

Provolone

Mozzarella

Parmesan

Scamorza

basil

dried oregano

parsley

Sartù di Riso
This rice mold, served with garnishes, is one of the more elaborate Neapolitan dishes.

Eggplants, artichokes, peppers
Vegetables are served as antipasti or with main courses.

Aromatic herbs
Basil and oregano (dried or fresh) are frequently used to flavor dishes based on tomato and mozzarella, while flat-leaved parsley is served with fish dishes.

Babà
(rum baba)

Sfogliatelle
(millefeuilles)

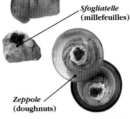

Pesce all'Acqua Pazza
For this dish, fresh fish is cooked in a little water, with tomatoes, garlic, and parsley.

Zeppole
(doughnuts)

Pastiera
(Easter cake)

Pastries
Sfogliatelle *are filled with ricotta, sugar, and candied fruit and come as sweet shortcrust pastry or shell-shaped puff pastry. Other special occasion cakes are* pastiera *(Christmas and Easter),* struffoli *(pastries with honey and fruit, for Christmas), and* zeppole *for San Giuseppe (see p40).*

Carne al Ragù
A typical Sunday meal is meat rolls served with savory tomato sauce.

Casatiello
This traditional country-style pie is made for Easter festivities, with salami, cheese, and egg stuffing.

Wines and Drinks
The white Lacryma Christi (see p138) wine, made for centuries by monks on the slopes of Vesuvius, goes well with fish dishes.

Lacryma Christi

Greco di Tufo is another good white wine. Limoncello is a lemon-flavored liqueur.

Limoncello

NEAPOLITAN COFFEE

The coffee made with a typical Neapolitan coffeemaker is excellent. It is lighter than espresso and tastes good even when reheated. The coffeemaker consists of two metal cylinders, one with a spout, the other a central container to hold finely ground roast coffee. The *caffettiera* is a percolator and not a steam pressure espresso machine.

Neapolitan *caffettiera*

Choosing a Restaurant

THE RESTAURANTS in this chart have been selected for their high quality of food and good value. They are listed by price category and district (Naples) or region (outside Naples). See the Street Finder on pp212–17 for map references in Naples; for those in other areas, see the Road Map on the inside back cover.

	CREDIT CARDS	OPEN AT MIDDAY	LATE OPENING	OUTDOOR TABLES	GOOD WINE LIST

NAPLES

	CREDIT CARDS	OPEN AT MIDDAY	LATE OPENING	OUTDOOR TABLES	GOOD WINE LIST
TOLEDO AND CASTEL NUOVO: *Amici Miei* ⓁⓁ Via Monte di Dio 78. **Map** 6 F2. 081-764 60 63. A classic menu with mainly meat dishes. Excellent first courses, especially pasta with vegetables and legumes. The atmosphere is cozy. ● *Sun eve, Mon; Aug.*	V AE DC	●	■		
TOLEDO AND CASTEL NUOVO: *Ciro a Santa Brigida* ⓁⓁⓁ Via Santa Brigida 71. **Map** 7 A2. 081-552 40 72. This temple of Neapolitan cuisine opened in the 1930s and has won its share of regular patrons. It features traditional fare such as *sartù di riso* and *minestra maritata* (vegetable soup), and its pizzas are exquisite. ● *Sun; 12 days at Ferragosto (15 Aug).* &	V AE DC	●	■		■
SPACCANAPOLI: *Da Michele* Ⓛ Via C Sersale 1/3. **Map** 4 D5 (10 F3). 081-553 92 04. This 19th-century establishment still has its original marble tables. It prepares only classic pizzas such as Margherita and Marinara. ● *Sun; 12 days in Aug.*		●			
SPACCANAPOLI: *Trianon* Ⓛ Via P Colletta 46. **Map** 4 D4 (10 F2). 081-553 94 26. The city's most popular pizzeria, in business since the 1930s, features three sizes of pizzas: "mignon," normal, and "maxi." ● *Sun lunch.*		●			
SPACCANAPOLI: *Lombardi a Santa Chiara* ⓁⓁ Via B Croce 59. **Map** 3 B5 (9 C4). 081-552 07 80. Situated in the heart of the old city, Lombardi's is known for its traditional cuisine and especially for its excellent pizzas. ● *Sun; 20 days in Aug.*	V AE	●	■		
SPACCANAPOLI: *La Taverna dell'Arte* ⓁⓁ Rampe San Giovanni Maggiore 1/a. **Map** 3 B5 (9 C4). 081-552 75 58. This restaurant in a pleasant setting has a limited number of tables, so book in advance. The menu is based on traditional Neapolitan recipes, including delectable desserts. In the summer, dinner is served outside under an arbor. ● *Sun; Aug.*	V		■	●	
DECUMANO MAGGIORE: *Da Carmine* Ⓛ Via dei Tribunali 330. **Map** 3 B5 (9 C3). 081-29 43 83. Don Carmine runs the kitchen, while the rest of the family sees to the table service; the result is wholesome, tasty food and a warm atmosphere. ● *Sun; 7 days in Aug.* &		●	■		
DECUMANO MAGGIORE: *Al 53* ⓁⓁ Piazza Dante 53. **Map** 3 A5 (9 B3). 081-549 93 72. Traditional cooking that varies according to the season. The antipasti alone are worth the trip; from seafood salad to macaroni omelette. ● *Wed.* &	V AE DC	●	■	●	
DECUMANO MAGGIORE: *Mimì alla Ferrovia* ⓁⓁⓁ Via A d'Aragona 21. **Map** 4 E4. 081-553 85 25. Traditional, tasty food popular with lawyers from the nearby law courts. ● *Sun; 12 days in Aug.*	V AE DC	●	■	●	
VOMERO: *Il Cortile* ⓁⓁ Viale A Albini 3/a. **Map** 4 D2. 081-560 40 48. Original, mainly vegetarian dishes – such as small pizzas with *friarelli* (broccoli), ravioli with *caciotta* cheese and marjoram, meat loaf with vegetable stuffing – are rounded off with fine homemade desserts. ● *Mon; 15 days in Aug.*	V AE	●	■	●	

| | | **Price categories** for a three-course evening meal for one, including a half-bottle of house wine, tax, and service:
Ⓛ under L35,000
ⓁⓁ L35,000 – 55,000
ⓁⓁⓁ L55,000 – 75,000
ⓁⓁⓁⓁ L75,000 – 100,000
ⓁⓁⓁⓁⓁ over L100,000. | **OPEN AT MIDDAY**
Often open all day, with a break in the late afternoon to prepare for the evening session.
LATE OPENING
Orders will be accepted until midnight.
OUTDOOR TABLES
Facilities for eating outdoors, on a terrace (often with a good view) or in a garden during the summer.
GOOD WINE LIST
A wide range of specially selected good wines – local, national, and international. |

	CREDIT CARDS	OPEN AT MIDDAY	LATE OPENING	OUTDOOR TABLES	GOOD WINE LIST
VOMERO: *Steak House* ⓁⓁ Piazzetta A Falcone 2. **Map** 1 C5. **[** 081-578 23 06. In rustic surroundings, choose from a menu consisting mostly of variations on the theme of grilled meat and fried potatoes. ● *Mon; 15 days in Aug.* &			■	●	
CASTEL DELL'OVO AND CHIAIA: *Osteria della Mattonella* Ⓛ Via Nicotera 13. **Map** 6 F1. **[** 081-41 65 41. This small, family-run trattoria with wooden tables and walls covered with tiles *(mattonelle)* conjures up traditional, tasty food. ● *Sun; 15 days in Aug.*	V	●	■		
CASTEL DELL'OVO AND CHIAIA: *La Cantina di Triunfo* ⓁⓁ Riviera di Chiaia 64. **Map** 5 C2. **[** 081-66 81 01. A century ago this was a wine shop. Today, while La Cantina's specialty continues to be its wines and liqueurs (try the *rosoli*), – it also offers a small, daily-changing menu of high-quality cooking. ● *Sun; Aug.*					■
CASTEL DELL'OVO AND CHIAIA: *Vadinchenia* ⓁⓁ Via Pontano 21. **Map** 5 C2. **[** 081-66 02 65. Delicate dishes, often based on fish, abound on the innovative, seasonal menu at this restaurant. The regional specialties are prepared with real passion, and the desserts are delicious. ● *Sun; Aug.*					■
CASTEL DELL'OVO AND CHIAIA: *La Bersagliera* ⓁⓁⓁ Borgo Marinaro. **Map** 7 A5. **[** 081-764 60 16. The location of this excellent fish restaurant is really special: right on the waterfront with views of Castel dell'Ovo and Mount Vesuvius. ● *Tue; 4 days at Ferragosto (Aug 15).*	V AE DC	●	■	●	
CASTEL DELL'OVO AND CHIAIA: *Ciro a Mergellina* ⓁⓁⓁ Via Mergellina 18. **Map** 5 B4. **[** 081-68 17 80. Noisy and crowded, an all-time favorite with Neapolitans, Ciro a Mergellina is known for its antipasti (for example, squid in sauce and mixed fried fish), really fresh fish as a main course, and excellent pizzas. ● *Mon; Fri in summer.*	V AE DC	●	■	●	
CASTEL DELL'OVO AND CHIAIA: *Da Dora* ⓁⓁⓁ Via F Palasciano 28. **Map** 5 C2. **[** 081-680 05 19. This family-run trattoria features delicious fish recipes. Try the *linguine alla Dora* with fresh clams, lobster, and shrimp. ● *Sun; 15 days in Aug.* &		●			
CASTEL DELL'OVO AND CHIAIA: *Don Salvatore* ⓁⓁⓁ Via Mergellina 5. **Map** 5 B4. **[** 081-68 18 17. Back to basics with carefully prepared traditional Neapolitan cuisine and a well-stocked wine cellar. The wide selection of antipasti is accompanied by tasty bread as well as pizza and wonderfully fresh fish. ● *Wed.* &	V AE DC	●		●	■
CASTEL DELL'OVO AND CHIAIA: *La Cantinella* ⓁⓁⓁⓁ Via Cuma 42. **Map** 7 A4. **[** 081-764 88 38. An elegant restaurant on the waterfront offering creative dishes, fish in particular. The house special is *tagliatelle alla Santa Lucia*. ● *Sun; 7 days in Aug.*	V AE DC	●	■		■
CASTEL DELL'OVO AND CHIAIA: *Caruso dell'Hotel Vesuvio* ⓁⓁⓁⓁ Via Partenope 45. **Map** 7 A4. **[** 081-764 00 44. On the top floor of this historic hotel, this elegant restaurant offers a splendid view of the bay and cooking based on the freshest local ingredients. ● *Sun.* &	V AE DC	●	■	●	■

For key to symbols see back flap

<table>
<tr><td rowspan="2">

Price categories for a three-course evening meal for one, including a half-bottle of house wine, tax and service:
Ⓛ under L35,000
ⓁⓁ L35,000 – 55,000
ⓁⓁⓁ L55,000 – 75,000
ⓁⓁⓁⓁ L75,000 – 100,000
ⓁⓁⓁⓁⓁ over L100,000.
</td></tr>
</table>

OPEN AT MIDDAY
Often open all day, with a break in the late afternoon to prepare for the evening session.

LATE OPENING
Orders will be accepted until midnight.

OUTDOOR TABLES
Facilities for eating outdoors, on a terrace (often with a good view), or in a garden during the summer.

GOOD WINE LIST
A wide range of specially selected good wines – local, national and international.

	CREDIT CARDS	OPEN AT MIDDAY	LATE OPENING	OUTDOOR TABLES	GOOD WINE LIST
POSILLIPO: *'A Fenestella* ⓁⓁ Calata del Ponticello a Marechiaro 23. 081-769 00 20. The window *(fenesta)* in this restaurant is celebrated in an Italian song by Salvatore di Giacomo. The house speciality is linguine with gurnard and cherry tomatoes. ● Wed; Sun in summer; 7 days at Ferragosto (15 Aug).	V AE DC	●	■		
POSILLIPO: *Al Poeta* ⓁⓁ Piazza S Di Giacomo 133. 081-575 69 36. This well-known fish restaurant is always crowded, especially throughout the summer. Try the excellent pizza. ● Mon; 15 days in Aug.	V AE DC	●	■	●	
POSILLIPO: *Giuseppone a Mare* ⓁⓁⓁ Via F Russo 13. 081-575 60 02. A classic Neapolitan restaurant, Giuseppone a Mare is famous both for its meticulous service and its excellent seafood. ● Mon; 7 days in Aug.	V AE DC	●	■		
POSILLIPO: *La Sacrestia* ⓁⓁⓁⓁ Via Orazio 116. 081-761 10 51. A view of the bay, elegant surroundings, imaginative presentation, excellent wine list and impeccable service make La Sacrestia the best restaurant in town. ● Mon; Sun in summer; 7 days in Aug.	V AE DC	●	■	●	■
PHLEGRAEAN FIELDS					
BACOLI: *La Misenetta* ⓁⓁⓁⓁ Via Lungolago 2. **Road map** B3. 081-523 41 69. An original, mainly fish, menu, combining tradition and creativity. ● Mon; 15 days in Aug; 23 Dec–4 Jan.	V AE	●	■		
POZZUOLI: *Michelemmà* ⓁⓁⓁ Via C Rosini 27. **Road map** B3. 081-526 27 49. There is no lack of choice at this establishment: a snack bar for light meals, a live music area and a full restaurant specializing in seafood. ● Tue & Wed; Mon in summer; 21 days in Aug.			■	●	
SORRENTO PENINSULA					
MASSA LUBRENSE: *Antico Franceschiello (da Peppino)* ⓁⓁⓁ Via Partenope 27. **Road map** C4. 081-533 97 80. A historic restaurant with a breathtaking view and a long tradition. This was where *delizia al limone*, a local lemon dessert, was invented. ● Wed (not in summer).	V AE DC	●			
MASSA LUBRENSE: *I 4 Passi* ⓁⓁⓁ Via Marina del Cantone, Nerano. **Road map** C4. 081-808 12 71. Tasty dishes cooked in the open kitchen. The *pappardelle* with courgette flowers, broad bean ravioli and fruit mousse are really special. ● Wed (not in summer); 8 Dec–8 Jan.	V AE	●	■	●	
MASSA LUBRENSE: *La Taverna del Capitano* ⓁⓁⓁ Via Marina del Cantone, Nerano. **Road map** C4. 081-808 10 28. La Taverna del Capitano is a restaurant with rooms. Its delicious, genuine cooking is a happy marriage of tradition and invention. ● Mon (not in summer); 7–31 Jan.	V AE DC	●		●	
SANT'AGATA SUI DUE GOLFI: *Don Alfonso 1890* ⓁⓁⓁⓁⓁ Piazza Sant'Agata 11. **Road map** C4. 081-878 00 26. One of Italy's most famous restaurants. An elegant setting, and unforgettable dishes prepared with produce grown on Alfonso and Livia Iaccarino's own farm. ● Mon, Tue (only Mon in summer); 10 Jan–25 Feb.	V AE DC	●			■

SORRENTO: *Emilia*   Ⓛ
Via Marina Grande 62. **Road map** C4. ☎ 081-807 27 20.
One of the typical, family-run trattorias on the Sorrento peninsula, featuring
a fine range of fish specialities prepared on the spot.
● *eve (not in summer); Tue.*

SORRENTO: *Antica Trattoria*   ⓁⓁ   V
Via Padre Reginaldo Giuliani 33. **Road map** C4. ☎ 081-807 10 82.   AE
The menu is strong on meat, rare for the peninsula, and also has unusual   DC
dishes such as *pappardelle* with porcini mushrooms and strawberries.
● *Mon; Jan.*

SORRENTO: *'O Parrucchiano*   ⓁⓁ   V
Corso Italia 71. **Road map** C4. ☎ 081-878 13 21.
Classic Sorrento cuisine is the offering from the kitchen of this restaurant,
whose doors first opened for business over 100 years ago.
● *Wed (not in summer).*

SORRENTO: *Caruso*   ⓁⓁⓁ   V
Via Sant'Antonino 12. **Road map** C4. ☎ 081-807 31 56.
A sophisticated setting, and imaginative cooking. The ravioli with prawn
or seafood stuffing are delicious, and the desserts excellent.
● *Mon (not in summer).* ♿

AMALFI COAST

AMALFI: *La Caravella*   ⓁⓁⓁ   V
Via M Camera 12. **Road map** D4. ☎ 089-87 10 29.   AE
Good, interesting, fish-based cooking. A recommended first course   DC
is the Amalfi pesto with anchovies, olives, capers and lemon zest.
● *Tue (not in Aug); Nov.*

AMALFI: *Da Gemma*   ⓁⓁⓁ   V
Via Fra Gerardo Sasso 9. **Road map** D4. ☎ 089-87 13 45.   AE
The wall is covered with newspaper clippings of this historic restaurant,   DC
which has been preparing mouthwatering seafood for over a century.
● *Wed (not in summer), Aug: midday, Jan–Feb.*

POSITANO: *Da Adolfo*   Ⓛ
Spiaggia di Laurito. **Road map** D4. ☎ 089-87 50 22.
Enjoy spaghetti with clams, squid and potatoes, grilled *fiordilatte* cheese and
almond cake while sitting at one of the shaded tables beneath the straw roof of
this restaurant – there is no need to change out of your swimming things.
● *Oct–May: evening.*

POSITANO: *Il Grottino Azzurro*   Ⓛ
Via G Marconi 158. **Road map** D4. ☎ 089-87 54 66.
The cuisine is distinctly rustic at Grottino Azzurro: typical dishes include
cannelloni, gnocchi, farmyard chicken and home-made desserts.
● *Wed (not in summer).*

POSITANO: *Scirocco*   Ⓛ   V
Loc. Montepertuso, Via Pestelle 126. **Road map** D4. ☎ 089-87 57 86.
Scirocco's hallmarks are its panoramic location and simple, good food such
as fresh fish, grilled vegetables and pizzas cooked in wood-fired ovens.
● *Tue (not in summer); Feb.*

POSITANO: *La Buca di Bacco*   ⓁⓁⓁ   V
Via Rampa Teglia 8. **Road map** D4. ☎ 089-87 56 99.   AE
Sooner or later everyone comes to this fashionable and timeless establishment   DC
for a drink at its bar or dinner at its restaurant on the beach.
● *Oct–Apr.*

POSITANO: *La Cambusa*   ⓁⓁⓁ   V
Piazza Amerigo Vespucci 4. **Road map** D4. ☎ 089-87 54 32.   AE
A fine location and super-fresh seafood. In winter the beach terrace   DC
is enclosed and the setting becomes even more romantic.
● *Tue (not in summer).*

POSITANO: *Carlo e Tanina*   ⓁⓁⓁ   V
Loc. Montepertuso, Via Montepertuso 97–9. **Road map** D4. ☎ 089-81 18 06.   AE
The kitchen is in full view, so you can watch the bread being made along   DC
with the adventurous new dishes that change every day.
● *Mon (not in summer); Nov–mid Mar.*

For key to symbols see back flap

	CREDIT CARDS	OPEN AT MIDDAY	LATE OPENING	OUTDOOR TABLES	GOOD WINE LIST

Price categories for a three-course evening meal for one, including a half-bottle of house wine, tax and service:

Ⓛ under L35,000
ⓁⓁ L35,000 – 55,000
ⓁⓁⓁ L55,000 – 75,000
ⓁⓁⓁⓁ L75,000 – 100,000
ⓁⓁⓁⓁⓁ over L100,000.

OPEN AT MIDDAY
Often open all day, with a break in the late afternoon to prepare for the evening session.

LATE OPENING
Orders will be accepted until midnight.

OUTDOOR TABLES
Facilities for eating outdoors, on a terrace (often with a good view), or in a garden during the summer.

GOOD WINE LIST
A wide range of specially selected good wines – local, national and international.

RAVELLO: *Cumpà Cosimo* ⓁⓁ
Via Roma 42–4. **Road map** D4. 🕻 089-85 71 56.
Originally a famous wine shop, Cumpà now offers good home-made food. The pasta dishes are recommended, especially the fusilli and gnocchi.
● *Mon (not in summer).*

| V AE DC | ● | ■ | | |

RAVELLO: *Palazzo della Marra* ⓁⓁ
Via della Marra 7/9. **Road map** D4. 🕻 089-85 83 02.
The arches and vaults of the building in which this restaurant is set were left intact during recent restoration, lending a certain elegance. The menu is a careful and successful blend of tradition and creativity.
● *Tue; Nov and Jan.* 🕭

| V AE DC | ● | | ● | |

CAPRI

ANACAPRI: *Da Gelsomina* ⓁⓁ
Via Migliara 72. **Road map** C4. 🕻 081-837 14 99.
The rustic surroundings may have disappeared, but the flavoursome food at Da Gelsomina has remained true to the countryside. Try the pasta with *cicerbie* and the *pollo al mattone.*
● *Tue (not in summer).*

| V AE DC | ● | | ● | |

ANACAPRI: *Add'o Riccio* ⓁⓁⓁ
Via Grotta Azzurra 11. **Road map** C4. 🕻 081-837 13 80.
Only a stairway separates Add'o Riccio from the famous Blue Grotto sea cave, a setting with undeniable fascination. It is a firm favourite with seafood lovers, offering dishes such as spaghetti with seafood, or linguine with lobster.
● *eve (except summer weekends); Nov–Feb.*

| V AE DC | ● | | ● | |

CAPRI: *Il Bocciodromo* Ⓛ
Traversa Lo Palazzo 2. **Road map** C5. 🕻 081-837 74 14.
A pleasant family atmosphere, large garden and delicious food reward the owners of Il Bocciodromo with regulars who keep coming back for more. The home-made lemon tart is excellent.
● *Mon (not in summer); 10 Nov–26 Dec, 15 Jan–18 Mar.*

| V AE DC | ● | ■ | ● | |

CAPRI: *La Savardina* Ⓛ
Via Lo Capo 8. **Road map** C5. 🕻 081-837 63 00.
An enjoyable walk takes you to this country trattoria. The simple but delicious home-cooked dishes such as ravioli come to your table in a garden filled with citrus fruit trees and herbs.
● *Tue (not in summer); Jan–Feb.*

| V | ● | ■ | ● | |

CAPRI: *Le Grottelle* ⓁⓁ
Via Arco Naturale 13. **Road map** C5. 🕻 081-837 57 19.
Le Grottelle offers you wholesome country cooking in a family-run trattoria with a magnificent view of the Arco Naturale and beyond.
● *Thu (not in summer); mid Nov–mid Mar.*

| V AE | ● | | | |

CAPRI: *Settanni* ⓁⓁ
Via Longano 5. **Road map** C5. 🕻 081-837 01 05.
A few steps from the square in the main town, this trattoria is well known for its *spaghetti alla chiummenzana*, with cherry tomatoes, oregano, basil and other aromatic herbs found on the island.
● *Thu (not in summer); 10 Jan–Feb.*

| V AE | ● | | | |

CAPRI: *La Canzone del Mare* ⓁⓁⓁ
Via Marina Piccola 93. **Road map** C5. 🕻 081-837 01 04.
Frequented in the 1960s by film stars, singers and other rich and beautiful characters from the world of show business, La Canzone del Mare is a famous restaurant attached to the most exclusive bathing establishment in Capri. Naturally, the house specials are fish and seafood dishes.
● *eve; Nov–Mar.*

| V AE DC | ● | | ● | |

CAPRI: *Faraglioni*
Via Camerelle 75. **Road map** C5. 081-837 03 20.
In the business of providing traditional fare for locals and visitors to Capri since the late 19th century, this restaurant, with its tables lined along the Via Camerelle, is ideal for those who don't mind, or perhaps even relish, being on view to the throngs who pass by.
● *Nov–Mar.*

CAPRI: *Da Gemma*
Via Madre Serafina 6. **Road map** C5. 081-837 04 61.
More than 50 years of experience have brought Da Gemma considerable praise, as can be seen by photographs on the wall with dedications by some of the restaurant's famous guests. The pizza is indeed wonderful.
● *20 days in Jan.*

CAPRI: *Luigi ai Faraglioni*
Strada dei Faraglioni. **Road map** C5. 081-837 05 91.
Here you can enjoy an extraordinary, panoramic view of the Faraglioni and the Monacone rock in the shade of a thatched-roof area while experiencing classic Capri cuisine.
● *eve; Oct–Easter.*

CAPRI: *Da Paolino*
Via Palazzo a Mare 11. **Road map** C5. 081-837 61 02.
Eating outside at Da Paolino in the summer evenings, surrounded by lemon trees, is a really special experience. A chance to tuck into the marvellous antipasto buffet alone is worth the trip.
● *Tue (not in summer); Nov–Easter.*

ISCHIA

CASAMICCIOLA TERME: *Il Focolare*
Via Cretaio 68. **Road map** A4. 081-98 06 04.
Come here for traditional Ischia cuisine cooked by Riccardo and Loretta D'Ambra, who also run a local winery of the same name.
● *Wed (not in summer), Mon, Tue, Thu at midday.*

FORIO: *Da Peppina di Renato*
Via Bocca 42. **Road map** A4. 081-99 83 12.
Good country cooking with local produce. The menu features soups, rabbit *all'ischitana* and first-rate, home-made desserts.
● *Wed (not in summer); mid Nov–mid Mar.*

ISCHIA PORTO: *Damiano*
Variante Esterna SS 270. **Road map** A4. 081-98 30 32.
Excellent fish and a magnificent view of the port are the highlights of this restaurant, unarguably one of the best on the island. Order the mixed fried fish appetizer to whet your taste buds.
● *Oct–Mar.*

ISCHIA PORTO: *Gennaro*
Via Porto 66. **Road map** A4. 081-99 29 17.
This restaurant has the best classic seafood that islands in the Bay of Naples have to offer, with a great selection of fresh fish, starting with the fine antipasti and marvellous soup, and continuing through each course.
● *Nov–Mar; Jul & Aug: midday.*

PROCIDA

MARINA CORRICELLA: *Gorgonia*
Marina Corricella 50. **Road map** B3. 081-810 10 60.
The *gorgonia* referred to in this establishment's name is a seaweed. The restaurant's menu is – unsurprisingly – based almost exclusively on fish. Try the pasta and beans with mussels.
● *Nov–Apr (not at weekends in Mar, Apr & Oct).*

MARINA DI SANCIO CATTOLICO: *Sent' Cò*
Via Roma 167. **Road map** B3. 081-810 11 20.
This restaurant's strange-looking name is a dialect form of Sancio Cattolico, which is the name of the port area where the restaurant is located. Naturally, the menu offers fish galore. The house speciality is a rather unusual dish – spaghetti with sea urchins.
● *at midday (not in summer).*

For key to symbols see back flap

Light Meals and Snacks in Naples

NAPLES IS FULL of bars, pastry shops, rosticcerie, and small places with stand-up counters where you can stop for a drink and a snack. It is an Italian habit to stop at a local bar to breakfast on a cappuccino and warm croissant, to pause for an apéritif before lunch, or have a coffee in the afternoon. An inexpensive and quick meal can be bought at the many fast food establishments that sell sandwiches, small pizzas, and filled rolls, as well as prepared meals like pasta with different sauces, to eat on the spot or to take out.

BARS AND CAFÉS

IN NAPLES, unlike most other European cities, the bars generally only have stand-up counters for customers to have a quick coffee. In bars and cafés where seating space is provided, there is usually an additional charge for service at the table. In the summer, however, all available outdoor space is packed with tables. Some of the cafés stay open until the wee hours and are equally popular with the young and the old. Many bars in Naples double as pastry shops (pasticceria), ice cream parlors (gelateria), quick self-service restaurants (tavola calda), or all these combined.

One historic Neapolitan café frequented by celebrities in the past is **Caffè Gambrinus**, one of the most elegant bars in the center (see p52). Here, a short distance from the Palazzo Reale, you can sit outside and admire the lovely Piazza del Plebiscito, which is closed to traffic. Other elegant cafés are **La Caffettiera** in Piazza dei Martiri, or the **Caffetteria Bernini** on Piazza Fanzago. Both of these are in the Vomero district and get very busy in the evenings, especially on weekends.

If you are walking along the waterfront (lungomare), stop for an apéritif at the **Bar dell'Ovo**. The small and elegant **Bar Prencipe** in Piazza Municipio, which retains its original Art Deco interior, is a good place to pause for breakfast in the city center. The **Gran Caffè Verdi** on Via Verdi and **Caffè Roma** on Via Toledo, with their spacious refreshment areas, are both popular with office workers during their breaks.

To taste an excellent coffee, try the **Caffè Mexico** in Piazza Dante with superb blends, or the **Café do Brasil** in the Vomero area opposite the Teatro Diana. In the old city center the **Bar Nilo** is known for its courteous and friendly service.

During the summer, popular spots for night owls are the **Caffè delle Arti**, opposite the Academy of Art, and the cafés in Piazza Bellini: the **Caffè 1799**, the **Caffè Arabo**, and the **Intra Moenia**, which also sells books and promotes cultural events.

PASTRY SHOPS AND ICE-CREAM PARLORS

NEAPOLITAN PASTRY shops, known throughout the world and descended from a centuries-old tradition, offer a number of specialties. Among these are the shortcrust or puff pastries called sfogliatelle, the pastiera eaten at Easter, babà, zeppola di San Giuseppe, and seasonal Christmas pastries such as rococò and struffoli (pastry rings with honey and candied fruit).

A favorite spot for the locals, particularly on Sundays, is **Scaturchio** in Piazza San Domenico Maggiore, one of the best cafés in the historic center. Also in Piazza San Domenico Maggiore, **L.U.I.S.E.** sells excellent pastries and sweets, as do **Augustus** in Via Toledo, **Daniele** and **Bellavia** in the Vomero, and **Moccia** in the Chiaia district. The **Gran Bar Riviera**, which opened in Chiaia in 1870, also offers many treats; the tartufo was invented here, a delectable semifreddo ice cream with chestnut cream filling. The best sfogliatella can be found

at **Pintauro** on Via Toledo or **La Sfogliatella** in the Galleria Umberto I. Good ice-cream parlors are **La Scimmia** in Piazza Carità, the **Bilancione** in Posillipo, **Soave** in Vomero, and **Häagen-Dazs** in Chiaia.

The so-called chalets along the waterfront in the Mergellina area are legendary among Neapolitans. The most famous of these is **Chalet Ciro**, specializing in home-made ice cream (artigianale). People come here for coffee or an apéritif. **Chiquito's**, on the nearby Via Mergellina, was once a water vendor and is now famous for his fruit cups and exotic fruit shakes.

TAKE-OUT FOOD

FOUNDED IN 1887 by Gaetano Cecere, the first Neapolitan fast food establishment is aptly named **Vaco 'e pressa** (I'm in a hurry). True to its founder's tradition, it still has marble furnishings and a quaint atmosphere. Rather than **McDonald's**, the locals usually prefer to drop in at a tavola calda, where they can eat a quick plate of pasta or buy a sandwich prepared in a delicatessen (salumeria), eat a local mozzarella, or have hot snacks from a rosticceria. Excellent take-outs are **Tavola Calda L.U.I.S.E.** in Via Toledo and **Imperatore** in the Vomero area, where you can also buy tasty roast chicken. **La Piazza**, next to Santa Maria La Nova church, offers a quick snack, and **Hot Stuff** in Via Schipa sells sandwiches or bruschette (toasted bread with garlic and oil).

If you like sweet or savory crêpes, **La Crêperie** in the Vomero area is the place for you. Then there are the many pizzetterie such as **Villa Pizza**, **Ciao Pizza**, **Le Focacce Moccia**, **Pizzette e Cornetti**, and the rosticcerie such as **Elettroforno** in Posillipo, which sells pizza by the slice as well as "crocché" (potato croquettes), arancini di riso (rice croquettes), and saltimbocca (veal). Many of these pizzerie, such as the **Cibo** chain, also sell roasted meats.

DIRECTORY

TOLEDO AND CASTEL NUOVO

Bars and Cafés

Bar Prencipe
Piazza Municipio 20.
Map 7 B2.

Caffé Gambrinus
Piazza Trieste e
Trento 38.
Map 7 A3.

Caffè Roma
Via Toledo 235.
Map 7 A2 (9 A5).

Gran Caffè Verdi
Via Verdi 23.
Map 7 A2.

Pastry Shops and Ice Cream Parlours

Augustus
Via Toledo 147.
Map 7 A2 (9 A5).

Pintauro
Via Toledo 275.
Map 7 A2 (9 A5).

La Scimmia
Piazza Carità 4.
Map 7 A1.

La Sfogliatella
Galleria Umberto I, 66.
Map 7 A2.

Take-Away Food

Cibo
Via Cervantes 70.
Map 7 A2.

Tavola Calda L.U.I.S.E.
Via Toledo 266.
Map 7 A1 (9 A5).

McDonald's
Via Sanfelice 16/20.
Map 7 B1 (9 C5).

SPACCANAPOLI

Bars and Cafés

Bar Nilo
Via San Biagio dei
Librai 129/130.
Map 3 C5.

Pastry Shops and Ice Cream Parlours

L.U.I.S.E.
Piazza San Domenico
Maggiore 5.
Map 3 B5 (9 C3).

Scaturchio
Piazza San Domenico
Maggiore 19.
Map 3 B5 (9 C3).

Take-Away Food

Ciao Pizza
Via Benedetto
Croce 42.
Map 3 B5 (9 C4).

Cibo
Piazza del Gesù 27.
Map 3 B5 (9 B4).

Le Focacce Moccia
Piazzetta Nilo 16 bis.
Map 3 B5 (10 E3).

La Piazza
Piazza Santa Maria La
Nova.
Map 7 B1 (9 C5).

Villa Pizza
Via Capitelli 28.
Map 3 A5.

DECUMANO MAGGIORE

Bars and Cafés

Caffè Arabo
Piazza Bellini 66.
Map 3 B5.

Caffè 1799
Piazza Bellini 71.
Map 3 B5.

Caffè delle Arti
Via Micco
Spadaro 4/5.
Map 7 B2.

Caffè Mexico
Piazza Dante 86.
Map 3 A5 (9 B3).

Intra Moenia
Piazza Bellini 70.
Map 3 B5.

Scaturchio
Via Portamedina 22.
Map 3 A5 (9 A4).

Take-Away Food

McDonald's
Piazza Dante 92.
Map 3 A5.

Vaco 'e Pressa
Piazza Dante 87.
Map 3 A5 (9 B3).

VOMERO

Bars and Cafés

Café do Brasil
Via Giordano 31.
Map 5 B2.

La Caffettiera
Piazza Vanvitelli 10.
Map 2 D5.

Caffetteria Bernini
Piazza Fanzago.
Map 2 D4.

Caffé Mexico
Via Scarlatti 69.
Map 2 D5.

Pastry Shops and Ice Cream Parlours

Bellavia
Via Giordano 158.
Map 1 C5.

Daniele
Via Scarlatti 104/106.
Map 2 D5.

Soave
Via Scarlatti 130.
Map 2 D5.

Take-Away Food

Cibo
Via Cimarosa 144.
Map 1 C5.

La Crêperie
Via Donadio 1/3.
Map 2 D4.

Imperatore
Via Scarlatti 180.
Map 2 D5.

McDonald's
Via Scarlatti 209.
Map 2 D5.

Pizzette e Cornetti
Via Kerbaker 4.
Map 2 D5.

CASTEL DELL'OVO AND CHIAIA

Bars and Cafés

Bar dell'Ovo
Via Partenope 6.
Map 7 A4.

La Caffettiera
Piazza dei Martiri 30.
Map 6 F2.

Pastry Shops and Ice Cream Parlours

Chalet Ciro
Via Caracciolo
(opposite Via Orazio).
Map 5 B4.

Chiquito's
Via Mergellina
(opposite the funicular).
Map 5 B3.

Häagen-Dazs
Via Nisco 3.
Map 6 E2.

Moccia
Via San Pasquale
21/22.
Map 6 E2.

Gran Bar Riviera
Riviera di Chiaia 183.
Map 5 C2.

Take-Away Food

Hot Stuff
Via Schipa 65.
Map 5 B2.

POSILLIPO

Pastry Shops and Ice Cream Parlours

Augustus
Via Petrarca 81 a/b.
Map 5 A4.

Bilancione
Via Posillipo 238/b.
Map 5 A5.

Take-Away Food

Elettroforno
Piazza San Luigi 12/b.

SHOPS AND MARKETS

SHOPPING IN NAPLES is an excellent way to explore the labyrinth of this fascinating city. Expensive boutiques line the main streets such as Via Toledo and Via Chiaia, where good quality, stylish clothes, shoes, and jewelry can be bought. However, don't limit yourself to the fashionable areas but wander around the alleyways in the old town to discover the small specialty shops and artisan workshops. Here visitors can find authentic and handmade souvenirs.

Nativity figure

These streets often bear the name of the trade practiced there, such as Piazza degli Orefici (Goldsmiths' Square).

Perhaps the most enjoyable way to shop is to follow the example of most Neapolitans and buy from the numerous markets and stands along the roadside. These *bancarelle* sell everything from clothes to kitchenware, and children's toys to jewelry. Many common items are seconds from the manufacturer or imitation designer labels.

Coral jewelry in a shop window

OPENING HOURS

STORES ARE OPEN from 10am to 2pm and from 4pm to 8pm. They are closed Sundays and Monday mornings in winter, Saturday afternoons and Sundays in summer. Food stores and markets are closed on Thursday afternoons. Before holiday periods like Christmas, many places are open on Sundays and extend their weekly opening hours. In summer most stores close for two weeks around August 15 (Ferragosto).

HOW TO PAY

MAJOR CREDIT CARDS are accepted in most boutiques and department stores. After you have made your purchase, make sure you are given the receipt (*ricevuta fiscale*). By law the police can make a spot check outside the shop, and if you are without a receipt, you may be fined.

SALES

FROM EARLY JULY to early September and mid-January to mid-March, sales are held in Naples. You can find excellent bargains with discounts of up to 50 percent and sometimes as much as 70 percent. It is a good idea to check goods before you leave the shop; refunds are unlikely.

FASHION AND ACCESSORIES

THE EXCLUSIVE STORES are concentrated in Via dei Mille and Via Calabritto, in the elegant Chiaia district. Here the great fashion designers have their stores, such as **Emporio Armani**, **Prada**, **Gianni Versace**, and **Mario Valentino**, whose shoes are exhibited at the Museum of Modern Art in New York. In Riviera di Chiaia, **Marinella** sells her famous ties worn by

The store window of the elegant Livio de Simone boutique

many VIPs.

At **Eddy Monetti** the emphasis is on elegant and classical fashion. Clothes with an innovative touch are offered by **Barbaro** in Galleria Umberto I, while avant-garde men's and women's wear is sold by **Maxi Ho**. **Livio De Simone**, a native of Naples, offers stylish clothes in bright Mediterranean colors, while **Amina Rubinacci** is known for her woollen and cashmere sweaters. Naples also has boutiques for **Max Mara** and **Max & Co**.

Clothing at more accessible prices is sold at **Camomilla** and **G.B. Pedrini**. Young people have no lack of choice with clothes from the **Benetton** outlets and the **Bamba** boutique in Via Chiaia, famous for its original designs. Modern fashion for young people is also offered in the **Magazzini Generali** (General Store) with a huge stock catering to all budgets. Original second-hand clothes and personalized T-shirts are sold at **Mu Mu Frequencies**, a multimedia cultural group.

The **Prénatal** chain caters to mothers-to-be and small children. Handbags, belts,and other accessories, mostly made by local craftsmen, are sold in the **Spatarella** and **Tramontano** stores.

In the old center between San Biagio dei Librai and Via degli Orefici there are many jewelers' and goldsmiths' shops. The age-old tradition of engraving and cameo work is still practiced in many shops.

Interior of the Colonnese bookshop in Via San Biagio dei Librai

Caso is unrivaled for its coral jewels, and other jewelry shops such as **Ventrella** and **Knight** stock original designs.

DEPARTMENT STORES AND SHOPPING CENTERS

Most Neapolitans prefer smaller, specialty shops where the service is more personal. However, some department stores such as **La Rinascente** and **Coin** offer a good variety of products from quality clothes, cosmetics, and perfumes to household goods and dishes. For specialists in household and kitchen goods, try the **Croff** chain, which also sells a wide variety of modern furnishings. The large chain stores, **Upim** and **Standa**, are generally less expensive and feature cosmetics, lingerie, household articles, and clothes.

The shopping centers, **Galleria Vanvitelli** and the elegant **Galleria Scarlatti,** are found in the Vomero district, and the chic 19th-century Galleria Umberto I, off Piazza Trieste e Trento, is an arcade of elegant stores.

Coin
Via Scarlatti 100.
[578 01 11.
Via Santa Caterina a
Chiaia 23.
[245 19 38.

Croff
Via Diaz 38/40.
[552 39 83.

Galleria Scarlatti
Via Scarlatti.

Galleria Vanvitelli
Piazza Vanvitelli.

La Rinascente
Via Toledo 343.
[41 15 11.

Standa
Via Solimene 143.
[578 04 80.
Viale Colli Aminei.
[743 06 33.

Upim
Piazza Matteotti 7.
[552 12 79.
Via dei Mille 59.
[41 75 20.
Via Scarlatti.
[556 28 17.

ART, ANTIQUES, AND INTERIOR DESIGN

Naples is famous for its fascinating antique and second-hand shops. The best-known antique dealers can be found in Via Domenico Morelli: **Brandi**, **D'Amodio**,

Falanga, and **Florida** are all specialists in 18th-century furniture and paintings. Shops with historic objects, such as **L'Antiquario** and **Affaitati**, are in Via Costantinopoli. Old engravings, prints and lithographs, picture frames, and other *objets d'art* are on sale at **Bowinkel**, the oldest shop in Piazza dei Martiri. Rare books, prints, and gouaches are sold at the **Casella** and **Regina** antiquarian booksellers, while the **Colonnese** bookstore stocks traditional Neapolitan articles. Among the second-hand dealers the most interesting is **Quagliozza**, which sells all kinds of objects, including lamps, frames, and telephones on the steps of the church of San

The traditional craft of making and restoring string instruments

Nicola a Nilo. The **Archivio Fotografico Parisio**, with about 100,000 photographs of Neapolitan life and characters, provides a unique record of the city's history. Art galleries with interesting work on display include the **Galleria Amelio**, **Lia Rumma**, **Studio Morra,** and **Studio Trisorio**.

Neapolitan second-hand dealer with goods on display in the street

Restoration of a puppet head in the Ospedale delle Bambole *(see p61)*

Leading interior design shops include **Agorà** in the Posillipo area and **Novelli** in Piazza Amedeo, featuring the latest styles in home furnishings. Simple, clean-cut design solutions for a younger generation are displayed at **IdeArredo**.

HANDICRAFTS

Tнᴇ ᴍᴀɴʏ ᴡᴏʀᴋsʜᴏᴘs and second-hand stores in the historic center offer a varied choice of articles, from the kitsch to the well-designed. In Via San Gregorio Armeno is the workshop of the famous nativity scene artisan, **Giuseppe Ferrigno**, while in Via San Biagio dei Librai is the **Ospedale delle Bambole** (hospital for dolls) where porcelain dolls, shepherds, marionettes, and puppets are repaired and restored. At the **Liuteria Calace**, in the historic center, violins, violas, mandolins, and lutes are made and restored. **Nel Regno di Pulcinella** is a workshop dedicated to the making of Neapolitan masks.

At **Lunarossa** you can buy objects made of wood, copper, ceramic, and stone. Book restoration, bookbinding, and elegant objects made from handmade Amalfi paper make the **Bottega Artigiana del Libro e della Carta** a fascinating place. If you are interested in ceramics, take a look at **Il Cantuccio della Ceramica** and the workshop of **Lisa Weber**.

FOOD, WINE, AND SPIRITS

Tнᴇ ʟᴇᴀᴅɪɴɢ delicatessens in Naples are **La Botteghina** and **Gastronomia L.U.I.S.E.**, all of which sell a variety of local specialties. **Codrington** is known for its large stock of international brands. **Gay Odin** has the finest chocolate in Naples, including the delicious *Vesuvio* chocolate with rum. The old-fashioned **Scaturchio** sells fine cakes and candy as well as ice cream. A good selection of wines can be found at the **Enoteca del Buon Bere** and the **Enoteca Belledonne**.

OPEN-AIR MARKETS

Street stalls and markets set up in the early morning and usually pack up after midday. Food stands selling seasonal fruit and vegetables generally have fresher and less expensive produce than the shops. Clothes and household items will be cheap and, although they may not be designer quality, they are perfectly good. Bargaining is not usually done when buying food, but for clothes and other items try asking for a discount *(sconto)*.

Market at Sant'Antonio Abate

Mercatino di Antignano
Piazza degli Artisti. ◻ *8am–1pm Mon–Sat.*
Clothing, shoes, household articles, fabrics.

Fiera Antiquaria Napoletana
Villa Comunale. ◻ *8am–4pm penultimate Sat & Sun of month.*
Antique market: silverware, jewelry, and ornaments.

Mercato del Casale di Posillipo
Posillipo. ◻ *8am–2pm Thu.*
Clothes, accessories, household articles.

Mercato del Ponte di Casanova
Porta Capuana. ◻ *8am–sunset Mon–Sat.*
New and used clothes.

Mercato dei Fiori
Castel Nuovo. ◻ *daily at dawn.*
Flowers.

Mercatino della Pignasecca
Near Piazza Carità. ◻ *8am–2pm Mon–Sat.*
Food.

Mercato di Sant'Antonio
Via Sant'Antonio Abate. ◻ *9am–8pm daily.*
Food market.

Mercato di Porta Nolana
Via Carmignano. ◻ *8am–6pm Mon–Sat (8am–2pm Sun).*
Fresh fish and seafood.

Mercatino della Torretta
Viale Gramsci. ◻ *8am–1pm Mon–Sat.*
Food market and clothing.

The inviting entrance of the famous Scaturchio *pasticceria*

SHOPS AND MARKETS

193

DIRECTORY

FASHION AND ACCESSORIES

Amina Rubinacci
Via dei Mille 16.
41 56 72.

Bamba
Via Chiaia 209.
41 47 67.

Barbaro
Galleria Umberto I.
41 12 84.
One of many branches.

Benetton
Via Chiaia 203/204.
40 53 85.
One of many branches.

Camomilla
Via A Scarlatti 185.
578 20 04.
One of many branches.

Caso
Piazza San Domenico
Maggiore 16.
551 67 33.

Eddy Monetti
Via dei Mille 45a/b/c.
40 70 64.

Emporio Armani
Piazza dei Mille 64.
42 58 16.

G.B. Pedrini
Via Toledo 330.
40 49 49.

Gianni Versace
Via Calabritto 7.
764 42 10.

Knight
Piazza dei Martiri 52.
764 38 37.

Livio De Simone
Via D Morelli 15.
764 38 27.

Magazzini Generali
Via dei Mille 26/28.
41 38 72.

Marinella
Riviera di Chiaia 287.
764 42 14.

Mario Valentino
Via Calabritto 9/10.
41 86 38.

Max & Co.
Corso Umberto I 28.
552 62 23.
One of many branches.

Max Mara
Corso Umberto I 134/136.
553 85 01.

Maxi Ho
Via N Nisco 20 bis, 23/27.
42 75 30.

Mu Mu Frequencies
Piazza Monteoliveto 10.
552 41 03.

Prada
Via Calabritto 9.
764 13 23.

Prénatal
Via A Scarlatti 184.
556 30 18.
One of many branches.

Spatarella
Via Calabritto 1.
764 37 94.

Tramontano
Via Chiaia 149/e.
41 47 58.

Ventrella
Via C Poerio 11.
764 37 12.

ART, ANTIQUES, AND INTERIOR DESIGN

Agorà
Via Orazio 138/a.
65 10 56.

Affaitati
Via Costantinopoli 18.
564 06 10.

L'Antiquariato
Via Costantinopoli 34.
564 06 07.

Archivio Fotografico Parisio
Largo Carolina 10.
764 51 22.

Bowinkel
Piazza dei Martiri 24.
764 43 44.

Brandi
Via D Morelli 21.
764 39 06.

Casella
Via C Poerio 92/e.
764 26 27.

Colonnese
Via S Pietro a Maiella 32.
45 98 58.

D'Amodio
Via D Morelli 6 bis.
764 38 72.

Falanga
Via D Morelli 6.
764 37 04.

Florida
Via D Morelli 13.
764 34 40.

Galleria Amelio
Piazza dei Martiri 58.
42 20 23.

IdeArredo
Via R Bracco 41/49.
551 09 92.

Lia Rumma
Via V Gaetani 12.
764 36 19.

Novelli
Piazza Amedeo 21/22.
41 32 33.

Quagliozza
Via San Biagio dei Librai 11 (Church of San Nicola a Nilo).

Regina
Via Costantinopoli 51/103.
45 99 83.

Studio Morra
Via Calabritto 20.
763 37 37.

Studio Trisorio
Riviera di Chiaia 215.
41 43 06.

HANDICRAFTS

Bottega Artigiana del Libro e della Carta
Calata Trinità Maggiore 4.
551 12 80.

Il Cantuccio della Ceramica
Via B Croce 38 (inside).
552 58 57.

Giuseppe Ferrigno
Via S Gregorio Armeno 10.
552 31 48.

Lisa Weber
Via G Paladino 4.

Liuteria Calace
Via San Domenico Maggiore 9.
551 59 83.

Lunarossa
Via B Croce 22.
551 70 05.

Ospedale delle Bambole
Via S Biagio dei Librai 81.
20 30 67.

Nel Regno di Pulcinella
Salita Arenella 56.
578 64 50.

FOOD, WINE, AND SPIRITS

La Botteghina
Via Orazio 104.
68 22 66.

Codrington
Via Chiaia 94.
41 82 57.

Enoteca Belledonne
Vico Belledonne a Chiaia 18.
40 31 62.

Enoteca del Buon Bere
Via M Turchi 13.
764 78 43.

Gastronomia L.U.I.S.E.
Via S Caterina a Chiaia 4.
41 77 35.

Gay Odin
Via Toledo 427/428.
551 34 91.

Scaturchio
Piazza San Domenico Maggiore.
551 69 44.

Shops and Markets along the Coast

EVERY TOWN AND VILLAGE in the region, from the islands to the coast, offer typical local handicrafts such as ceramics or glassware as well as foods and wines associated with the history and culture of each place. Wandering through the narrow streets in these lovely seaside spots, you will find many things to buy.

FASHION AND ACCESSORIES

BESIDES SHOPS with designer wear, there are still several old local fashion houses. You can find the top names in Italian and foreign fashion at places such as **Adario & Fiorentino**, which has a shop at Sant'Agata sui due Golfi, or **Dominique** in Ischia and **Elle et Lui** at Lacco Ameno. The shopping street in Capri, Via Camerelle, boasts the elegant **Marcello Rubinacci** boutique, known for top-quality cashmere sweaters. Elegant apparel, mostly made of silk, and typical Capri shoes are among the specialties of **Laura Merola**. Two top jewelers in Capri are **La Campanina** and **Chantecler**, located in Via Vittorio Emanuele, which stock precious stones in every color as well as diamonds and coral necklaces of very fine quality.

Fashion styles in Positano are famous for their originality. Among the town's leading houses is **Maria Lampo**, well known for making their items quickly (*lampo* meaning "in a flash"). Top designer wear as well as handmade patchwork clothing and quilts are sold at **Nadir's**, while **La Bottega di Brunella** and **La Tartana** are distinguished for their fine fabrics and original patterns. If you want the bikini of your dreams, go to **Susy** on Capri, where you can order swimwear made to measure.

Sorrento, Positano, and Capri are famous for their handmade sandals; to have a pair made especially for you, go to **Siniscalchi** in Sorrento, **Costanzo Avitabile** in Positano, the imaginative **Canfora** in Capri, or Antonio Viva's shop at Anacapri, aptly called **L'Arte del Sandalo**

Caprese. Again in Anacapri, **Costanzo e Anna Arcucci** make canvas and rope-soled shoes to order. On the mainland, cloth shoes decorated in weird and wonderful ways can be found at **La Gabella** in Amalfi.

ART AND HANDICRAFTS

BY EXPLORING the craftsmen's shops in the towns and villages outside Naples you can really get to know the heart of a place and discover its cultural and artistic traditions. The boats known as *gozzi* are built by the **Aprea Mare** company in Sorrento and are world famous. The ancient tradition of marquetry in the Sorrento peninsula is carried on by craftsmen such as **Giuseppe Gargiulo**, **Peppe Rocco**, and **Giliberto Attardi**.

Vietri sul Mare is famous for its decorated ceramics; the **Solimene** factory employs at least 40 craftsmen who, despite the large output of the place, make fine handmade products. The **Perrotti** brothers make splendid stained glass and accept commissions. Other high-quality ceramics are produced by **Taki** in Ischia and **Artigiò** in Procida, while **La Bottega dell'Arte** in Capri – thanks to the well-known ceramicist Sergio Rubini – now has more than 200 outlets in the United States alone. Again in Capri, **Carmelina** offers classic primitive paintings.

In Amalfi, visit the **Cartiere Amatruda** and **Cavaliere** mills, where fine quality paper is produced. As a souvenir of Capri there are the **Carthusia** perfumes, sold only on the island (you can also visit their laboratories at No. 2 Via Parco Augusto). On the island of Procida, **Maria**

Rosaria Intartaglia makes lovely embroidered lingerie to order. Lastly, the **Emporio Scialò** at Ischia sells raffia dolls and Pulcinella puppets, all made by hand.

FOOD, WINE, AND LIQUEURS

MANY FINE DAIRY products such as cheese come from the area around Naples. In Sorrento you can visit the **Apreda** dairy and buy fresh braids of *fiordilatte*, a type of mozzarella made from cow's milk, in the nearby shop. The **Caseificio Isola di Capri** and **Gabriele** in Vico Equense are also excellent dairies. In Capri, **Sfizi di Pane** offers 15 different types of *tarallini* biscuits as well as various kinds of bread. For the sweet-toothed, Ischia's **Caffè Calise** has orange *sfogliatelle*, and in Positano the **La Zagara** pastry shop has delicious fruit tarts called *crostate*. While in Amalfi, try the delightful lemon pastries at **Andrea Pansa**.

Some wine shops also sell local products such as jam, honey, and spices: **Piemme** in Sorrento, **Ischia Sapori** on Ischia, and **Gusti e Delizie** in Ravello. A good range of wine is on sale at **La Valle dei Mulini** in Amalfi, **I Sapori di Positano** in Positano and **Enoteca Casa D'Ambra** in Ischia. **Limoncello di Capri** is the most famous source of limoncello, or lemon-flavored liqueur, and **I Giardini di Ravello** also stocks wines.

MARKETS

THERE ARE numerous markets in the outlying areas. The most important in size and tradition is the secondhand market in Resina at Ercolano (Herculaneum), where you will find used clothes and accessories. It is half an hour from the central train station in Naples: take the Circumvesuviana line and get off at Ercolano.

DIRECTORY

FASHION AND ACCESSORIES

Adario & Fiorentino
Via Nastro Azzurro 1–3
(Sant'Agata sui Due Golfi).
081-878 00 65.
One of two shops.

L'Arte del Sandalo Caprese
Via G Orlandi 75
(Anacapri).
081-837 35 83.

La Bottega di Brunella
Via Pasitea 76
(Positano).
081-837 06 43.

La Campanina
Via V Emanuele 18
(Capri).
081-837 06 43.

Canfora
Via Camerelle 3
(Capri).
081-837 04 87.

Chantecler
Via V Emanuele 51
(Capri).
081-837 05 44.

Costanzo Avitabile
Piazza A Vespucci 1–5
(Positano).
081-87 53 66.

Costanzo e Anna Arcucci
Via Vigna 46
(Anacapri).
081-837 13 08.

Dominique
Corso V Colonna 180
(Ischia).
081-99 12 21.
One of two shops.

Elle et Lui
Piazza Santa Restituta 8
(Lacco Ameno).
081-90 02 28.

La Gabella
Via P Comite 37
(Amalfi).
0330-67 54 03.

Laura Merola
Via Fuorlovado 2
(Capri).
081-837 04 03.

Marcello Rubinacci
Via Camerelle 9
(Capri).
081-837 72 95.

Maria Lampo
Via Pasitea 12–16
(Positano).
089-87 50 21.

Nadir
Via Pasitea 44
(Positano).
089-87 54 46.

Siniscalchi
Via San Cesareo 83
(Sorrento).
081-877 15 15.
One of two shops.

Susy
Via Le Botteghe 61
(Capri).

La Tartana
Via della Tartana 5
(Positano).
098-87 56 45.

ART AND HANDICRAFTS

Aprea Mare
Via Santa Lucia 15
(Sorrento).
081-807 28 18.

Artigiò
Via V Emanuele 10
(Procida).
081-896 96 69.

Giliberto Attardi
Via Padre R Giuliani 45–49
(Sorrento).
081-878 12 91.

La Bottega dell'Arte
Via Catena 2–4
(Capri).
081-837 18 78.

Carmelina
Via Roma (Capri).

Carthusia
Via Camerelle 10
(Capri).
081-837 05 29.
One of two shops.

Cartiera Amatruda
Via Fiume 100
(Amalfi).
089-87 13 15.

Cartiera Cavaliere
Via M del Giudice 2.
(Amalfi).

Ceramiche Artistiche Solimene
Via Madonna degli Angeli 7
(Vietri sul Mare).
089-21 02 43.

Emporio Scialò
Corso Umberto I, 21
(Forio d'Ischia).
081-99 75 92.

Giuseppe Gargiulo
Via Fuoro 33
(Sorrento).
081-878 24 20.

Maria Rosaria Intartaglia
Via Lubrano di Vavarla 12
(Procida).
081-896 86 74.

Peppe Rocco
Via San Nicola 12
(Sorrento).
081-878 48 74.

Perrotti
Via Nazionale Costiera 32
(Vietri sul Mare).
089-76 15 76.

Taki
Via Marina 20
(Forio d'Ischia).
081-98 91 49.

FOOD, WINE, AND LIQUEURS

Andrea Pansa
Piazza Duomo 40
(Amalfi).
089-87 10 65.

Apreda
Via del Mare 20
(Sorrento).
081-878 13 34.
One of two shops.

Caffè Calise
Via A Sogliuzzo 69
(Ischia Porto).
081-99 12 70.

Caseificio Isola di Capri
Via Roma 38
(Capri).
081-837 68 75.

Enoteca Casa D'Ambra
Via Porto 24
(Ischia Porto).
081-99 10 46.

Gabriele
Corso Umberto I, 5–7
(Vico Equense).
081-879 87 44.

I Giardini di Ravello
Via Civiltà 14
(Ravello).
089-87 22 64.

Ravello Gusti e Delizie
Via Roma 28–30
(Ravello).
089-85 77 16.

Ischia Sapori
Via Gianturco 2
(Ischia Porto).
081-98 44 82.

Limoncello di Capri
Via Roma 79
(Capri).
081-837 55 61.

Piemme
Corso Italia 161
(Sorrento).
081-807 29 27.

I Sapori di Positano
Via Mulini 6
(Positano).
089-81 11 16.

Sfizi di Pane
Via delle Botteghe 4
(Capri).
081-837 01 06.

La Valle dei Mulini
Via delle Cartiere 55
(Amalfi).
089-87 32 11.

La Zagara
Via Mulini 10
(Positano).
089-87 59 64.

ENTERTAINMENT

AS YOU MIGHT EXPECT of a major city, Naples offers an exciting range of entertainment, including cultural and sports events as well as other leisure activities. The nightlife is dynamic, the cafés, nightspots and cultural venues are always open late, and just about every taste is catered to. Music and theater performances take place throughout the year, bolstered by some important international festivals held in summertime, mostly in the vacation resorts.

Tennis at Villa Comunale

For film buffs there are two multiplexes and many film clubs. During the week people usually go to the movies or out to eat; on weekends the piazzas are buzzing with life, as it is customary for Neapolitans to meet up to have a drink before going on to the nearby nightspots, pubs, or discos. No one goes dancing before midnight, and those who dance the night away can always have a hot brioche and coffee for breakfast at dawn in one of the all-night bars.

Nighttime illuminations in a city that is happy to party until dawn

INFORMATION AND BUYING TICKETS

TO FIND OUT WHAT'S on in Naples, check the listings (and supplements) in the local newspaper *Il Mattino*, or the Naples inserts in the national newspapers. You will also find free entertainment guides in most hotels.

There are two official booking offices: **Concerteria** and **Box Office**. Tickets are usually sold at the door on the day of performance. It might be more difficult, however, to get seats at short notice for premieres; very important events; at theaters like the Diana and Bellini for chamber music concerts; and for the opera season at the Teatro San Carlo.

You can also find out more information via the Internet; the regional website is: www.na.flashnet.it/prov.htm., which provides details on museums, movies, and parks.

Classical ballet dancers at the Teatro San Carlo

The cultural association called Napoli Porte Aperte provides cultural itineraries in town and also has a website with more information: www.cib.na.cnr.it/Napoli/indice.html.

DANCE, THEATER, AND OPERA

NATIONAL and international touring productions as well as performances by local companies make Naples one of the leading cities for theater in Italy *(see p39)*. Each theater has a published program (the season runs from October through May),

although there are exceptions such as the **Augusteo**, which will put on the occasional concert or visiting theater company production as "extras." Mainstream theater and musicals are featured at the **Bellini,** and leading Italian companies perform at the **Diana** and the historic **Mercadante**, now restored to its former glory after 30 years of neglect. New small companies·play at the **Sancarluccio**, while fringe and experimental theater are featured at the **Nuovo** and **Galleria Toledo**.

Traditional Neapolitan comedy survives at the **Sannazaro**, a typical 19th-century theater where Eleonora Duse, Eduardo Scarpetta, and the De Filippo brothers performed. The **Totò** was recently opened and is a venue for variety shows. The best place for opera and ballet as well as for Neapolitan social occasions, is the **Teatro San Carlo** *(see pp37, 39, 53)*; the opera is world class and top singers perform. A premiere here is always an important international event.

Interior of Teatro San Carlo

FILM

THE TWO multiplexes are the **Plaza** and the **Modernissimo**. New films are shown at reduced prices on Wednesdays, while on Mondays some of the art-houses feature older movies at half-price. In the summer, retrospectives are held in historic sites in and around Naples, including the court-yards of the Maschio Angioino (see pp54–5) and Palazzo Reale (see pp50–51).

NIGHTSPOTS

THE TRENDY discos are **La Mela** and **Chez Moi**, which were once decidedly traditional but are now open to avant-garde influences. Two very popular multi-purpose nightspots are **Mephisto** and **S'Move** (two levels, high-volume music, and five of the best DJs in Naples). **Queen Victoria**, with a piano bar, offers a mixed bag of live music, South American dances, belly dancing, and flamenco. For the latest in dance music there are three good night-clubs: **Velvet Underground**, which offers an interactive, varied program with theme evenings; **Riot**, a multimedia club that often hosts exhibitions and concerts; and the recently opened **Vibes Café**, which has a small square at the back for outdoor entertainment.

Lead singer in the Almamegretta group (see p37)

LIVE MUSIC

THE CITY that is home to the prestigious San Pietro a Maiella Conservatoire offers plenty of opportunities to listen to masterpieces of classical music. For instance, the symphony season at Teatro San Carlo draws huge numbers of people each year. Furthermore, excellent concerts are organized by the **Associazione Alessandro Scarlatti**, where old and new classical pieces are performed to great critical acclaim.

Pop, rock, and jazz show up at the **Antica Birreria Kronenbourg**, **Lido Pola**, and the historic **Otto Jazz Club**. Another excellent live music spot is **Rude Pravo**, which opened in 1995 and features new groups. **Pala-partenope** is the only auditorium that can handle huge audiences.

Carousel at the Edenlandia park

AMUSEMENT PARKS

THE MAIN amusement park in Naples is **Edenlandia**. It features the world of fables and Walt Disney favorites, and there are over 200 attractions, with models of settings from the Disney stories and themed merry-go-rounds. The **Q-Zar** park attracts the more competitive, while the lively **Bowling Oltremare** has table tennis and bars as well as bowling.

INTERNET

FOR THOSE ADDICTED TO surfing the net, there are internet monitors and terminals for rent at the **City Hall Café** and **Internet Bar**. You can always consult the website devoted to Naples (see opposite page).

Trotting races at Agnano

SPORTS

THE ITALIAN soccerl championship is the sporting event that most fires the passions of Neapolitans. The ritual at the **San Paolo Stadium** (see p42) is repeat-ed every time the Naples team plays at home. Tickets always sell out quickly.

The **Ippodromo di Agnano** (race track), where the famous Gran Premio is held every April, lies in a splendid natural location. Tennis is also popular, and courts are in abundance.

But Naples is first and foremost a seaside city. Nautical sports, especially canoeing and sailing, are organized by the waterfront clubs. Although reserved for members only, they will be happy to accept the foreign guests of a member, so if you are lucky enough to know one, don't miss the chance to enjoy a unique experience. Swimming, diving, and especially water polo are extremely popular sports in Naples. All of them are practiced at the recently opened **Piscina Scandone**, the public swimming pool.

A fast-paced game of water polo, popular in Naples

Reed thickets surrounding a lake at the WWF nature preserve on Vesuvius, a popular destination with hikers

WALKING

THE PLEASURE of hiking through lovely countryside is now a popular vacation idea. Maps with suggested routes are distributed free at the **EPT** offices *(see p203)*, and information is also given by associations like the **Naples WWF**, which runs the Cratere degli Astroni nature preserve on Vesuvius. You can reach this crater by taking the Agnano exit on the *tangenziale* (by-pass road); the paths in its thick woods lead to stretches of water inhabited by herons and other birds. Another hiking route is in the Vesuvius park, where the **Guide Alpine della Campania** organizes guided tours. For information on the various routes up Mount Vesuvius, contact the **Ente Parco del Vesuvio**.

OUTSIDE NAPLES

THE FESTIVALS are the real highlights in the calendar of cultural events in the area around Naples. Concerts are very popular as a result, so it is best to book seats well in advance. Among these are the **Estate Musicale Sorrentina**, held in the cloister of the church of San Francesco in Sorrento, and the prestigious **Festival Internazionale di Ravello** *(see p41)*.

There is plenty of nightlife in the Phlegraean Fields area, with its nightspots, bars, and discos; the best known is **Michelemmà**, a garden in the heart of Pozzuoli, with a jazz club and pizzeria. In the

The Festival Internazionale at Ravello

same town, the **Havana Club** has three dance floors, an outdoor pool, and a pine grove. Toward Licola and in the Sorrento peninsula, the beach bars turn into beach discotheques on summer

evenings. In Sorrento there are the **Kan Kan** disco and the **Filou Club** piano bar. Positano offers good entertainment, such as drinks and conversation at the **Buca di Bacco** and then off to **Music on the Rocks**, a disco and piano bar.

In Capri, after a stroll around the square you could try **Number Two** or **New Penthotal** for a night of energetic dancing, or else go to the taverna **Anema e Core** to sing classical Neapolitan songs. Evenings in Procida are spent in the bars in the Marina or Chiaiolella, while Ischia has at least two dance spots that stay open until the wee hours – **New Valentino** and **Jane**.

SCUBA AND SKIN DIVING

A GLIMPSE OF marine life and the features of the ocean floor in the two bays is an experience you shouldn't miss: make inquiries at the **Capri Diving Club** and **Ischia Diving Center** or **Teresa Lucibello** at Positano's Marina Grande. You can also explore the magnificent coastal and island ocean floor with the small **Sottomarino Tritone** submarine.

Fireworks, a popular tradition in Naples and the Campania region

DIRECTORY

INFORMATION

Box Office
Galleria Umberto I.
☎ 551 91 88.

Concerteria
Via M Schipa 23.
☎ 761 12 21.

DANCE, THEATER, AND OPERA

Galleria Toledo
Via Concezione a
Montecalvario 34.
☎ 42 58 24.

**Teatro
Augusteo**
Piazzetta Duca d'Aosta
263.
☎ 41 42 43.

Teatro Bellini
Via Conte di Ruvo 14.
☎ 549 96 88.

Teatro Diana
Via L Giordano 69.
☎ 556 75 27.

**Teatro
San Carlo**
Via San Carlo 93/f.
☎ 797 21 11.

**Teatro
Mercadante**
Piazza Municipio 74.
☎ 551 33 96.

Teatro Nuovo
Via Montecalvario.
☎ 40 60 62.

**Teatro
Sancarluccio**
Via San Pasquale a
Chiaia 49.
☎ 40 50 00.

**Teatro
Sannazaro**
Via Chiaia 157.
☎ 41 17 23.

Teatro Totò
Via F Cavara 12/a.
☎ 29 60 51.

FILM

**Multicinema
Modernissimo**
Via Cisterna dell'Olio 59.
☎ 551 12 47.

Plaza Multisala
Via Kerbaker 85.
☎ 556 35 55.

NIGHTSPOTS

Chez Moi
Via Parco Margherita 13.
☎ 40 75 26.

La Mela
Via dei Mille 40 bis.
☎ 41 38 81.

Mephisto
Via Medina 12.
☎ 551 66 42.

Queen Victoria
Via V Fornari 15.
☎ 42 23 34.

Riot
Via S Biagio dei Librai 39.

S'Move
Vico dei Sospiri 10.
☎ 0330-99 54 49.

**Velvet
Underground**
Via Cisterna dell'Olio 11.

Vibes Café
Largo San Giovanni
Maggiore 26–7.
☎ 551 39 84.

LIVE MUSIC

**Antica Birreria
Kronenbourg**
Parco Edenlandia.
☎ 239 40 90.

**Associazione
Alessandro
Scarlatti**
Piazza dei Martiri 58.
☎ 40 60 11.

Lido Pola
Via Nisida 34.
☎ 570 19 50.

Otto Jazz Club
Piazzetta Cariati.
☎ 551 74 53.

Palapartenope
Via Barbagallo.
☎ 762 82 16.

Rude Pravo
Piazza Fanzago 111.
☎ 556 01 82.

AMUSEMENT PARKS

**Bowling
Oltremare**
Viale J F Kennedy.
☎ 62 44 44.

Edenlandia
Viale J F Kennedy.
☎ 239 40 90.

Q-Zar
Via Lomonaco 1.
☎ 40 18 15.

INTERNET

City Hall Café
Corso V Emanuele 137a.
☎ 68 17 80.

Internet Bar
Piazza V Bellini 74.
☎ 29 50 35.

SPORTS

**Ippodromo di
Agnano**
Via Ippodromo.
☎ 570 16 60.

**Piscina
Scandone**
Viale Giochi del
Mediterraneo.
☎ 570 91 59.

**Stadio
San Paolo**
Fuorigrotta.
☎ 239 56 23.

WALKING

**Ente Parco del
Vesuvio**
Municipio di San
Sebastiano al Vesuvio.
☎ 786 71 11.

**Guide Alpine della
Campania**
☎ 777 57 20.

Naples WWF
☎ 560 10 04.

OUTSIDE NAPLES

Anema e Core
Via Sella Orta 39/a (Capri).
☎ 837 64 61.

Buca di Bacco
Spiaggia Grande (Positano).
☎ 089-87 50 67.

Filou Club
Via Santa Maria della Pietà
12 (Sorrento).
☎ 878 20 83.

Jane
Via Arenile Pagoda (Ischia).
☎ 99 32 96.

Kan Kan
Piazza Sant'Antonino
(Sorrento). ☎ 878 11 14.

Michelemmà
Via Rossini 27 (Pozzuoli).
☎ 326 01 52.

**Music On The
Rocks**
Grotte dell'Incanto
(Positano).
☎ 089-87 58 74.

New Penthotal
Via V Emanuele 45 (Capri).
☎ 837 67 93.

New Valentino
Corso V Colonna 97
(Ischia). ☎ 98 25 69.

Number Two
Via Camerelle 1 (Capri).
☎ 837 70 78.

DIVING

Capri Diving Club
Località Punta Carena 8.
(Anacapri). ☎ 837 85 94.

**Ischia Diving
Center**
Via Jasolino 8 (Ischia).
☎ 98 50 08.

Teresa Lucibello
Spiaggia Marina Grande
(Positano).
☎ 089-87 50 32.

**Sottomarino
Tritone**
Via delle Rose 50/A
(Piano di Sorrento).
☎ 808 66 18.

SURVIVAL
GUIDE

PRACTICAL INFORMATION

NAPLES is a lively and somewhat chaotic city that may seem bewildering to visitors. However, over the past few years the city has undergone something of a rebirth. Its rich historic and artistic wealth has been reassessed, with more monuments open at regular hours and reorganization of the major museums to make the most of their world-class collections. Improved facilities and new pedestrian areas have revived public spaces, and cultural and social activities, advertised in the tourist offices, abound.

Visitors will still find the city has its frustrating aspects, with crippling bureaucracy at banks and public offices. It is wise to be on the lookout for petty crime, keeping money and valuables well out of sight. However, only simple guidelines and some forward planning are needed to make the most of this fascinating city and its past.

ITALIA

ENTE NAZIONALE ITALIANO PER IL TURISMO

The ENIT logo

Looking over Piazza Mercato, one of Naples's liveliest squares

TOURIST INFORMATION

YOU CAN BEGIN to organize your own itineraries before you leave for Italy by making inquiries at the **ENIT** office (the Italian National Tourist Office) in your home country. Once you are in Italy, the network of local tourist offices, known as **EPT** (Ente Provinciale per il Turismo), can provide useful information concerning accommodations, guided tours, and excursions in the surrounding area. These information offices are found at key arrival points such as the airport and the main train station in Naples as well as in the city center.

Outside Naples, the **Azienda Autonoma di Soggiorno, Cura e Turismo**, which is organized by the regional administration, has offices in Naples and the main tourist resorts. They are reliable sources of information and will provide free maps and guide books. Smaller towns will also have an information office, called a *Pro Loco*, often based in the town hall.

INFORMATION FOR STUDENT TRAVELERS

STUDENTS AND young people under 26 can obtain air, train, and ferry discount tickets at the local Centro Turistico Studentesco (**CTS**). The membership card costs L43,000 and includes the ISIC international student identity card and the Italian *Carta Giovani*. This card offers discounts at theaters, bookstores, and other businesses in Naples. CTS will also help with car rentals and courses for its members. Students can purchase the ISIC card or the *Carta Giovani* separately for L15,000 each. The ISIC card offers a 24-hour telephone helpline providing general advice and information.

The **Associazione Italiana Alberghi per la Gioventù** (Youth hosteling association) operates hostels for members of the YHA (Youth Hostel Association). If you are not already a member, the card can be purchased directly from the hostel for L25,000. There is one youth hostel in Naples, the Ostello Mergellina, which is conveniently located and open all year round. For information on hostels outside Naples, inquire at the youth hostel association office.

ENTERTAINMENT

THE MONTHLY magazine called *Qui Napoli*, published by the **Azienda Autonoma di Soggiorno, Cura e Turismo** and available from most hotels and information offices, is a free guide to events in and around Naples. It lists opening hours for monuments and museums, and each issue has an updated *Agenda* in both Italian and English with information on exhibitions, theater, concerts, and conferences. More detailed information on lectures, seminars, sports, and entertainment can be found in the national magazines or in the relevant supplements of the daily newspapers.

Luglio / July 1996

Qui Napoli

Mensile per il turista · A monthly magazine for tourists

Regione Campania - Azienda autonoma di soggiorno cura e turismo

Qui Napoli, a free tourist monthly for Naples and Campania

◁ **Bird's-eye view of busy Piazza Municipio**

Modern Neapolitan skyscrapers, a striking contrast with the old city

MUSEUMS AND MONUMENTS

SOME STREETS and squares in the old center of Naples have information display panels with a map of the area showing the position of museums, monuments, and churches. Museums are usually open in the morning and closed on Mondays. Admission is free for under 18s or those over 60.

Churches are usually free, although there may be a charge for certain areas like cloisters. Visits to underground Naples are organized by **L.A.E.S.** and **Napoli Sotterranea** on Thursdays at 9pm, Saturdays at 10am and noon, and Sundays from 10am to noon. Archaeological sites are open every day from the morning to one hour before sunset.

Display panel with local map and tourist information

IMMIGRATION AND CUSTOMS

EUROPEAN UNION (EU) residents and visitors from the United States, Canada, Australia, New Zealand, and Japan do not need a visa for visits of up to three months but must have one for a longer stay.

US citizens can bring in 200 cigarettes or 100 cigars or 250 grams of tobacco, 2 liters of alcohol, 2 liters of wine, 50 cc of perfume, and 500 grams of coffee. US tourists may also claim an IVA rebate provided their purchases total more than L300,000. Please remember to have the receipt stamped by Italian customs before leaving Europe. If you need help, call the appropriate consulate or EPT office.

Street clock with the city arms

ITALIAN TIME

ITALY IS SIX HOURS ahead of Eastern Standard Time (EST). The clocks are put forward one hour in March and back one hour in September (like Daylight Savings Time). From Italy New York and Ottawa are -6 hours; London is -1 hour; Tokyo is +8 hours; and Sydney is +10 hours.

ELECTRIC ADAPTORS

ELECTRIC CURRENT is 220 volts, with two-pin or three-pin round-pronged plugs.

Security and Public Services

WHILE THE COUNTRYSIDE around Naples does not pose particular problems, petty crime is quite widespread in Naples itself. By taking a few simple precautions you will be able to protect yourself from pickpockets and purse snatchers: don't wear valuable jewelry or watches; handbags are easy targets, so hold onto them tightly and carry your money in your pockets. If possible, keep cameras and video cameras hidden from sight. It's best to be wary in Naples, but don't let apprehension ruin your trip.

Logo of the bank of Naples

LOOKING AFTER YOUR PROPERTY

IT'S BEST NOT to carry large sums of money on you while walking around town – leave it in your hotel safe. Always make photocopies of your vital documents like passports, or at least make a note of the number. Report any loss or theft to the police; lost or stolen traveler's checks and credit cards should also be reported immediately to the issuing bank. If you are traveling by car, always park in supervised parking lots, and do not leave items visible inside the vehicle. In crowded public areas or on public transportation, watch out for pickpockets; they are very agile. Purse snatchers on mopeds prefer to take jewels and handbags from strolling pedestrians. The train station is best avoided at night, and it is not advisable for single women to go around alone after dark.

A team of policemen

the water is polluted. Tap water is drinkable in Naples, but many Italians generally prefer to drink bottled mineral water. Neapolitan cuisine includes many seafood dishes,

so be careful not to eat closed shellfish and avoid raw seafood.

If you should need urgent medical assistance, call the **Pronto Soccorso** (emergency room) or the **Guardia Medica** at night and on weekends. All pharmacies will have a list of branches open at night and on public holidays *(farmacia di turno)* posted on their door. The **Farmacia Almasalus** in Piazza Dante, in the center of Naples, is open 24 hours a day.

CREDIT CARDS

MAJOR CREDIT CARDS – Visa, Access/MasterCard, American Express, and Diners Card – are accepted by larger businesses and restaurants. Smaller trattorias may only accept cash. Traveler's checks are the safest way to carry large sums of money..

Italian pharmacy sign

HEALTH

IN THE SUMMER, if you go to the seaside, watch out for the no swimming signs *(divieto di balneazione)* on the beaches. This means that

CURRENCY

You can exchange currency at an automatic cash dispenser at certain bank branches in Naples, such as at the airport, but it's best to have Italian money with you when you arrive. Italy's currency is the *lira* (plural *lire*). Bills are issued in denominations of L1,000, L2,000, L5,000, L10,000, L50,000, and L100,000. The small denomination bills come in handy in bars and small shops. If you prefer traveler's checks, choose a well-known name or checks issues through a major bank. There is a minimum charge on each transaction, so changing small sums is not economical. Banks offer better exchange rates than hotels. Foreign exchange offices have the same opening hours as stores – useful to know when banks are closed.

Italian notes: L100,000, L50,000, L10,000, L5,000, L2,000, and L1,000

BANKING HOURS

BANKS ARE OPEN from Monday to Friday. Opening hours vary but generally run from 8:30am to 1:20pm and 2:45pm to 3:45pm. Lines may be very long, and identification is required for any transaction. Cash cards for US bank accounts may be used at Bancomats (ATMs) displaying the appropriate system logos.

Banco di Napoli
Via Toledo 177–178.
(791 11 11.
Banca di Roma
Via Toledo 352/a.
(785 41 11.
Cariplo
Via Nuova Marina 20.
(550 71 11.

An Italian mail box

POSTAL SERVICES

POST OFFICES in Naples are open Monday to Saturday from 8:30am to 1:20pm (noon on the last day of the month). The central post office in Piazza Matteotti is open from 8:15am to 7:20pm (8:15am–2pm on Sundays). Branch post offices are situated all over the city, in the train stations, and at Capodichino airport. The Italian postal service is by no means a model of efficiency, so for urgent communications, whether you are sending letters or packages, it is advisable to use the *Posta celere* express service. This is a fast and reliable service for a fee. Stamps can be bought at the tobacconist *(tabaccaio)* as well as in the post office itself. The zip code for Naples is 80100.

Posta Centrale
Piazza Matteotti.
Operator (551 19 47.
Information (551 14 56.

Automatic cash machine

PUBLIC TELEPHONES

Public telephones in the street or in bars accept coins, telephone cards (which can be bought from a *tabaccaio* or a bar), and, at times, credit cards. Some bars have a *telefono a scatti*, or metered phone. The phone call is paid for at the end. Offices run by Telecom Italia (the state telephone company) also use this system; you can also place reverse charge and credit card calls here.

For international directory inquiries, dial 176. For international operator assistance, dial 170. General information is given on 1400. With Country-direct service you can call an operator in another country, who will connect you to the number you want: dial 172, followed by the country code (codes are listed in the Telecom directory). With credit card phones you can have your calls charged to your home phone bill; dial 187 for this service. The area code for Naples is 081. Note that hotel phones can be expensive.

A telephone card phone

Telecom Italia Office
Via Depretis 4. ⬤ 9:30am–1pm, 2–5:30pm daily. (551 09 21.

TRAVEL INFORMATION

IN THE WAKE of a campaign to improve transportation in Naples, plans are being made to restructure and develop existing flight, rail, and ferry links. The airport, Capodichino, is close to the city and is used for domestic, European, and charter flights, with the nearest international airport in Rome to the north. The fastest means of reaching Naples by land is to travel by

An Alitalia airplane

train, since there are no direct long-distance bus connections with European cities, and cars are far from ideal because of parking and traffic problems in town. Naples also has a large maritime passenger terminal with ferry connections to the islands in the Bay of Naples. Buses, funiculars, and two subway lines link all the main sites in the city of Naples itself.

The elegant Campi Flegrei train station

ARRIVING BY AIR

If you are flying from the US, TWA, **Continental, Delta,** and **American** operate direct scheduled flights to Rome and Milan, with connecting flights via **Alitalia** to Naples. Alitalia also runs regular services between many Italian cities, so passengers can easily transfer from major European cities to domestic flights. It may be a better bargain and more convenient for passengers to take a budget flight to London, Frankfurt, Paris, Rome, or Amsterdam, and then continue their trip to Naples by plane, train, rental car, or bus.

Capodichino airport bus service

The **C.L.P.** company offers direct bus connections from the airport to the center of town (Piazza Municipio, on the corner of Via Medina); departures are hourly from 6:30am to 11:30pm (from the airport) and from 7am to midnight (from Piazza Municipio); tickets cost L3,000 and can be bought on board.

If you go by taxi, go to the official taxi stand and be sure that the meter is on. The trip lasts about 20 minutes; the fare should be around L40,000.

Package tours are often less expensive than independent travel. Most operators will arrange your domestic travel and accomodations, plus any special tours you may wish..

Many travel agents and car-rental firms will organize fly-drive packages that allow you to book a flight and have a rental car waiting for you at your destination. It is usually less expensive and involves fewer formalities than renting a car on arrival..

ARRIVING BY TRAIN

THERE ARE THREE MAIN train stations in Naples – **Napoli Centrale** (Piazza Garibaldi), **Mergellina** (on the water), and **Campi Flegrei** (at Fuorigrotta).

The main station in Piazza Garibaldi is also the main interchange for the city's transit systems. Access to the subway (*metropolitana*) and the Circumvesuviana line (for trains to Pompei-Villa dei Misteri and the coast) is from inside the station. In the square in front you will find the main terminal for the city and suburban buses as well as buses for destinations in Southern Italy.

A plan for the development of high-speed trains called **TAV** (*Treni ad Alta Velocità*) is now under way; it will connect all the major stations. In the meantime, the fastest and most convenient way of traveling by train is the Intercity line (IC), for which you pay a supplement. There is a train every hour on the Naples-Rome line. For trips of less than 200 km (120

The Mergellina train station

The passenger terminal in the Naples seaport

miles) you can purchase a discount ticket *(biglietto a fasce chilometriche)* at newsstands in all stations.

Toll booths on the highway

ARRIVING BY CAR

SHOULD YOU decide to travel into Naples by car, be prepared for highly stressful driving, heavy traffic, and parking problems. A car may be convenient for visiting other sites in the region, but in Naples itself it is advisable to use the public transportation system or walk.

The **Automobile Club d'Italia** (ACI) provides maps and a towing-and-repair service to its members as well as to members of affiliated foreign associations. Tolls are charged on the *autostrada* (highway) and can be paid in cash or with a Viacard magnetic card, available at a

tabaccaio (tobacconist's) or an ACI agency. Emergency telephones are located at intervals along the highway.

Autostrada A2 exits into the Naples bypass road *(tangenziale)*, which takes you quickly to the center or the outskirts. For the coastal resorts, follow signs for Autostrada A3, going toward Salerno. The state road 163 runs the length of the beautiful Amalfi coastline.

ARRIVING BY BOAT

THE MAIN MARITIME passenger terminal (Stazione Marittima), used by large and medium-sized ships, is the **Molo Angioino**, opposite Piazza Municipio. Ferries and hydrofoils for connections to the islands in the bay and the Sorrento peninsula depart from the nearby **Molo Beverello** and **Mergellina** *(see p119)* passenger terminals.

The **Tirrenia** ship line offers direct connections between Naples and Sardinia, Sicily, and Tunisia. The **Linee Lauro** company sails twice-weekly to Sardinia, and **Siremar** operates the route from Naples to the Aeolian Islands. **Aliscafi SNAV** runs a high-speed hydrofoil service for the Aeolian islands, Ponza, and Ventotene. This route is operated only in the summer.

A SNAV express hydrofoil to the Aeolian Islands and Ponza

Getting Around Naples

THE CITY TRANSPORTATION system is being improved and expanded in stages, but it is still unreliable and often rather slow. In fact, it will usually take you less time to travel around the central districts on foot rather than on a bus or tram With the exception of the subway system *(metropolitana)*, public transportation is recommended only for longer distances. In the main squares in the city center there are display panels with a map of Naples that indicate the main bus, tram, and metro (subway) stops.

The funicular

transportation. Buses and trams are generally crowded and have their share of pickpockets, so be aler, and keep valuables tucked away. Recently, three new bus lines (R1, R2, R3) were created to improve the general standards of service; they depart every 5 or 10 minutes from 6am to 10pm. There are also **ANM** night buses.

Via G Marino 1.
Information ☎ 763 11 11.

A Naples city (ANM) bus

SUBWAY SYSTEM

NAPLES HAS TWO subway lines *(metropolitana)*: one is part of the Ferrovie dello Stato (FS, or state railroad), and the other is the hill metro *(collinare)*. The FS uses regular train routes and is often subject to delays. It runs from 5:30am to 10:20pm, with departures every 8 minutes. It goes through the main areas in Naples. The hill metro links Vomero with the hospital and the Chiaiano and Secondigliano quarters. It runs from 6:40am to 10:54pm, with departures every 12 minutes.

FUNICULARS

THERE ARE FOUR funicular routes. Three are run by the Azienda Napoletana Mobilità (ANM), the city's transportation system. These and Funicolare Centrale,

Funicolare di Montesanto, and Funicolare di Chiaia. They connect the center of the city with the Vomero district, where the museum of San Martino and the museum of Duca di Martina are located.. The Mergellina funicular, run by a separate company, connects the waterfront area (Via Mergellina) with Via Manzoni. The funiculars are reliable and fast and run from 7am to 10pm, with departures every 10 minutes.

BUSES AND TRAMS

BUS AND TRAM networks are run by the ANM. You need patience to travel by bus in Naples; even short trips take time because of the heavy and famously chaotic traffic, a situation aggravated by the fact that Neapolitan drivers often use lanes reserved for public

TICKETS AND MONTHLY PASSES

THE "GIRANAPOLI" system of tickets operates in Naples for all local buses, trams, funiculars, the hill metro, and the FS metro. A Giranapoli ticket that costs L1,200 is valid for 90 minutes.

Giranapoli tickets

A ticket costing L4,000 can be used all day. On the metros and funiculars a single ticket is valid for only one trip.

THE STATE (FS) SUBWAY SYSTEM (METROPOLITANA)

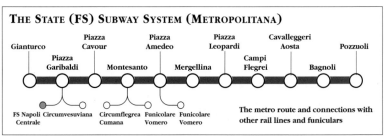

Gianturco — Piazza Garibaldi — Piazza Cavour — Montesanto — Piazza Amedeo — Mergellina — Piazza Leopardi — Campi Flegrei — Cavalleggeri Aosta — Bagnoli — Pozzuoli

FS Napoli Centrale · Circumvesuviana · Circumflegrea Cumana · Funicolare Vomero · Funicolare Vomero

The metro route and connections with other rail lines and funiculars

A taxi stand

Giranapoli tickets are sold in the stations, at newsstands and tobacco shops. You must validate each ticket before departure by stamping it in a machine. If you are in Naples for several weeks, it is worth buying the monthly Giranapoli pass, which costs L35,000.

TAXIS

IF YOU TAKE A TAXI, make sure it is one from an official taxi stand. The meter should read L4,000 at the beginning of the ride, which is the local tax. The fare is double for rides from the airport to town and for out-of-town trips. There is an additional charge of L2,000 on weekends and on public holidays; an extra L3,000 from 10pm to 7am; and L500 for each item of luggage.

The Neapolitan taxi logo

You can easily find taxis in the official stands outside the train and metro stations and in the main squares of Naples. You can also reserve a taxi by telephone, but a supplement of L1,500 is charged for this service.
Cotana
[570 70 70.
Napoli
[556 44 44.
Partenope
[556 02 02.

WALKING

THE PEDESTRIAN ZONES are a recent, much-needed development in a city with immense traffic problems. You can now walk along streets in the historic center and admire the monuments in relative peace and quiet. To shop away from traffic, go to the pedestrian-only Via Chiaia or Via Scarlatti (in Vomero). Every Sunday part of Via Partenope is closed to traffic, enabling you to admire Vesuvius and Castel dell'Ovo. However, be careful crossing the street elsewhere: drivers often ignore traffic lights and people waiting at crosswalks, and fast-moving scooters appear from nowhere. Fortunately, Neapolitans have quick reflexes and usually manage to avoid accidents.

Traffic policeman

DIRECTORY

PARKING

Parcheggio di Interscambio
Via B Brin.
[763 28 32.

Grilli
Via G Ferraris 40.
[26 43 44.

Mergellina
Via Mergellina 112.
[761 34 70.

Santa Chiara
Pallonetto Santa Chiara 30.
[551 63 03.

Supergarage
Via Shelley 11.
[551 31 04.

Turistico
Via A De Gasperi 14.
[552 54 42.

PARKING

IT IS BOTH DIFFICULT and dangerous to park your car in Naples. Double parking is a common practice, and you may very well find your car hemmed in by other vehicles. Out-of-town license plates may also attract the attention of thieves. Park only in authorized and, if possible, supervised parking areas, such as those near the Centrale and Mergellina train stations and in the port area.

SCOOTER AND MOPED RENTAL

The brave may find that mopeds and scooters are the best method of negotiating the heavy Naples traffic. At least you can easily find parking space.
You can find these at some car-rental agencies:
Italrent
Via Comunale Tavernola 166–7.
[763 11 11.
Capodichino Airport.
[599 13 16.

Motorcycle rental: **Bernini**
Via Torrione San Martino 29.
[556 71 12.

A scooter, the most practical way of getting around Naples

Traveling Outside Naples

SEPSA buses
logo

EVEN IF YOU ARE BASED IN NAPLES it is not difficult to visit ancient sites such as the Phlegraean Fields, the archaeological sites at Pompeii and Herculaneum, the towns on the Amalfi coast (Amalfi, Positano, and Ravello), and the enchanting islands of Capri, Ischia, and Procida. Most places are accessible by local train or bus, and excursions are available from larger hotels and local travel agents.

Interior of the Centrale station

A Circumvesuviana train

LOCAL TRAINS

THE CIRCUMVESUVIANA train service connects Naples with the towns around Mount Vesuvius (including ancient Pompeii) and those on the Sorrento peninsula. The main terminal is in Corso Garibaldi, with the next stop in Piazza Garibaldi (at underground level), where moving walkways connect the metro station to the **Circumvesuviana**. There are four routes: Naples-Sorrento, Naples-Pompei-Poggiomarino, Naples-Ottaviano-Sarno, and Naples-Nola-Baiano. In addition there are three types of trains: the *accelerato* (ACC), which stops at all stations, the *diretto* (DIR), stopping

only at the main ones, and the *direttissimo* (DD), stopping at even fewer. Services run from 4am to midnight, with trains departing roughly every 20 minutes. You may want to avoid traveling late at night, though, because trains are infrequent, and there are fewer people around. From March 1 to November 1 there is a seasonal service run by the Funivia di Monte Faito cableway, starting from Castellammare di Stabia station. To reach the towns on the Phlegraean Fields and the coast you can take the **Ferrovia Cumana**, and the **Ferrovia Circumflegrea** serves the towns in the interior. The main station is in Piazza Montesanto; the service is fast and efficient. The Cumana service has departures every 10 minutes for Bagnoli and every 20 for Pozzuoli and runs from 5:21am to 9:41pm. The main stops on the Circumflegrea

line are Montesanto, Soccavo, Quarto, Licola, and Torregaveta; departures are every 20 minutes until 9:43pm. Six trains per day stop at Cuma, Lido Fusaro, and Torregaveta.

HYDROFOILS AND FERRIES

VARIOUS SHIPPING LINES offer frequent crossings from Naples to the islands in the bay. The Sorrento peninsula and some Amalfi coast towns can also be reached by boat. Ferries and hydrofoils depart from the Molo Beverello in Piazza Municipio, near the Stazione Marittima, and from Mergellina (hydrofoils only). From the port of Pozzuoli the crossing to Procida and Ischia is shorter and cheaper; you can also take your car on board, but check on available space beforehand. The **Caremar** line operates a ferry to Procida, Ischia, and Capri that departs from the Molo Beverello and from Pozzuoli. **Linee Lauro** serves the Naples-Ischia route with ferries and hydrofoils departing from the Molo Beverello; Sorrento and Capri are served by hydrofoil from the port of Mergellina.

SNAV logo

A hydrofoil in the Bay of Naples

Bus for the Amalfi coast

Mergellina is also the departure point for the **SNAV** line's hydrofoils for Procida, Ischia (Casamicciola), and Capri. **Alilauro** offers a hydrofoil service to Ischia, Sorrento, and Capri from the Molo Beverello and to Ischia, Capri, and the Amalfi coast (Amalfi, Positano, and Salerno) from Mergellina. Hydrofoils run by **Navigazione Libera del Golfo** go to all the islands from Mergellina and to Capri, Amalfi, and Positano from the Molo Beverello.

towns in the Phlegrean Fields area (Baia and Bacoli). The blue SITA buses go to various towns and resorts on the Sorrento peninsula, the tourist sights on the Amalfi coast (Amalfi, Maiori, Minori, Positano, Ravello, and so on), and Salerno. The **SITA** terminal is located at Nos. 3–7 Via Pisanelli (near Piazza Municipio). Departures are every half an hour on weekdays and Saturdays and every two hours on Sundays and public holidays.

Three of the main car rental firms

CAR HIRE

IN ITALY CAR HIRE is quite expensive, and driving in Naples is highly stressful. If you are determined to drive, it is best to pre-book through an international agency or organize a fly-drive deal and use the vehicle only for visiting the tourist attractions outside the city. To rent a car you must be over 21 and have held a valid driver's licence for at least a year. Agencies are listed in the Yellow Pages *(Pagine Gialle)* under Autonoleggio.

TRAVELING BY BUS

YOU CAN ALSO reach towns and resorts in the region by bus. Local companies depart from the terminal in Piazza Garibaldi or from the airport at Capodichino. The bus company **ACTP** serves the towns in the Vesuvius area and Caserta, with departures every 20 minutes on weekdays and every 40 minutes on Sundays and public holidays. The **SEPSA** bus company covers the

---

CIRCUMVESUVIANA

Napoli — Torre Annunziata — Castellammare — Sorrento

Torre del Greco — Pompei — Meta

The main stations on the Circumvesuviana line

NAPLES STREET FINDER

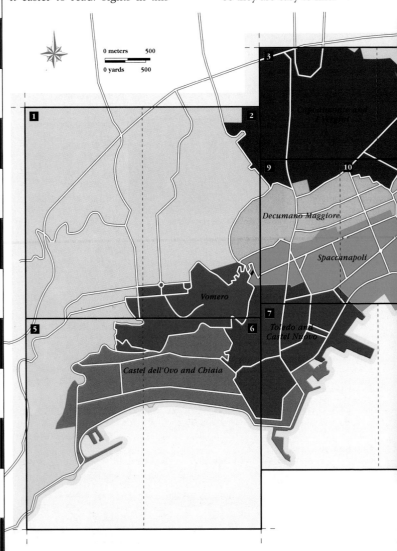

THE PAGE GRID superimposed on the *Area by Area* map below shows which parts of Naples are covered by this Street Finder. The map references given for the restaurants, hotels, and sights in Naples refer to the maps in this section. Central Naples has been enlarged on map pages 9 and 10 to make it easier to read. Sights in this area will give both map references. A complete index of the street names and major sights in the city follows on pages 214–17. The key on the opposite page shows the scales of the maps and explains the symbols. 'All the main sights in the city are clearly indicated in pink so they are easy to find.

0 meters   500

0 yards   500

Capodimonte and I Vergini

Decumano Maggiore

Spaccanapoli

Vomero

Toledo and Castel Nuovo

Castel dell'Ovo and Chiaia

How to Use the Maps

The first number corresponds to the Street Finder map.

Gesù Nuovo ❸

Piazza del Gesù Nuovo. **Map** 3 B5 (9 B4).
📞 *44 05 11.* ⬤ *6:30am–12:45pm
(1:30pm Sun), 4:15–7:30pm daily.*

The letters and numbers form the map coordinates. Letters are along the top, numbers are along the sides.

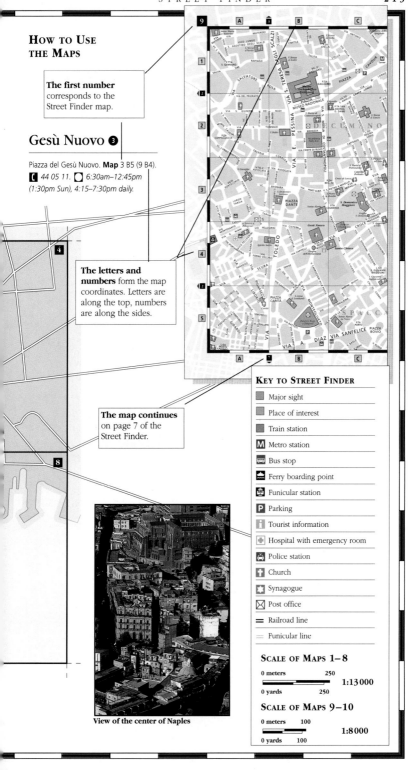

The map continues on page 7 of the Street Finder.

KEY TO STREET FINDER

🟧	Major sight
🟫	Place of interest
🟦	Train station
M	Metro station
🚌	Bus stop
⛴	Ferry boarding point
🚠	Funicular station
P	Parking
i	Tourist information
➕	Hospital with emergency room
🚓	Police station
✝	Church
✡	Synagogue
⊠	Post office
=	Railroad line
=	Funicular line

SCALE OF MAPS 1–8

0 meters   250
0 yards   250   1:13 000

SCALE OF MAPS 9–10

0 meters   100
0 yards   100   1:8 000

View of the center of Naples

Street Finder Index

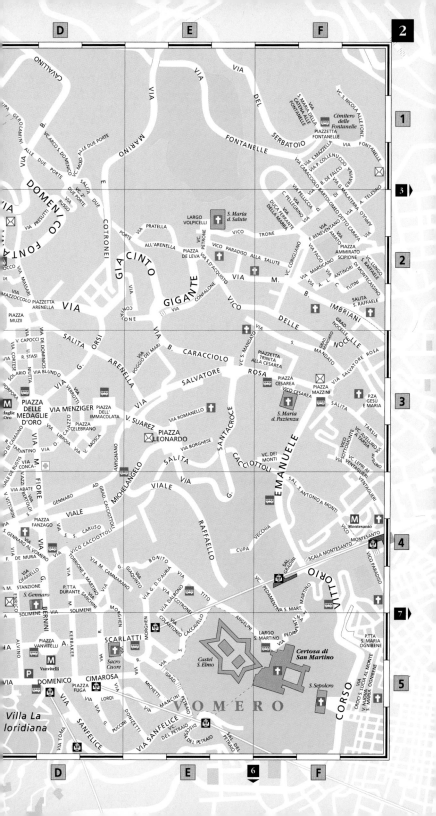

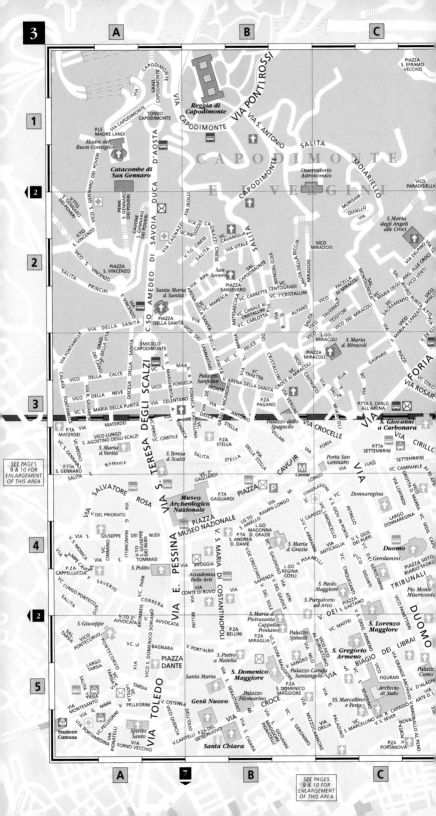

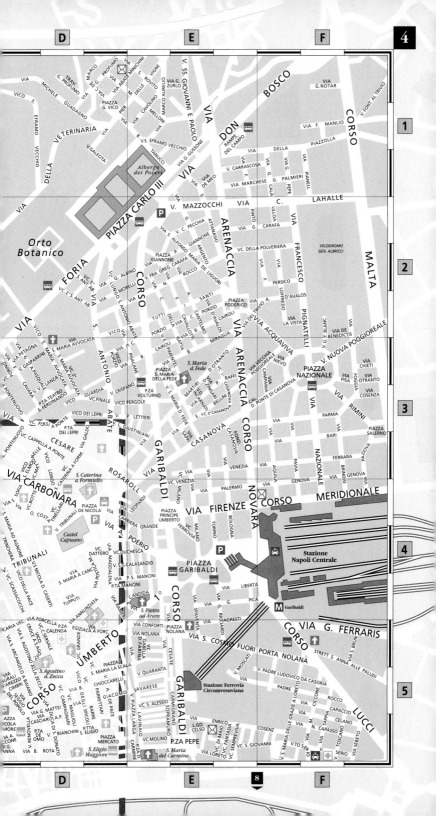

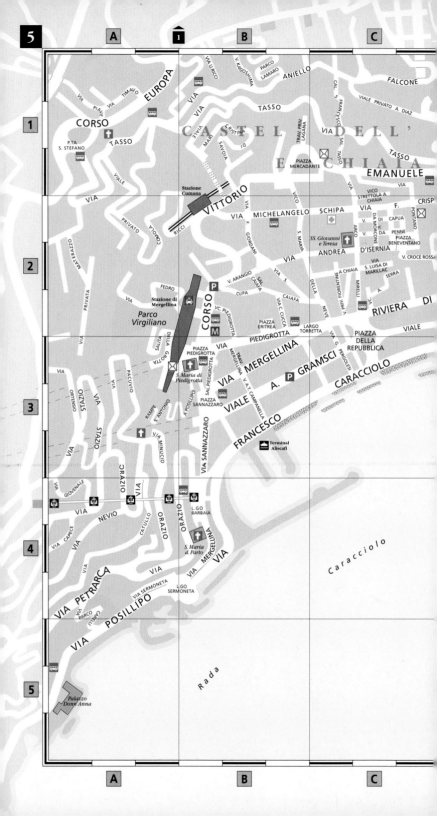

SEE PAGES
9 & 10 FOR
ENLARGEMENT
OF THIS AREA

SEE PAGES
9 & 10 FOR
ENLARGEMENT
OF THIS AREA

A   B   C

1
2
3
4
5

A   B   C

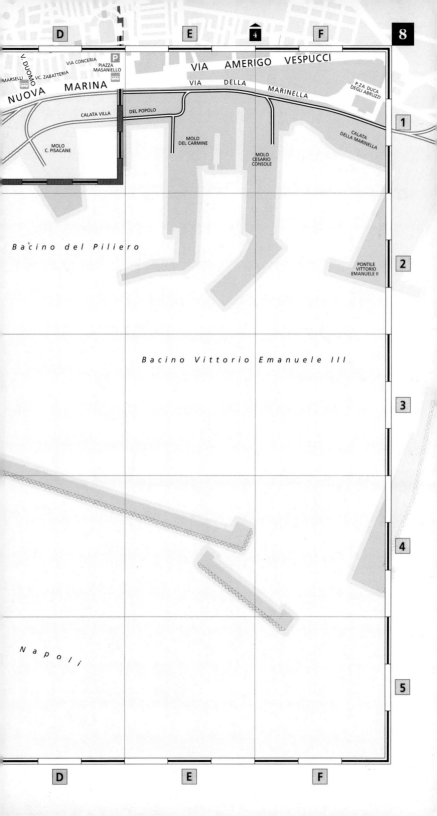

D   E   4   F

V. DUOMO

MARSELLI

VIA CONCERIA

VC. ZABATTERIA

PIAZZA
MASANIELLO

NUOVA   MARINA

CALATA VILLA

DEL POPOLO

VIA   AMERIGO   VESPUCCI

VIA   DELLA   MARINELLA

P.ZA. DUCA
DEGLI ABRUZZI

MOLO
C. PISACANE

MOLO
DEL CARMINE

MOLO
CESARIO
CONSOLE

CALATA
DELLA MARINELLA

1

Bacino del Piliero

PONTILE
VITTORIO
EMANUELE II

2

Bacino Vittorio Emanuele III

3

4

Napoli

5

D   E   F

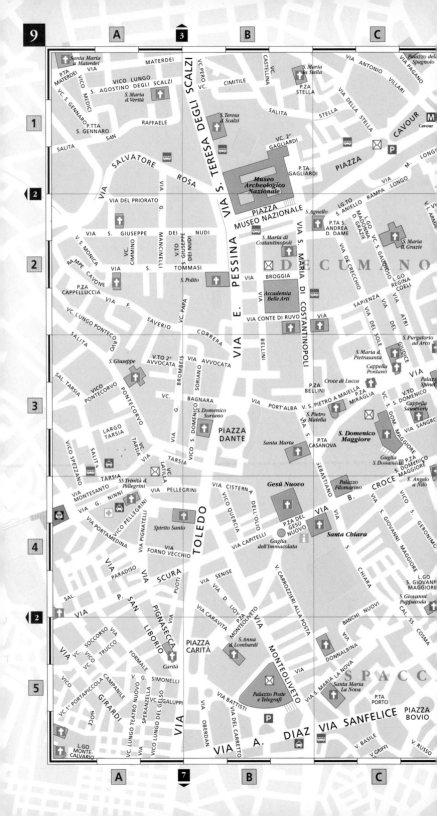

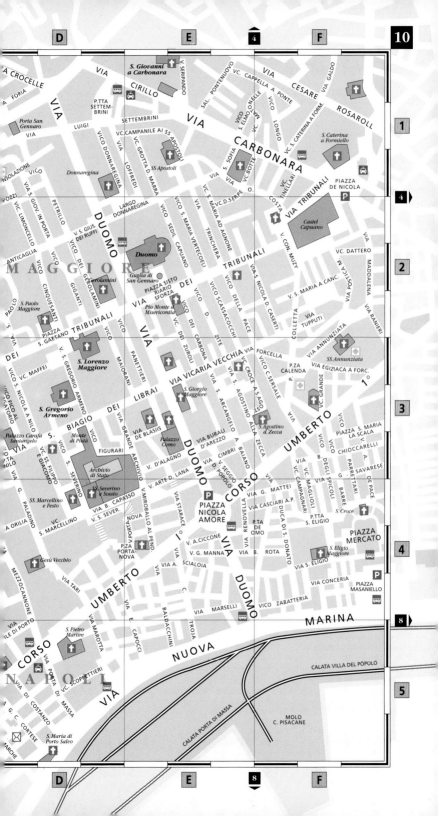

General Index

Acknowledgments

DORLING KINDERSLEY WOULD LIKE to thank the
following people whose contributions and
assistance have made the preparation of
this book possible: Guido Bevilacqua, Luigi
Consiglio, Diana Georgiacodis, Costantino
Pantano, Adriana Sandrini Maione. Dorling
Kindersley would also like to thank all the
museums and tourist information offices,
too numerous to mention individually, for
their assistance and kind permission to
photograph at their establishments.

EDITORIAL ASSISTANCE
Riccardo Baldini, Felicity Laughton, Ferdie
McDonald, Giorgio Padovani, Iris Rosoff.

PICTURE CREDITS
Key: t = top; tl = top left; tlc = top left
center; tc = top center; trc = top right
center; tr = top right; cla = center left
above; ca = center above; cra = center right
above; cl = center left; c = center; cr =
center right; clb = center left below; crb =
center right below; cb = center below; bl =
bottom left; br = bottom right; b = bottom;
bc = bottom center; bcl = bottom center
left; bcr = bottom center right.

Every effort has been made to trace the
copyright holders. The publisher
apologizes for any unintentional omissions
and would be pleased, in such cases, to
add an acknowledgment in future editions.

All the photographs reproduced in this
book are from the Overseas S.r.l. Milano
picture library except for the following:

ASSOCIAZIONE CULTURALE ARCHIVIO PARISIO,
NAPLES: 22br, 24c, 24bl, 25tl, 26bc, 42tr,
55cl, 85cl, 125c, 127c, 130c, 139cr.

GIUSEPPE AVALLONE, NAPLES: 1, 19cr, 21cr,
27cr, 29bl, 31tl, 33tl, 34tl, 34tr, 35tr, 37tr,
37cl, 38cl, 38br, 41tl, 41br, 55cr, 60, 62bc,
63tl, 65tc, 76tr, 77bc, 89bl, 92br, 102, 120,
124, 130bc, 130cl, 131br, 136cl, 140cl,
150tl, 152tr, 153tr, 153bl, 155tr, 155b,
163tl, 165b, 166b, 191cl, 192c, 196c,
196tc, 196cl, 198c.

FORNASS s.a.s., Portici (Napoli) 83cr, 192tl,
196br.

IMAGE BANK, MILAN: 2–3, 10–11, 28–29, 30tr,
30cl, 38tr, 38tl, 39cl, 40cr, 42br, 44–45,
105cl, 107tl, 112, 115c, 117b, 126–127,
131tl, 132bc, 132cl, 133ca, 139bl, 142tr,
145tl, 149br, 150tr, 151tr, 151cl, 154tr, 154br,
156cl, 159cl, 159tr, 160tl, 162tl, 163bl,
163br, 164cl, 164bl, 165tl, 165cr, 200.

MIMMO JODICE, NAPLES: 40tc, 68bc, 80tc, 96bc.

LUCIANO PEDICINI, NAPLES: 19tc, 68c, 69tl, 71c,
81cl, 84c, 84bl, 97bl, 147br, 156tr, 157cl,
157tr, 157tc, 160bl, 161cr, 203tr.

Phrase Book

IN EMERGENCY

Help!	**Aiuto!**	*eye-yoo-toh*
Stop!	**Fermate!**	*fair-mah-teh*
Call a	**Chiama un**	*kee-ah-mah oon*
doctor.	**medico.**	*meh-dee-koh*
Call an	**Chiama un'**	*kee-ah-mah oon*
ambulance.	**ambulanza.**	*am-boo-lan-tsa*
Call the	**Chiama la**	*kee-ah-mah lah*
police.	**polizia.**	*pol-ee-tsee-ah*
Call the fire	**Chiama i**	*kee-ah-mah ee*
department.	**pompieri.**	*pom-pee-air-ee*
Where is the	**Dov'è il telefono?**	*dov-eh eel teh-leh-*
telephone?		*foh-noh?*
The nearest	**L'ospedale**	*loss-peh-dah-leh pee-*
hospital?	**più vicino?**	*oo vee-chee-noh?*

COMMUNICATION ESSENTIALS

Yes/No	**Si/No**	*see/noh*
Please	**Per favore**	*pair fah-vor-eh*
Thank you	**Grazie**	*grah-tsee-eh*
Excuse me	**Mi scusi**	*mee skoo-zee*
Hello	**Buon giorno**	*bwon jor-noh*
Goodbye	**Arrivederci**	*ah-ree-veh-dair-chee*
Good evening	**Buona sera**	*bwon-ah sair-ah*
morning	**la mattina**	*lah mah-tee-nah*
afternoon	**il pomeriggio**	*eel poh-meh-ree-joh*
evening	**la sera**	*lah sair-ah*
yesterday	**ieri**	*ee-air-ee*
today	**oggi**	*oh-jee*
tomorrow	**domani**	*doh-mah-nee*
here	**qui**	*kwee*
there	**la**	*lah*
What?	**Quale?**	*kwah-leh?*
When?	**Quando?**	*kwan-doh?*
Why?	**Perchè?**	*pair-keh?*
Where?	**Dove?**	*doh-veh?*

USEFUL PHRASES

How are you?	**Come sta?**	*koh-meh stah?*
Very well,	**Molto bene,**	*moll-toh beh-neh*
thank you.	**grazie.**	*grah-tsee-eh*
Pleased to	**Piacere di**	*pee-ah-chair-eh dee*
meet you.	**conoscerla.**	*coh-noh-shair-lah*
See you later.	**A più tardi.**	*ah pee-oo tar-dee*
That's fine.	**Va bene.**	*va beh-neh*
Where is/are ...?	**Dov'è/Dove sono ...?**	*dov-eh/doveh soh-noh?*
How long does	**Quanto tempo ci**	*kwan-toh tem-poh*
it take to get to ...?	**vuole per**	*chee voo-oh-leh pair*
	andare a ...?	*an-dar-eh ah ...?*
How do I	**Come faccio per**	*koh-meh fah-choh*
get to ...?	**arrivare a ...?**	*pair arri-var-eh ah..?*
Do you speak	**Parla inglese?**	*par-lah een-gleh-zeh?*
English?		
I don't	**Non capisco.**	*non ka-pee-skoh*
understand.		
Could you speak	**Può parlare**	*pwoh par-lah-reh*
more slowly,	**più lentamente,**	*pee-oo len-ta-men-teh*
please?	**per favore?**	*pair fah-vor-eh?*
I'm sorry.	**Mi dispiace.**	*mee dee-spee-ah-cheh*

USEFUL WORDS

big	**grande**	*gran-deh*
small	**piccolo**	*pee-koh-loh*
hot	**caldo**	*kal-doh*
cold	**freddo**	*fred-doh*
good	**buono**	*bwoh-noh*
bad	**cattivo**	*kat-tee-voh*
enough	**basta**	*bas-tah*
well	**bene**	*beh-neh*
open	**aperto**	*ah-pair-toh*
closed	**chiuso**	*kee-oo-zoh*
left	**a sinistra**	*ah see-nee-strah*
right	**a destra**	*ah dess-trah*
straight on	**sempre dritto**	*sem-preh dree-toh*
near	**vicino**	*vee-chee-noh*
far	**lontano**	*lon-tah-noh*
up	**su**	*soo*
down	**giù**	*joo*
early	**presto**	*press-toh*
late	**tardi**	*tar-dee*
entrance	**entrata**	*en-trah-tah*
exit	**uscita**	*oo-shee-ta*
toilet	**il gabinetto**	*eel gah-bee-net-toh*
free, unoccupied	**libero**	*lee-bair-oh*
free, no charge	**gratuito**	*grah-too-ee-toh*

MAKING A TELEPHONE CALL

I'd like to place a	**Vorrei fare**	*vor-ray far-eh oona*
long-distance call.	**una interurbana.**	*in-tair-oor-bah-nah*
I'd like to make	**Vorrei fare una**	*vor-ray far-eh oona*
a reverse-charge	**telefonata a carico**	*teh-leh-fon-ah-tah ah*
call.	**del destinatario.**	*kar-ee-koh dell dess-*
		tee-nah-tar-ree-oh
Could I speak to...	**Potrei parlare con...**	*po-tray par-lah-reh con*
I'll try again later.	**Ritelefono più**	*ree-teh-leh-foh-noh*
	tardi.	*pee-oo tar-dee*
May I leave a	**Posso lasciare**	*poss-oh lash-ah-reh*
message?	**un messaggio?**	*oon mess-sah-joh?*
Hold on.	**Un attimo,**	*oon ah-tee-moh,*
	per favore.	*pair fah-vor-eh*
Could you speak	**Può parlare più**	*pwoh par-lah-reh*
up a little, please?	**forte?**	*pee-oo for-teh?*
local call	**telefonata locale**	*te-leh-fon-ah-tah*
		loh-cah-leh

SHOPPING

How much	**Quant'è,**	*kwan-teh*
does this cost?	**per favore?**	*pair fah-vor-eh?*
I would like ...	**Vorrei ...**	*vor-ray...*
Do you have ...?	**Avete ...?**	*ah-veh-teh...?*
I'm just looking.	**Sto soltanto**	*stoh sol-tan-toh*
	guardando.	*gwar-dan-doh*
Do you take	**Accettate**	*ah-chet-tah-teh kar-teh*
credit cards?	**carte di credito?**	*dee creh-dee-toh?*
What time do	**A che ora apre/**	*ah keh or-ah*
you open/close?	**chiude?**	*ah-preh/kee-oo-deh?*
this one	**questo**	*kweh-stoh*
that one	**quello**	*kwell-oh*
expensive	**caro**	*kar-oh*
cheap	**a buon prezzo**	*ah bwon pret-soh*
size, clothes	**la taglia**	*lah tah-lee-ah*
size, shoes	**il numero**	*eel noo-mair-oh*
white	**bianco**	*bee-ang-koh*
black	**nero**	*neh-roh*
red	**rosso**	*ross-oh*
yellow	**giallo**	*jal-loh*
green	**verde**	*vair-deh*
blue	**blu**	*bloo*

TYPES OF SHOP

antique dealer	**l'antiquario**	*lan-tee-kwah-ree-oh*
bakery	**il forno/**	*eel forn-oh/*
	il panificio	*eel pan-ee-fee-choh*
bank	**la banca**	*lah bang-kah*
bookstore	**la libreria**	*lah lee-breh-ree-ah*
butcher	**la macelleria**	*lah mah-chell-eh-ree-ah*
cake shop	**la pasticceria**	*lah pas-tee-chair-ee-ah*
delicatessen	**la salumeria**	*lah sah-loo-meh-ree-ah*
department store	**il grande**	*eel gran-deh*
	magazzino	*mag-gad-zee-noh*
drugstore	**la farmacia**	*lah far-mah-chee-ah*
fishseller	**il pescivendolo**	*eel pesh-ee-ven-doh-loh*
florist	**il fioraio**	*eel fee-or-eye-oh*
greengrocer	**il fruttivendolo**	*eel froo-tee-ven-dob-loh*
grocery	**alimentari**	*ah-lee-men-tah-ree*
hairdresser	**il parrucchiere**	*eel par-oo-kee-air-eh*
ice cream parlor	**la gelateria**	*lah jel-lah-tair-ee-ah*
market	**il mercato**	*eel mair-kah-toh*
newsstand	**l'edicola**	*leh-dee-koh-lah*
post office	**l'ufficio postale**	*loo-fee-choh pos-tah-leh*
shoe shop	**il negozio di**	*eel neh-goh-tsioh dee*
	scarpe	*skar-peh*
supermarket	**il supermercato**	*eel su-pair-mair-kah-toh*
tobacconist	**il tabaccaio**	*eel tah-bak-eye-oh*
travel agency	**l'agenzia di viaggi**	*lah-jen-tsee-ah dee*
		vee-ad-jee

SIGHTSEEING

art gallery	**la pinacoteca**	*lah peena-koh-teh-kah*
bus stop	**la fermata**	*lah fair-mah-tah*
	dell'autobus	*dell ow-toh-booss*
church	**la chiesa/**	*lah kee-eh-zah/*
	la basilica	*lah bah-seel-i-kah*
closed for	**chiuso per le**	*kee-oo-zoh pair leh*
holidays	**ferie**	*fair-ee-eh*
garden	**il giardino**	*eel jar-dee-no*
library	**la biblioteca**	*lah beeb-lee-oh-teh-kah*
museum	**il museo**	*eel moo-zeh-oh*
train station	**la stazione**	*lah stat-tsee-oh-neh*
tourist	**l'ufficio**	*loo-fee-choh*
information	**di turismo**	*dee too-ree-smoh*

STAYING IN A HOTEL

Do you have any vacant rooms?	**Avete camere libere?**	*ah-veh-teh kah-mair-eh lee-bair-eh?*
double room	**una camera doppia**	*oona kab-mair-ah dob-pee-ah*
with double bed	**con letto matrimoniale**	*kon let-toh mah-tree-moh-nee-ab-leh*
twin room	**una camera con due letti**	*oona kab-mair-ah kon doo-eh let-tee*
single room	**una camera singola**	*oona kab-mair-ah sing-gob-lah*
room with a bath, shower	**una camera con bagno, con doccia**	*oona kab-mair-ah kon ban-yob, kon dot-chah*
porter	**il facchino**	*eel fab-kee-nob*
key	**la chiave**	*lah kee-ab-veh*
I have a reservation.	**Ho fatto una prenotazione.**	*ob fat-toh oona preh-nob-tah-tsee-ob-neh*

EATING OUT

Do you have a table for ...?	**Avete una tavola per ... ?**	*ah-veh-teh oona tah-vob-lah pair ...?*
I'd like to reserve a table.	**Vorrei riservare una tavola.**	*vor-ray ree-sair-vah-reh oona tab-vob-lah*
breakfast	**colazione**	*kob-lah-tsee-ob-neh*
lunch	**pranzo**	*pran-tsob*
dinner	**cena**	*cheb-nah*
The bill, please.	**Il conto, per favore.**	*eel kon-toh pair fah-vor-eh*
I am a vegetarian.	**Sono vegetariano/a.**	*soh-nob veb-jeb-tar-ee-ah-nob/nab*
waitress	**cameriera**	*kab-mair-ee-air-ah*
waiter	**cameriere**	*kab-mair-ee-air-eh*
fixed-price menu	**il menù a prezzo fisso**	*eel meb-noo ah pret-sob fee-sob*
dish of the day	**piatto del giorno**	*pee-ab-toh dell jor-no*
appetizer	**antipasto**	*an-tee-pass-tob*
first course	**il primo**	*eel pree-mob*
main course	**il secondo**	*eel seb-kon-dob*
vegetables	**il contorno**	*eel kon-tor-nob*
dessert	**il dolce**	*eel doll-cheh*
cover charge	**il coperto**	*eel kob-pair-tob*
wine list	**la lista dei vini**	*lah lee-stab day vee-nee*
rare	**al sangue**	*al sang-gweh*
medium	**al puntino**	*al poon-tee-nob*
well done	**ben cotto**	*ben kot-tob*
glass	**il bicchiere**	*eel beck-kee-air-eh*
bottle	**la bottiglia**	*lah bot-teel-yah*
knife	**il coltello**	*eel kol-tell-ob*
fork	**la forchetta**	*lah for-ket-tah*
spoon	**il cucchiaio**	*eel koo-kee-eye-ob*

MENU DECODER

l'acqua minerale gassata/naturale	*lab-kwab mee-nair-ab-leh gab-zab-tab/ nab-too-rah-leh*	mineral water fizzy/still
aceto	*ab-cheb-tob*	vinegar
aglio	*al-ee-ob*	garlic
l'agnello	*lab-niell-ob*	lamb
al forno	*al for-nob*	baked/roasted
alla griglia	*ab-lah greel-yah*	grilled
l'aragosta	*lah-rah-goss-tab*	lobster
arrosto	*ar-ross-tob*	roast
basilico	*bab-zee-lee-kob*	basil
la birra	*lah beer-rah*	beer
la bistecca	*lah bee-stek-kab*	steak
il brodo	*eel brob-dob*	broth
il burro	*eel boor-ob*	butter
il caffè	*eel kab-feb*	coffee
i calamari	*ee kab-lah-mab-ree*	squid
i carciofi	*ee kar-choff-ee*	artichokes
la carne	*la kar-neb*	meat
la cipolla	*la chip-ob-lab*	onion
i contorni	*ee kon-tor-nee*	vegetables
le cozze	*leb cob-tzeb*	mussels
i fagioli	*ee fab-job-lee*	beans
il fegato	*eel fay-gab-tob*	liver
il finocchio	*eel fee-nok-ee-ob*	fennel
il formaggio	*eel for-mad-job*	cheese
le fragole	*leb frab-gob-leb*	strawberries
il fritto misto	*eel free-tob mees-tob*	mixed fried dish
la frutta	*lah froot-tob*	fruit
frutti di mare	*froo-tee deemab-reb*	seafood
i funghi	*eefoon-ghee*	mushrooms
i gamberi	*ee gam-bair-ee*	shrimp
il gelato	*eel jeb-lab-tob*	ice cream
l'insalata	*leen-sab-lab-tab*	salad

il latte	*eel labt-teb*	milk
lesso	*less-ob*	boiled
la melanzana	*lah meb-lan-tsab-nab*	eggplant
la minestra	*lah mee-ness-trab*	soup
l'olio	*lob-lee-ob*	oil
il pane	*eel pab-neb*	bread
le patate	*leb pah-tab-teb*	potatoes
le patatine fritte	*leb pab-tah-teen-eb free-teb*	French fries
il pepe	*eel peb-peh*	pepper
la pesca	*lah pess-kab*	peach
il pesce	*eel pesb-eh*	fish
il polipo	*eel pob-lee-pob*	octopus
il pollo	*eel poll-ob*	chicken
il pomodoro	*eel pob-mob-dor-ob*	tomato
il prosciutto cotto/crudo	*eel pro-shoo-tob kot-tob/kroo-dob*	ham cooked/cured
il riso	*eel ree-zob*	rice
il sale	*eel sab-leb*	salt
la salsiccia	*lah sal-see-chab*	sausage
le seppie	*leh sep-pee-eh*	cuttlefish
secco	*sek-kob*	dry
la sogliola	*lah soll-yob-lab*	sole
i spinaci	*ee speenab-chee*	spinach
succo d'arancia/ di limone	*soo-kob dab-ran-chab/ dee lee-moh-neb*	orange/lemon juice
il tè	*eelteb*	tea
la tisana	*lah tee-zab-nab*	herbal tea
il tonno	*eelton-nob*	tuna
la torta	*lab tor-tab*	cake/tart
l'uovo	*loo-ob-vob*	egg
vino bianco	*vee-nob bee-ang-kob*	white wine
vino rosso	*vee-nob ross-ob*	red wine
il vitello	*eel vee-tell-ob*	veal
le vongole	*leb von-gob-leb*	clams
lo zucchero	*lob zoo-kair-ob*	sugar
gli zucchini	*lyee dzu-kee-nee*	zucchini
la zuppa	*lab tsoo-pab*	soup

NUMBERS

1	**uno**	*oo-nob*
2	**due**	*doo-eb*
3	**tre**	*treb*
4	**quattro**	*kwat-rob*
5	**cinque**	*ching-kweb*
6	**sei**	*say-ee*
7	**sette**	*set-teb*
8	**otto**	*ot-tob*
9	**nove**	*nob-veb*
10	**dieci**	*dee-eb-chee*
11	**undici**	*oon-dee-chee*
12	**dodici**	*dob-dee-chee*
13	**tredici**	*tray-dee-chee*
14	**quattordici**	*kwat-tor-dee-chee*
15	**quindici**	*kwin-dee-chee*
16	**sedici**	*say-dee-chee*
17	**diciassette**	*dee-chab-set-teb*
18	**diciotto**	*dee-chot-tob*
19	**diciannove**	*dee-chab-nob-veb*
20	**venti**	*ven-tee*
30	**trenta**	*tren-tab*
40	**quaranta**	*kwab-ran-tab*
50	**cinquanta**	*ching-kwan-tab*
60	**sessanta**	*sess-an-tab*
70	**settanta**	*set-tan-tab*
80	**ottanta**	*ot-tan-tab*
90	**novanta**	*nob-van-tab*
100	**cento**	*chen-tob*
1,000	**mille**	*mee-leb*
2,000	**duemila**	*doo-eb mee-lab*
5,000	**cinquemila**	*ching-kweb mee-lab*
1,000,000	**un milione**	*oon meel-yob-neb*

TIME

one minute	**un minuto**	*oon mee-noo-tob*
one hour	**un'ora**	*oon or-ab*
half an hour	**mezz'ora**	*medz-or-ab*
a day	**un giorno**	*oonjor-nob*
a week	**una settimana**	*oona set-tee-mab-nab*
Monday	**lunedì**	*loo-neb-dee*
Tuesday	**martedì**	*mar-teb-dee*
Wednesday	**mercoledì**	*mair-kob-leb-dee*
Thursday	**giovedì**	*job-veb-dee*
Friday	**venerdì**	*ven-air-dee*
Saturday	**sabato**	*sah-bab-tob*
Sunday	**domenica**	*dob-meb-nee-kab*